THUCYDIDES AND THE PURSUIT OF FREEDOM

THUCYDIDES AND THE PURSUIT OF FREEDOM

MARY P. NICHOLS

CORNELL UNIVERSITY PRESS
Ithaca and London

Copyright © 2015 by Cornell University

First published 2015 by Cornell University Press

Printed in the United States of America

Library of Congress Cataloging-in-Publication Data

Nichols, Mary P., author.
   Thucydides and the pursuit of freedom / Mary P. Nichols.
       pages cm
   Includes bibliographical references and index.
   ISBN 978-0-8014-5316-8 (cloth : alk. paper)
   1. Thucydides—Political and social views. 2. Liberty.
3. Thucydides. History of the Peloponnesian War. I. Title.
   DF229.T6N53   2015
   938'.05092—dc23   2014024626

Cornell University Press strives to use environmentally responsible suppliers and materials to the fullest extent possible in the publishing of its books. Such materials include vegetable-based, low-VOC inks and acid-free papers that are recycled, totally chlorine-free, or partly composed of nonwood fibers. For further information, visit our website at www.cornellpress.cornell.edu.

Cloth printing   10 9 8 7 6 5 4 3 2 1

❦ CONTENTS

THUCYDIDES AND THE PURSUIT OF FREEDOM

Introduction

Thucydides as Historian

In this book I explore Thucydides' commitment to the cause of freedom. Historians are not ordinarily thought of as embracing a cause. The historian, as Aristotle **was** one of the first to assert, describes what happens (*Poetics* 1451b4–6). If a historian has a cause, it would be accuracy about the facts. Thucydides describes his own work in just such terms. Early in his account of the war between the Athenians and the Peloponnesians he criticizes how little effort others make in "searching for the truth" (1.20.3) and describes his own efforts to obtain clarity and precision for his work in the face of faulty memory and goodwill toward (*eunoia*) one side or the other. He asks us to judge what is said by the facts or the deeds (*erga*), as he struggles to get them straight (1.21.2, 1.22). His writing appears to be defined by what happens, insofar as he can understand it through his investigations. As to the events of the war that he is recounting, they seem more the result of necessity or compulsion than of freedom. As Thucydides famously observes, Athens's increasing greatness and the fear it caused made war inevitable (1.23.6). As Thucydides' writing is determined by what happens, which he faithfully records, what happens is also determined by prior events.

A closer look at *History of the Peloponnesian War*, however, demonstrates the extent to which freedom was a central theme for Thucydides.[1] Cities

---

1. Although I refer to Thucydides' work as *History of the Peloponnesian War*, he left it untitled. Nor did he refer to his work as a history, saying simply that he "wrote up the war between the

and individuals in his account take freedom as their goal, whether they claim to possess it and want to maintain it, or desire to attain it for themselves or others. Freedom is the goal of both antagonists in the Peloponnesian War, Sparta and Athens, although in different ways. Sparta has ruled itself under good laws, without tyrants, Thucydides tells us, for almost four hundred years, and has become powerful enough to put down tyrants elsewhere in the Hellenic world (1.18.1–2). Now that Athens has extended its empire, the Hellenic world looks to Sparta to defend freedom against this "tyrant city" (e.g., 1.122.3, 1.124.3).[2] Athens, for its part, takes pride in a free government, especially as Pericles describes it in his famous funeral oration. Because of Athens's free way of life, Pericles claims, his city serves as a model for other cities. Indeed, he argues that Athens is entitled to rule others, especially since it demonstrates a liberality or generosity in ruling that few cities would in similar circumstances (2.37.1, 2.40.3). At the same time, Thucydides shows the extent to which both cities and individuals fall short of their claims to act freely and for the sake of freedom.

In defending freedom as a goal of political action, while demonstrating throughout his work both the failures and excesses of its pursuit, Thucydides himself is taking freedom as his cause. On the one hand, he demonstrates that freedom makes possible human excellence, including courage, self-restraint, deliberation, and judgment, which support freedom in turn. On the other, the pursuit of freedom, in one's own regime and in the world at large, clashes with interests and material necessity, and indeed the very passions required for its support. Athens's free way of life gives rise to the desire to conquer and rule Sicily and the suffering that follows, for example, while the expectation that Sparta will liberate the Hellenic world from Athenian tyranny leads

---

Peloponnesians and the Athenians" (1.1.1). "History" was not an established or identified genre when Thucydides wrote, and was not therefore a ready way in which he might have identified his work. Herodotus, who wrote about the Persian War prior to Thucydides, does describe his work as a *historia*, but he uses the word to refer not to his work itself, or to the events that he describes, but to the inquiry on which his work is based. When Aristotle distinguishes poetry from history in the *Poetics*, the former describing universals in particulars, the latter recounting what happens (*Poetics* 1451a37–b11), he comes closer to, and perhaps even establishes, our usage. See Simon Hornblower, *Thucydides* (Baltimore: Johns Hopkins University Press, 1987), 7–12. I will follow the long tradition of calling Thucydides a historian, and his work a history.

2. Translations of Thucydides are my own, based on the Oxford Classical Text: Thucydides, *Historiae*, ed. Henricus Stuart Jones (Oxford: Oxford University Press, 1966). I have, however, consulted the translation of Steven Lattimore, *The Peloponnesian War*, with an introduction, notes, and glossary (Indianapolis: Hackett, 1998); and also *The Landmark Thucydides*, rev. ed. of the Richard Crawley translation, ed. Robert B. Strassler, with an introduction by Victor Davis Hanson (New York: Simon & Schuster, 1996).

❧ Acknowledgments

I have had two occasions over the years to teach Thucydides as a graduate seminar, once at Fordham University and once at Baylor. Both classes stand out in my experience of over forty years of teaching, for the insights and the encouragement that my students gave me. Their good spirit, intelligence, and humor will always remain with me, as will the image of a "Save Plataea" T-shirt they promised. I have been blessed for so many years with my graduate students, from whom I have received more than they can imagine. To them all, I would like to dedicate this book.

Two presentations of my work on Thucydides, at the University of Notre Dame and the College of the Holy Cross, helped me refine my thoughts, as did the questions and conversations that followed. I am also grateful to the friends who read and criticized versions of my manuscript, including Christine Basil, Susan Benfield, Steve Block, Kevin Burns, William Mathie, and most of all David Nichols, whose support and love made this book possible. Thanks also to the anonymous readers who made suggestions for improving the manuscript, and to Peter J. Potter and his staff at Cornell University Press, who guided this process with competence and care. This book was supported in part by funds from the College and Dean of Arts and Sciences of Baylor University and from the Arts & Humanities Faculty Research Program and the Vice Provost for Research.

many to suffer from this unfounded hope. Thucydides' work, a possession for all time as he calls it, therefore speaks very much to our time, encouraging the defense of freedom while warning of the limits and dangers that arise in its defense. The powerful must defend freedom, Thucydides teaches, but they must beware lest they end up paying for the defense of freedom with freedom itself.

Political Freedom in Thucydides' History

Freedom, for Thucydides, means, in the first place, freedom from subjection to others. Freedom is opposed to slavery, and Thucydides often distinguishes the free (*eleutheros*, in Greek) inhabitants of a city from the slave population (e.g., 2.78.4, 4.118.7, 8.15.2, 8.28.4, 8.62.2, 8.73.5). Thucydides applies the distinction to cities as well as to individuals. The Hellenes, several decades before the Peloponnesian War, repelled the Persians, who had come "to enslave" the cities of Hellas (1.18.2). The Syracusan leader Hermocrates warns his city that just as the Persians tried to enslave the Hellenic world, the Athenians are now coming to do the same to Sicily (6.33.5–6). According to representatives of Mytilene, who revolted from Athenian rule early in the war, Athens has in fact "enslaved" a large part of the Hellenic world, leaving only a few cities in its alliance "autonomous and free" (3.10.4–5). Freedom means "autonomy" from the rule of other cities, that is, living under one's own laws rather than those imposed by another. At the outset of the war, Sparta claims to wage war against Athens in order to liberate Hellas from Athenian rule. The verb "to liberate" (*eleutheroun*) means literally "to make free." Spartan purpose creates goodwill, Thucydides says, in those wanting to be free, and others fearing their subjection (2.8.4–5). When the Spartan general Brasidas tells the cities in Thrace that he has come to liberate them from Athens, he insists that Sparta promises their "autonomy" and so will not impose any particular form of government on them (4.86.1–5).

Freedom for Thucydides does not mean merely freedom from subjection to others, or autonomy; it also refers to the free way of life within cities that autonomy makes possible and that supports it in turn. Human beings who are not slaves are not slavish. Thus Thucydides speaks of Sparta's good laws, stability, freedom from tyranny, and struggle against tyrants in the Hellenic world (1.18.1–2). Archidamus, a Spartan king at the outset of the war, defends Sparta's way of life, especially the moderation and deference to law that made it a free city for so long (1.84.1–3; see Herodotus 7.104).

Pericles is even more emphatic that freedom belongs to the Athenian regime and way of life. "In political life we conduct our common affairs with freedom," he explains in his funeral oration (2.37.1). Freedom for him consists first and foremost in participation in public life. Athenians consider useless a citizen who is not active in politics, some propounding policy, others judging it. Participation takes different forms. And so, Pericles says, Athenians do not think that speech and action are at odds, but that it is beneficial to be taught about what should be done before they act (2.40.2–3). Rather than being forced to act by their circumstances, Athenians are guided by speech and therewith reasons for acting in one way rather than in another. Thucydides demonstrates his agreement with Pericles by recording in his history more speeches in Athens than in any other city, and more opposing speeches in Athens than in any other city. Freedom lies in thinking about the reasons for acting and judging which actions in a given situation best serve the goods one wants to achieve. In all these ways, for Pericles, the past does not determine the future, for reason or speech has an effect on what happens. Pericles also explains the democratic principle of equality in light of his understanding of Athens as a free city, for in Athens equality allows merit to rise in public life. Nor does poverty or obscurity of birth prevent one from serving the city (2.37.1–2). Prominence is therefore attached to individual accomplishment rather than to wealth or privilege. Equality in a free city makes possible such distinction, and the past—in this case, class or birth—does not determine human action.

Athenians are unlike their antagonists, Pericles says, in opening their city to foreigners, rather than driving them away, even though "some enemy may benefit from seeing and learning what we do not hide" (2.39.1). The funeral at which Pericles is speaking is a public one, and Pericles addresses both citizens and foreigners who are present (2.36.4; also 2.34.2). A free city is a strong city, and a strong city does not have to hide itself. And Athens acts liberally toward other cities, Pericles says, presumably those it rules, acquiring friends by conferring benefits rather than by receiving them (2.40.4). Not least, Athenians act liberally toward one another. They are not suspicious, or angry at their neighbors, but allow one another to do what they please in their daily affairs (2.37.2). A free man and city are not merely free from subjection to others, but manifest deeds appropriate to freedom. Athenians' virtue, according to Pericles, comes from "within" themselves unlike that of the Spartans, whose courage is compelled by harsh discipline and training (2.39.1, 2.39.4). Athenians "willingly" (ethelein) risk their lives on behalf of their city and toil for its sake (2.41.5). Those who fall in battle therefore deserve everlasting fame (2.42.4). It is their free way of life, Pericles "teaches" his audience, that is at stake in the struggle with Sparta (2.42.1).

Although cities and individuals in Thucydides present themselves as free and their purposes in terms of freedom, there are also good reasons to question whether Thucydides himself concurs. If Athens's critics are correct that it is "a tyrant city" (and not only its critics, see 2.63.3 and 3.37.2), could such tyranny be consistent, or at least long consistent, with the city's vaunted freedom? And while Sparta has long enjoyed a freedom from tyranny, the city has a large subject population, the Helots, who, like the Hellenic cities subject to Athens, also desire their freedom (4.80.3–4). Sparta is not simply free of tyrants.

Moreover, Thucydides explains that while there are various allegations about the cause of war, the truest cause is Athens's increase of power and Spartan fear, which made the war inevitable (1.23.6). Cities and individuals may be blamed, and they are throughout Thucydides' history, but is that blame justified if they are not free to act, but rather compelled by their passions, their interests, and circumstances they do not control (such as the increase of power)? The Athenian envoys at Sparta trace the growth of the Athenian empire to the compulsions of fear, honor, and advantage (1.75.3, 1.76.2). Freedom is opposed to slavery and tyranny, and also to compulsion or necessity. When human beings and cities enslave others, the Athenian envoys suggest, they are simply following necessity. The Athenian representatives at Melos claim that even the gods yield to "a necessity of nature" to rule wherever they can (5.105.1–2). From this perspective, the "cause" of freedom is nothing more than a deception (Spartans, for example, claim that their goal is liberating cities from Athenian subjection when they are merely acting in their own interest) or a self-deception (human beings believe that they are free to choose when they act subject to necessity). Necessity—not freedom—may be the cause of human action. Individuals and cities in Thucydides' history are often "blamed" (*aitiasthai*), literally, held to be a cause (*aitia*) of what they do or do not do, and therefore responsible (*aitioi*) (e.g., 1.39.3, 1.66.1, 1.82.1, 2.59.2, 3.55.1, etc.). But in a deeper sense blame is just only if individuals are free to choose and to act.

Throughout his history of the Peloponnesian War, I will show, Thucydides portrays speeches and deeds that do make a difference, for better or worse.[3]

---

3. Paul Ludwig similarly argues that Thucydides entertains but does not embrace the view that individuals and cities are mastered by forces greater than themselves. "Fitting *ananke* [necessity] together with human will" becomes "a dialectical problem in the history." *Eros and Polis* (Cambridge: Cambridge University Press, 2002), 159. My approach is also indebted to Laurie M. Johnson's analysis of how both national and personal character in Thucydides' work qualify the realist and determinist position that many espouse in and about his history. *Thucydides, Hobbes, and the Interpretation of Realism* (DeKalb: Northern Illinois University Press, 1991), especially 3–4, 28, 29, 34, 42, 61, 166, and 209–17; and Paul A. Rahe, "Thucydides' Critique of Realpolitik," in *Roots of Realism: Philosophical and Historical Dimensions*, ed. Benjamin Frankel (London: Frank Cass, 1996), 105–41, esp. 110, 120, and 125.

He thereby affirms that freedom is a cause of human action, without denying limits to freedom. Indeed, it is Alcibiades who denies any limits to his actions, as Thucydides suggests when he points out that Alcibiades indulges his desires beyond his existing resources (*huparchousa ousia*) and that the people fear the extent of his "lawlessness" (6.15.3–4). When he is exiled from Athens and advises Sparta how to win the war against Athens, he goes so far as to claim that he is so great a lover of his city as to want to repossess (*anaktashai*) it (6.92.4). Although his expression suggests the conquest of Athens and the tyranny the Athenians fear from him, it also suggests that freedom requires a home in time and place where it can be realized and manifest.[4] Alcibiades at least needs a home, a base from which to act and from which to derive support. Thucydides documents time after time Alcibiades' failures once he breaks away from Athens. Perhaps this is why Thucydides never describes Alcibiades as free, although he operates "outside the law" of any regime, and even conspires with the Persians against both Athens and Sparta. By the end of the history, homecoming becomes a prominent theme, both that of the expedition to Sicily Alcibiades advocated and that of Alcibiades himself.[5] Although Nicias would like to lead the expedition home, "few out of many returned home" (*ep' oikou aponostein*), Thucydides observes (7.87.6).[6] Alcibiades' intrigues with the Persians, with the Athenian army at Samos, and with the leaders within Athens aim at his being recalled home from exile. Home

---

4. Martha C. Taylor points out the importance of home for Thucydides, connecting home with the land and the ancestral gods. She argues that Pericles scants the realities of home, devaluing Attica and the land in his vision of the city as a naval power and in his policy of moving the people from the countryside into the city and of allowing the Spartans to ravage the land. *Thucydides, Pericles, and the Idea of Athens in the Peloponnesian War* (Cambridge: Cambridge University Press, 2010), 7–91. Although Taylor reminds us of the importance of home for Thucydides' understanding of human life, she gives too little weight to the Athenian regime and the goods that it promotes for Thucydides.

5. Bernard J. Dobski also notes a similar movement in Thucydides' work, leading to a "return to the conventions of Athenian politics" that is "at once occasioned *and* conditioned by an awareness and acceptance of the fundamental limits (intelligible and otherwise) to the moral and political categories that define human life" (emphasis Dobski's). "The Incomplete Whole: The Structural Integrity of Thucydides' History," in *Socrates and Dionysus: Philosophy and Art in Dialogue*, ed. Ann Ward (Newcastle: Cambridge Scholars, 2013), 14.

6. Thucydides' phrase for returning home, *ep' oikou aponostein*, as several scholars discuss, recalls the Homeric heroes and the difficulties they faced with their homecomings (*nostoi*) from Troy. Useful discussions can be found in June W. Allison, "Homeric Allusions at the Close of Thucydides' Sicilian Narrative," *American Journal of Philology* 118, no. 4 (1997): 512 and 502; W. Robert Connor, *Thucydides* (Princeton: Princeton University Press, 1984), 161–62n9; and Hornblower, *Thucydides* 115–16. They do not, however, connect the failed homecoming of the Athenians from Sicily with Alcibiades' more convoluted efforts to return home after leaving with the expedition, or with the broader themes of Thucydides' work.

for Thucydides, I argue, does not merely circumscribe freedom, but by circumscribing it makes it possible.

Thucydides' Freedom as a Historian

Thucydides raises the question of his own freedom as a historian of the war when he contrasts his work with that of previous poets and prose writers, who "embellish" and "exaggerate" and offer "what is pleasing to hear at the expense of the truth." Warning his readers how little effort most people make in "searching for the truth," he tells us about his herculean efforts to be as "accurate as possible" in his writing, inasmuch as those present at events gave different accounts, sometimes due to memory, sometimes to their goodwill for one side or the other (1.20.3–22). When Thucydides tells us that the truest cause of the war is the growth of Athenian power and Spartan fear, he says that this cause was "least clear in what was said" about the war (1.23.6). Speech obstructs the truth, whether it be the speech of poets and prose writers or that of political actors who allege the causes of war by referring to violations of treaties and by appealing to justice (e.g., 1.67.1–4, 1.68.4). Words must be tested by facts or deeds (*erga*) (1.21.2).

Such statements lend credence to the view that Thucydides is the first scientific or objective historian, who attempts "to bring all human action within the realm of natural causes."[7] Science may free us from supernatural or unintelligible causes, but it also binds us to necessity. The scientific historian is limited to the facts, and to explaining their causes. The question of Thucydides' task—and accomplishment—as a historian thus parallels the question of the freedom that is possible for the individuals and cities that he describes in his history and of the limits that they face. Just as a scientific historian is constrained by the facts, the political actor pursues his goals within the confines of a reality constrained by the pursuit of power. Moreover, the limits of science require the limits of politics, inasmuch as a scientific account

---

7. Charles N. Cochrane, *Thucydides and the Science of History* (Oxford: Oxford University Press, 1929), 1; John H. Finley, Jr. *Thucydides* (Cambridge, MA: Harvard University Press, 1942), 69–70; F. E. Adcock, *Thucydides and His History* (Cambridge: Cambridge University Press, 1963), 109; William T. Bluhm, "Causal Theory in Thucydides' Peloponnesian War," *Political Studies* 10 (1962): 15–35; Robert Gilpin, "The Theory of Hegemonic War," *Journal of Interdisciplinary History* 18, no. 4 (1988): 591–613, esp. 593, 594, 596; and Hornblower, *Thucydides*, 73–109. Herodotus preceded Thucydides as historian, and is often called the father of history, but Herodotus takes "refuge in supernaturalism," when plausible natural explanations fail. More particularly, according to Cochrane, Thucydides adapts "the principles and methods of Hippocratic medicine to the interpretation of history." *Thucydides and the Science of History*, 15–17.

of human behavior requires that human action be grounded in necessity: only if there are compulsions will scientific laws of explanation hold.[8] William T. Bluhm therefore argues that Thucydides, as scientist, "view[s] political man in the category of necessity rather than that of freedom."[9] Even though Thucydides must be free from prejudice in order to pursue the facts with accuracy and clarity, his writing is determined by the facts.

In spite of his criticisms of the misleading character of speech and his inclusion of prose writers (*logographoi*) along with poets in the group of writers who, he says, embellish the facts, Thucydides calls attention to the fact that he himself is a writer of speeches. Even in the first sentence of his work, he tells us that he "wrote up" (*xuggraphein*) the war between the Peloponnesians and the Athenians (1.1.1). And throughout his work, he uses this same verb to describe his activity (see 2.70.4, 2.103.1, 3.25.2, 3.88.4, etc.). The prefix of the verb suggests that in writing he brings events "together," and thus indicates his active role as a historian. He is not simply a scientific recorder of facts whose writing is determined by them. It is Thucydides' account, or *logos,* that examines the things said in light of the deeds. His freedom in writing his history lies not merely in his pursuit of the facts with a clear mind, but in his evaluation of them. Facts serve as a test of speech, but speech also interprets the facts, or speaks for them. Pericles claims that he is able to advise the Athenians and to interpret (*hermeneuein*) his advice for them (2.60.5). This ability of which he boasts is a reflection of that of Thucydides, who interprets without boasting. Thucydides thus acknowledges that like the chroniclers of the past whom he criticizes, he too is a prose writer—literally, a writer of words (*logographos*).

Moreover, Thucydides may be described as "a speech writer" not only because he "wrote up" the war between the Peloponnesians and the Athenians. His writing includes numerous speeches that he attributes to statesmen, generals, and envoys and that play a part in our understanding of the war. He presents their speeches in direct discourse; we hear their words to their addressees. He faced greater difficulties with accuracy, he admits, in the case of the speeches than of the deeds, for even when he himself was present he could not remember the speeches verbatim. It therefore seemed best to

---

8. Steven Forde, "International Realism and the Science of Politics: Thucydides, Machiavelli, and Neorealism," *International Studies Quarterly* 39, no. 2 (1995): 150–52. Realist international relations theorists therefore find support in Thucydides the "scientist" for understanding the relations among states in terms of power, which states try to maximize especially for the sake of security or survival.

9. Bluhm, "Causal Theory," 16.

him to attribute to the speakers what was required (*deonta*) in the circumstances, while coming as close as possible to the complete sense of what they truly said (1.22.1). Victor Davis Hanson infers from this that Thucydides had "two contrary agendas"—"historical exactitude" and "contrivance," and he finds in Thucydides himself the "cleft between 'objective' and 'subjective' truth" of current academic discourse.[10] Thucydides' very inclusion of these speeches in his history, however, raises questions about the extent to which "historical exactitude" could be his standard for the accuracy or truth he seeks to convey in writing his history. Were he seeking historical exactitude, his purpose might weigh against including the speeches at all, since Thucydides cannot accurately reproduce them, as he acknowledges.[11] Should he aim at simple historical exactitude, moreover, he would lack any standard for deciding which speeches to include and which not.

Such considerations suggest that Thucydides works more like an artist than a scientist, and that his history is less an empirical account of what happened than a carefully organized and unified text. W. Robert Connor points out that "we have come to recognize that facts never speak for themselves unless selected and arranged by the narrator and that behind the shaping of any narration lie principles or assumptions that are vital for the understanding of the work." Indeed, according to Connor, Thucydides "shapes and guides the readers' responses" by expressing "attitudes, assumptions, and ideas that are eventually modified, restated, subverted, or totally controverted." Thucydides' very stance of impartiality or objectivity is therefore ironic—a "pose or literary device" that forces the reader to see things as he does.[12] Darien Shanske argues that Thucydides founds or creates a world whose metaphysics is a Heraclitean "continuous unfolding of contraries," rather than one of "mechanical or natural process." Through the "warring that we do in time," we create identities that make effective action possible, although "no solution is ever stable because there is no bedrock."[13] As Connor observes, our

10. Hanson, introduction to *Landmark Thucydides*, xvi.

11. There are approximately forty-four separate speeches in direct discourse in Thucydides' work. Of course some are longer than others, but this number offers a sense of how central they are to the work.

12. W. Robert Connor, "A Post Modernist Thucydides?" *Classical Journal* 72, no. 4 (April 1977): 298 and 291; also Connor, *Thucydides*, 18; Tim Rood, *Thucydides: Narrative and Explanation* (Oxford: Clarendon Press), 1998, e.g., 4–5, 9, 11, 14, 22; and David Gribble's discussion of Thucydides' "narratorial interventions" in *Alcibiades and Athens* (Oxford: Oxford University Press, 1999), 159–213, esp. 166, 170, 175, 194.

13. Darien Shanske, *Thucydides and the Philosophic Origins of History* (Cambridge: Cambridge University Press, 2007), e.g., 9–10, 32, 115, 133–38, 142–47, 163.

"thoroughly modernist Thucydides," a "disengaged, dispassionate, detached observer," has come to be viewed as "a post modernist."[14]

A variation of this view presents Thucydides as a constructivist, which is meant to refer to the position that the social world and conventions—and the language, speech, and shared meanings that shape them—have more effect on how human beings act than nature or necessity does. Whereas for science and for realism, according to Richard Ned Lebow, "phusis [nature] trumps nomos [law or convention]," for the constructivist, convention trumps nature, or at least leaves more room for human freedom. Human relations are "an expression of culturally determined and ever evolving conventions," but if conventions evolve, there may be room for human beings to affect their evolution. Human beings are not only the products of their societies and its conventions, they are also their source. For Thucydides, "both deeds and words are social constructions, but he gives pride of place to logoi."[15]

In a Heraclitean world of contraries in which we struggle to create our identities, however, there is no obvious ground for preferring one identity to another, unless it is one that acknowledges its own lack of bedrock and consequent ephemerality. Nor is it clear on what basis a constructivist Thucydides could choose what ends his narrative should serve, or what conventions, norms, and shared meanings political actors should seek to preserve or promote. Lebow nevertheless argues that Thucydides supports the construction of "conventions that maintain domestic and international order."[16] Constructivism serves political realism. His appeal to James Boyd White's work on Thucydides, however, is ominous. White derives the title for his work *When Words Lose Their Meaning: Constitutions and Reconstitutions of Language, Character, and Community* from Thucydides' description of the effect on speech of the brutal domestic conflict in Corcyra, where "words change their ordinary meaning and take that which is then given to them." Recklessness

---

14. Connor, *Thucydides*, 18.

15. Richard Ned Lebow, "Thucydides the Constructivist," *American Political Science Review* 95 (September 2001): 547–560, esp. 553, 556, 577, 558; Lebow, "Play It Again Pericles: Agents, Structures and the Peloponnesian War," *European Journal of International Relations* 2, no. 2 (1996): 231–58, esp. 232, 242–48; and Daniel Garst, "Thucydides and Neorealism," *International Studies Quarterly* 33, no. 1 (1989): 3–27, esp. 5, 6, 7, 12, 25.

16. Lebow, "Thucydides the Constructivist," 557. S. Sara Monoson and Michael Loriaux similarly claim that Thucydides approves of statesmen who *craft* and maintain norms of international action for the sake of survival. Their realist interpretation of Thucydides, they claim, thus "intersects with the new constructivist literature on norms and law." "The Illusion of Power and the Disruption of Moral Norms: Thucydides' Critique of Periclean Policy," *American Political Science Review* 92, no. 2 (June 1998): 294–95.

comes to be called courage, foresight cowardice, and moderation lack of manliness (3.82.4).[17] A fluid world, in which speech trumps nature, may mean moral and political anarchy, where laws and conventions are ineffective, as they are at Corcyra. Moreover, a fluid world, not just one of natural necessity, may conduce to the rule of the strong over the weak. Alcibiades has long been recognized as practicing a politics of image-making, reconstructing past events as well as constructing present ones to suit his purposes.[18] One can easily fear, as the Athenian people came to do, that such a freedom from conventions opens the door to a tyrannical politics (6.60.1).

Given Thucydides' portrayal of Alcibiades' politics, it is possible that the view of the world that postmodern interpretations attribute to Thucydides belongs more to Alcibiades than to Thucydides himself. The very notion of "subjective truth" that Hanson introduces to explain Thucydides' contrivance of speeches for his history is itself ambiguous. If Thucydides reconstructs speeches "more or less according to [his] own particular historical sense of what was likely, appropriate, and necessary,"[19] the truth that emerges is subjective not because it proceeds from a subject pursuing purposes or preferences of his own, but because it proceeds from one trying to understand and to reproduce what the circumstances require. As Thucydides suggests, he is seeking not mere historical accuracy—what happens to have taken place—but something that fits the situation. The latter could prove beneficial, Thucydides says, to those wishing to consider clearly other things that have occurred or will do so in the future, which will in the course of human affairs resemble what Thucydides recounts. It is this resemblance that makes his work "a possession for all time" (1.22.4).

An "artful" historian therefore may use his art in the service of conveying the truth that he has come to understand by his observations and reflections on the world. Virginia Hunter, who calls Thucydides an "artful reporter" in the title of her book, suggests such a task for the artist when she observes "the almost architectonic quality of [Thucydides'] mind, which grasped in a single vision not just the war which he claimed to record but all of human history,

---

17. James Boyd White, *When Words Lose Their Meaning: Constitutions and Reconstitutions of Language, Character, and Community* (Chicago: University of Chicago Press, 1984).

18. For example, C. W. Macleod, "Rhetoric and History," in *Collected Essays* (Oxford: Clarendon Press, 1983), 73, 75; H. D. Westlake, *Individuals in Thucydides* (Cambridge: Cambridge University Press, 1968), 251; Steven Forde, *The Ambition to Rule: Alcibiades and the Politics of Athenian Imperialism in Thucydides* (Ithaca, NY: Cornell University Press, 1989), 190–92; and Gribble, *Alcibiades and Athens*, 198, 202.

19. Hanson, Introduction, *Landmark Thucydides*, xvi.

as it were."[20] Such an artful reporter would recognize a reality by which his text can be judged. He is therefore freer than the scientific historian who is bound to the facts, but more dependent than the postmodern historian, who is bound primarily to his own vision.

Leo Strauss reminds us of the classical understanding of the artist—or, as the ancients said, the poet—who expresses what is universally true through his particular stories and characters. He refers us to Aristotle's distinction between the poet, who describes "what might happen," and the historian who describes "what happens." Because the historian presents only the "singulars" or particulars, whereas the poet shows universals in his particular stories, according to Aristotle, the historian is less "philosophic and serious" than the poet (*Poetics* 1451b6–7). But this task that Aristotle ascribes to the poet describes what Thucydides does in Strauss's view. Strauss's masterful analysis in *City and Man* of Thucydides' work establishes the extent to which Thucydides organized it around such philosophic issues as rest and motion, justice and necessity, and speech and deeds. In demonstrating how the particulars illustrate such universals, Strauss points out, Thucydides resembles Plato, who, he says, "discovered in a singular event—in the singular life of Socrates—the universal and thus [became] able to present the universal through presenting a singular."[21] As philosophic historian, Thucydides resembles the poet whom Aristotle contrasts with the historian.

The history that records merely what is seen and heard as accurately as possible has less to teach because it does not interpret what it sees and hears.[22] At the same time, for Thucydides, everything cannot be interpretation. If it were, interpretation would be neither necessary nor possible. When Thucydides asks us to judge what he says by the facts, he is not being ironic, as he would be if he were himself creating them. When Thucydides interprets, he is not merely speaking, he is letting the facts speak to us. A postmodern historian who did merely the former would be as bound to the particular as the scientific historian. In presenting a world as it appears to him, he too is presenting happenstance, inasmuch as it is he—and his idiosyncratic vision—that happens to have come into existence. It is both the

---

20. Virginia Hunter, *Thucydides the Artful Reporter* (Toronto: Hakkert, 1973), 183. Also Donald Kagan, "The Speeches in Thucydides and the Mytilene Debate," *Yale Classical Studies* 24 (1975): 72.

21. Leo Strauss, *City and Man* (Chicago: Rand McNally, 1964), 236, 142–43.

22. As C. W. Macleod says, an author's drawing out the significance through interpretation "is more faithful to reality" than if he or she shies away from interpretation altogether. "Rhetoric and History," 69.

scientific and postmodern historian whom Aristotle would find less serious and philosophic than poetry.

Even if Thucydides' work as a historian resembles that which Aristotle attributes to the poet—showing a truth for all time in the particulars he recounts—we should not expect his work to be exactly the same as the poet's, just as what occurs in the future will resemble but not be the same as what occurs in the past. The former follows from the latter. If the particulars in which the universals are manifest are mere manifestations of those universals, the future would in all essentials reproduce the past, and the work of Thucydides about the war would collapse into poetry. But the singularity of the particulars we experience means that they cannot be reduced to universals, which can therefore explain them only in part. Thucydides is constrained in a way that the poet is not, for Thucydides is writing not about what may occur, but about what has occurred. His work does not have the wholeness or completeness that Aristotle says good poets achieve by making universals appear in their stories. In distinguishing his work from the embellished work of the poets and prose writers, and acknowledging that his is less pleasant "for hearing" than theirs, Thucydides recognizes this difference. Perhaps when Thucydides identifies himself as an Athenian at the outset of his work, he recognizes the dependence of his own achievement on accident, the chance that he was born in a particular time and place that made it possible for him to record the war. Whether this makes his work less philosophic and serious than theirs, however, remains an open question, especially if the truth lies not simply in the universals that particulars illustrate—that is, if universals hold only for the most part (see Aristotle, NE 1094b20–23).

Moreover, Thucydides' very restraint in the face of chance—including his work as a historian rather than as a poet such as Aristotle describes—proceeds from his own freedom. His work originates in freedom, and thereby illustrates its possibility. Whereas the poet who offers the particular events and characters of his stories in order to reveal universals to this extent frees himself from time and place, the historian's freedom, limited as it is by chance, serves as a better model than the poet's for citizens and statesmen. In this, Thucydides is reflected in his Pericles, who, we will see, presents himself to the Athenians as an exemplar of the freedom he urges them to assume, and in Brasidas, who undertakes a liberation of Hellas.

My argument therefore addresses the views of Strauss and others influenced by his reading, when they conclude that the freedom possible for thought or understanding, and manifest in Thucydides' writing about the war, is not possible for political communities and political actors, with their necessarily limited and partial perspectives.[23] Whereas Clifford Orwin emphasizes the gulf between the city's self-understanding and the one available to Thucydides, I find Thucydides more cognizant of the restraints of time and place on his own thought and work, and the political community more able to share in his freedom.[24] Thucydides provides not universal propositions, but models, the "use" of which in other circumstances necessarily demands deliberation and judgment—evaluations of similarity and dissimilarity of circumstances, for example—which is needed for political freedom. Thucydides' work as historian therefore can provide guidance for statesmen without determining matters and events. Thucydides, I argue, is neither a "scientist" who demonstrates universal laws nor a postmodern who provides no guidance. Because he thinks that politics itself is worthy of wonder (e.g., 1.38.3, 2.39.4), he has much to say to statesmen.

My own analysis, much indebted to the efforts of the past, understands the freedom that Thucydides achieves as a historian to reflect that of the political actors in his history. Because human beings can act freely, they are responsible for doing so, and when they do, they can be blamed (see, e.g., 2.59.2, 2.65.10) or praised and admired (see, e.g., 1.138.3, 2.65.5–9). Thucydides generously does the latter, and justly does the former, in writing his history. At the same

---

23. Strauss, *City and Man*, 166, 226–38.

24. Clifford Orwin thus refers to "Thucydidean wisdom" that "perceives folly, willfulness, and perversity as the rule for human beings." Thucydides' perspective is therefore one of detachment and resignation. *The Humanity of Thucydides* (Princeton: University of Princeton Press, 1994), 162, 203–4. See also Christopher Bruell, "Thucydides' View of Athenian Imperialism," *American Political Science Review* 68 (1974): 16–17; David Bolotin, "Thucydides," in *The History of Political Philosophy*, ed. Leo Strauss and Joseph Cropsey, 3rd ed. (Chicago: University of Chicago Press, 1987), 31–32; Forde, *Ambition to Rule*, 209–10; Michael Palmer, *Love of Glory and the Common Good* (Lanham, MD: Rowman and Littlefield, 1992), 116; Thomas L. Pangle and Peter J. Ahrensdorf, "Classical Realism," in *Justice Among Nations: On the Moral Basis of Peace and Power* (Lawrence: University of Kansas Press, 2002), 13–32, esp. 31–32; and Timothy Burns, "The Virtue of Thucydides' Brasidas," *Journal of Politics* 73, no. 2 (April 2011): 508–23, esp. 520–22. This view in a way comes back around to the earlier view of Thucydides as scientist. Not only does it attribute to Thucydides a realist position on politics—and one that suggests minimal control of our political lives—it also returns to Thucydides as the "disengaged, dispassionate, detached observer," whom Connor argues has been displaced in the scholarship. Strauss indicates that Thucydides might seem to differ from Plato in allowing less scope to choice than to fatality in human affairs, inasmuch as Plato traces the transformation of Athens's ancestral regime into an extreme democracy to a "wilful disregard of ancestral law regarding music and the theater." In Thucydides' work, in contrast, "Athens was compelled to become a democracy," when the threat of Persia forced it to build a powerful navy, which required the poorest to become sailors and thus gain a higher status and greater power than previously. Strauss argues that this appearance of the difference between the two thinkers is incorrect. This is not, however, because Thucydides gives more room to choice than it may seem, but because Plato gives greater place to necessity. *City and Man*, 237–38.

time, Thucydides acknowledges that limits belong to the one who recounts the deeds of others, just as limits belong to those whose deeds he recounts. His own writing, for example, is limited by what he can know about events and their causes, as well as blessed by the chance that made those events available for his reflection. Thucydides therefore teaches his readers both their freedom and dependence. His doing so demonstrates his own dependence on the deeds of politics as well as the freedom of his thought. Whether political actions serve as proof of the philosophic historian's freedom and dependence, or whether the historian himself serves as a model for what is humanly possible, free and responsible history and politics stand or fall together. It is my contention that, for Thucydides, they stand together.

The Unfolding of Thucydides' History

Throughout the rest of the book, I will explore the individuals and events in which freedom finds its greatest expressions and its greatest failures. Achievement and defeat, however, are never far apart. Achievement in Thucydides' world may be tenuous and temporary, but defeat does not remove the hope of unrealized possibility. I begin with Athenian democracy, and its potential for freedom, manifest in self-rule, liberality, and deliberative judgment in the assembly. Sparta, in contrast, holds the promise of freedom through the stability and moderation of its customs and ways of life, both for its own citizens and others in the Hellenic world. Thucydides nevertheless shows us the dark side of Sparta's resistance to change, as well as of Athens's inclination to innovation, dark sides that make their achievements for Thucydides even more worthy of wonder.

Thucydides presents Pericles as one of Athens's greatest leaders, "the most able Athenian of his time in speaking and acting" (1.139.4). Both his words and deeds serve as the measure for others, just as he himself presents Athens as the measure of human virtue. Thucydides' portrayal of Pericles, both his speeches and his deeds, is the focus of my first chapter. The virtues of Athens, as Pericles understands them, are daring (*tolma*) and intelligence or judgment (*gnōmē*) (e.g., 2.40.3; also 1.144.3, 2.62.5), the very virtues that he himself embodies.[25] They are made possible by and serve Athens's freedom. In his funeral oration, he claims that the soldiers who fell, by giving their lives for

---

25. E.g., Adam Parry, "Thucydides' Historical Perspective," *Yale Classical Studies* (1972): 60; Lowell Edmunds, *Chance and Intelligence in Thucydides* (Cambridge, MA: Harvard University Press, 1975), 209–10.

such a city, departed in a brief moment at their peak, when their deeds will be "remembered forever" (2.42.4, 2.43.2).

So too does Athens itself reach a peak in this brief moment of Pericles' rhetoric. Immediately after Thucydides records Pericles' speech, he describes the less noble deaths of Athenians dying from the plague and the ignoble deeds of many when confronted with its terrors. Blaming Pericles for the war and its hardships, the Athenians attempt to negotiate peace with Sparta. The people's accusation revisits the issue of the cause of the war. To the extent that the people are correct in blaming Pericles for the war, the war is less necessary, less inevitable. Indeed, Thucydides' own account of events before the outbreak of the war gives weight to the people's claim. The growth of Athens's power and Sparta's fear of it made going to war necessary (1.23.6), but Thucydides shows us that that growth followed from choices and actions Athenians made. So too did the war. In his speech addressing their concerns, Pericles does not ask the Athenians to be resigned to the war's necessity, but rather to embrace the war with a new vision of their power (2.62.1–2). To be sure, he tells them that they can no longer withdraw from their rule of their allies, for they hold their rule like a tyranny that may seem unjust to have acquired but that is too dangerous to let go (2.63.3). Their past actions limit their present choices, but if the acquisition of their rule can be blamed as unjust, it was not necessary. Athens, like Pericles himself, is to blame. Pericles models Athens's freedom on his own.

Thucydides contrasts Pericles favorably with those who came after him. There is no longer "a first man" among the Athenians, as Thucydides describes Pericles (1.139.4, 2.65.9), only many who compete to be first. In chapter 2, I discuss Thucydides' presentation of Athenian politics in the years immediately after the death of Pericles, including the two Athenians who first come to the fore, Cleon and Diodotus. The two debate the fate of the captured city of Mytilene, in the first pair of speeches in Thucydides' history in which two Athenians take different positions. In the first of the two speeches, Cleon criticizes the seductive speeches of rhetoricians who mislead the people in a democracy. The Athenian who responds to Cleon, Diodotus, defends speech both explicitly in his speech and implicitly by his deed of delivering his speech in the face of Cleon's criticism. He therefore illustrates the conjunction between speaking or deliberation and action that Pericles associated with Athenian freedom. In contrast to Pericles, the "violent" Cleon rails at speech as harmful to action. In presenting the debate, Thucydides shows that speech can articulate alternatives so that deeds are chosen rather than compelled, dramatizing the connection between speeches in the democratic assembly and the freedom that Pericles implies when he says that speech should teach about what should be done before action is taken. Although speaking after Cleon's criticism of speech presents specific challenges for Diodotus, what Harvey Yunis says of Pericles' rhetoric is true of Diodotus's as well: his is "instructive rhetoric," which explains policy to the people "in such a way that they are persuaded to adopt it because they understand it."[26]

Cleon appeals to an "everlasting" distinction between friends and enemies in insisting on destroying Mytilene. The Athenians, in other words, must understand that they have no choice. Diodotus, in contrast, urges that deeds can make others friends and thus serve Athenian interests. Whereas Cleon presents an insular notion of "us and them," Diodotus imagines building new relationships through leniency (cf. 3.40.2 with 3.47). For him, reflection or speech helps the Athenians understand in a different way the circumstances in which they act. In so doing, his speech constructs for his addressees models of themselves in light of which they *might* act. In this way, choice becomes possible. It is for this reason that in this debate Athenian freedom lies in the balance. Diodotus offers Athens an alternative to the violence Cleon recommends, and Thucydides presents Diodotus himself as an alternative to Cleon. The vote in the Athenian assembly favors leniency. Although the Athenians had already dispatched a ship with the order to destroy Mytilene, its "monstrous" mission, Thucydides reports, made for a slow sail, and a second ship arrives in the wake of the first in time to reverse its order. Although Diodotus's triumph over Cleon in the Athenian assembly is limited—he is never mentioned again in Thucydides' history—it reflects Thucydides' own triumph over Cleon, which he achieves by presenting more attractive alternatives to Cleon in his history.

Thucydides contrasts the fall of Mytilene to Athens with the fall of Plataea to Sparta, and how each victorious city treats the one it conquers. By juxtaposing the two events in book 3, Thucydides continues to draw out his reflections on the antagonists in the war—a contrast that the Corinthians introduce in their speech at Sparta in the first book. Thucydides tests the words of the Corinthians about Athens and Sparta by the deeds of each city. And the difference between them involves the effect of speech on their deeds, and thus the extent to which their deeds are the result of freedom. In the "Plataean debate," the Plataeans are forced to speak first, defending themselves before they hear the charges, while the Thebans, their accusers and long-time enemies, get the last word. Thucydides confirms the

---

26. Harvey Yunis, *Taming Democracy: Models of Political Rhetoric in Classical Athens* (Ithaca, NY: Cornell University Press, 1996), 85, 77–86; also 93.

Plataeans' complaint that their trial is a sham, and their words useless. Even the Thebans' advice to their Spartan allies not to trust the noble but deceptive rhetoric of the Plataeans—advice that we have already heard Cleon give to the Athenians about all speech—is not necessary: Sparta has decided beforehand to gratify its Theban allies (3.68.4). The Spartans only pretend to listen to speech. Friendship between Sparta and Thebes may be strengthened by the deeds of the former, but they are partners in a deception—a sham trial—and their complicity facilitates the destruction of Plataea.

The contrast between Athens and Sparta that Thucydides draws over the fates of Mytilene and Plataea, however, raises questions about Sparta's commitment to the goal of liberating the Hellenic world from Athenian domination. In chapter 3, I discuss Sparta and especially Brasidas, who easily appears as the greatest Spartan leader of Thucydides' history. It is Brasidas who does most to achieve the liberation of cities from Athenian rule. Like Pericles, Brasidas interprets and represents his city to the world. Cities allied to Athens, either seeing Brasidas or hearing about him, are impressed by his virtue, and become more favorable to the Spartan side in the belief that other Spartans will be like him (4.81.2). But no one else quite like Brasidas comes forth from Sparta in Thucydides' history. The cities that embrace the liberation Brasidas offers them are mistaken about Sparta, and they suffer badly for their mistake (e.g., 5.32.1).

When Brasidas promises freedom to the citizens of cities he attempts to liberate from Athenian rule (e.g., 4.85.1, 4.86.1), and even freedom from Spartan interference in their domestic affairs (4.86.4–5), he lacks the resources to make good his promises. The vision of freedom he holds out to his addressees is not confirmed by the deeds that follow. Sparta's refusal to send him reinforcements (4.108.6–7), to say nothing of Sparta's using the "liberated" cities as bargaining chips in negotiations with Athens (4.81.2, 5.18), make a mockery of Brasidas's freedom, both the freedom he promises others and his own ability to act (4.123.4–124.1).

Whereas Pericles represents Athens at its best, Brasidas barely represents Sparta at all. All three of Pericles' speeches in Thucydides' history are delivered in Athens, public addresses to the people in one form or another. Brasidas's speeches are always in the field and never in Sparta, whether they are to his own troops or the people of the cities he is attempting to free from Athens. He is a man without a city, eventually refusing to follow Sparta's orders (4.122.2–3, 4.123.1). The troops he leads to Thrace are primarily mercenaries and members of Sparta's subject population, Helots, rather than Spartans (4.80.4). Forcing his way there through Thessaly, he in effect cuts off his return route to Sparta, at least by land (cf. 4.11.4–4.12.1). He finds a home elsewhere, but only after his death—in Amphipolis, one of the cities he liberates from Athenian rule and where he is buried and worshipped (5.11). That Brasidas is a man without a city may suggest his freedom, but Thucydides shows us that Brasidas's freedom from his city undermines his ability to accomplish anything lasting. Whereas Pericles describes Athens in terms of its noblest potential, Brasidas is so alien from his city that he misrepresents it to the world. Thucydides accuses Brasidas of something he never accuses Pericles of—lying (4.108.5).

Like Brasidas, Alcibiades, to whom I turn in chapter 4, breaks free of his city. He brags that his own preeminence reflects on his city and gives it glory, reversing the relation between the Athenian and his city (6.16) that Pericles describes in his funeral oration. The political act that Thucydides most associates with Alcibiades is urging and then leading an Athenian expedition against Sicily. Thucydides attributes the Sicilian expedition less to a desire to possess the goods of Sicily than "an *erōs* for sailing away," which he claims fell upon everyone in Athens (6.24.3). The general Nicias, who opposes the expedition and who opposes Alcibiades, claims that Athens's desire for the faraway is a diseased *erōs* (*duserōs*) (6.13.1). The freedom that Pericles declared arose from Athens's regime and way of life now pulls Athens outside itself. The faraway (*aponta*) that Nicias warns against is, literally, "the absent." What is absent is infinite, for it is everything that is not present. The claim of the Athenians at Melos that they are able in effect to command the sea (5.109), I argue, is a reflection of Alcibiades' politics. It is fitting that the impiety of which Alcibiades is accused in Athens is that of mocking the sacred mysteries. For Alcibiades, there are no boundaries. Nothing remains faraway.

When he is summoned home from his command in Sicily to stand trial for impiety, Alcibiades escapes prosecution by taking refuge in Sparta, where he advises Sparta how to defeat Athens. Thucydides presents Alcibiades' masterful and successful defense of himself before the Spartans and observes that he succeeds in motivating them in a way that Sparta's allies have difficulty doing. His two speeches in direct discourse in Thucydides' work are antithetical, the first successfully urging Athens to undertake the conquest of Sicily, the second advising Sparta how to prevent Athens from succeeding in doing so. Alcibiades may speak opposite Nicias at Athens, but his two speeches can be paired against each other. He alone in Thucydides' work delivers speeches on both sides of the same issue—the one promoting, the other undermining Athenian imperialism.[27] In contrast to the three speeches

---

27. See Gribble's analysis of how Alcibiades' two speeches are tailored to the different interests of his audience, and how "he addresses both groups with equal facility." *Alcibiades and Athens*, 209.

Thucydides attributes to Pericles, which are all delivered in Athens, and to the three he attributes to Brasidas, which all take place in the field of action outside of Sparta, Alcibiades gives two speeches, one in Athens, the other in Sparta. Whereas Pericles' identity is allied with his city, and Brasidas's identity is allied with his mission to liberate Hellas regardless of his city's support, Alcibiades seems to have no identity of his own. Thucydides shows him speaking just as successfully at Sparta as at Athens. So too does he ally himself with both democratic and oligarchic factions (e.g., 5.84.1, 6.50.1, 6.61.3, 6.74.1, 8.48.4). As Diodotus urges Athens to do, Alcibiades is always making new friends. Yet he makes new enemies at the same time. He makes nothing that lasts.

Alcibiades nevertheless struggles throughout his exile to be recalled to Athens. Like the homecoming of the expedition he once led to Sicily, his own homecoming becomes both a goal and a problem. In his treasonous speech at Sparta he claims that he wants to repossess his city (6.92.4), but could an Athens fallen to Spartan forces still be the Athens he loved? If yes, what he loves has no identity, and Athenian freedom and Pericles' vision of Athens are lost. If no, Alcibiades fails to repossess Athens, because he destroys it in his act of repossessing it. Alcibiades most benefits his city, Thucydides says, when he refuses to lead the Athenian army back to Athens when he has the opportunity to do so (8.86.4–7). The best thing he can do for Athens is to remain faraway.

In chapter 5, I discuss homecomings, or at least the unfulfilled desire for homecoming, on the part of Nicias and the soldiers he commands in Sicily, and on the part of Alcibiades. The issue of individual leaders' relations to their respective cities has been a theme of Thucydides' work from the beginning, as in his presentation of Pericles, who leaves Athens only in his service with the Athenian army, and in his presentation of Brasidas, who never appears at home in Sparta.[28] In the last two books of the history, the problems for the homecoming of the Athenian expedition in Sicily and for that of the exiled Alcibiades become explicit. Nicias, who commands the Athenian forces, would like to withdraw, but fears the reaction of the Athenian people if he does so without accomplishing their goals in Sicily. He asks the Athenians to

---

28. There may seem to be two exceptions. After his exploit at Methone, Thucydides reports, Brasidas was the first to be commended for his daring during the war (2.25.2). But it is not clear whether he received this commendation in absentia. Later the Spartans "send away" (*apostellein*) Brasidas with a force of Helots on a campaign to Thrace "above all because he wished it" (4.81.1). No sooner do we learn he was at home than we find out he has been "sent away," and we learn this well after he departs (4.70–81).

decide whether he should lead the army home, even though they are faraway from the situation at hand. Then when that situation worsens, and the threat from Syracuse and its allies demands immediate withdrawal, Nicias delays because of unfavorable omens. After yielding his judgment to the Athenian assembly, he then allows the gods, or rather the seers, to decide their fate. In doing so, he surrenders any last hope of homecoming, for both himself and his soldiers, just as he soon surrenders to the enemy. Their homecoming is thwarted not by the gods, as happens to many trying to return home from Troy in the poetic accounts, but by Nicias's ceding judgment first to the people and then to the seers. In doing so, he becomes unable to act, and so to return home. Homecoming, it turns out, must be earned, along with freedom. Nicias is not independent enough of his home to make it his own.

Thucydides criticizes both Nicias's subservience to his city and its gods (the seers) and also Alcibiades' godlike hubris. Both consequently have difficult relations with their city, one because of his dependence, the other because of his independence. Whereas Nicias does not avail himself of the freedom that Athens makes possible, Alcibiades does not appreciate the extent to which his freedom depends on Athens's regime. Pericles, who asks Athenians to become lovers of their city (2.43.1), connects freedom with Athens's regime rather than with a liberation of *erōs* for the faraway. He has an appreciation of Athens as a free regime that he shares with Thucydides (see 8.68.4).

In my concluding chapter, I discuss the ways in which Thucydides reconciles being a historian with being an Athenian, or the freedom implied in pursuing the truth with having a home. Thucydides includes two digressions in his work, both involving Athens's past, which play no necessary part in the events of the war that he recounts. One concerns the mistaken belief about Aristogeiton and Harmodius, whom Athenians incorrectly regard as freeing their city from tyranny (6.54–61); the other recounts the accusations of treason made against the Athenian leader Themistocles and his exile in Persia (1.128–38). Scholars have found these digressions gratuitous and irrelevant. But in each Thucydides looks back to the past, the past of his own city, as if reflecting on the relevance of the past to the present, and of a city's past to its identity. Thucydides in this way reflects on the relevance of his own history of the war to future generations, and to his own identity as an Athenian who records his city's history. Insofar as they are digressions, they belong to Thucydides more than do other speeches he includes in his history. Moreover, Thucydides' story of Themistocles provides a model of an Athenian who, like Thucydides, remains an Athenian in spite of his distance from his city.

Thucydides identifies himself as an Athenian when he mentions his writing up the war, as we have seen. However, he identifies himself by his patronymic—the son of Olorus—only when he discusses his own military command during the war (4.104.4). After that command, and his own failure to relieve Amphipolis, Thucydides tells us, he is exiled, and he remains in exile for twenty years. That Thucydides holds a command for his city in the war strengthens Hegel's including him among the "original historians," who "have themselves witnessed, experienced and lived through the deeds, events, and situations they describe, who have themselves participated in these events." The "first concern" of the original historian, whose spirit is the same as the events he relates, is not "to reflect upon his subject; for he is immersed in the spirit of the event he describes, and does not rise above it to reflect upon it."[29] That Thucydides' primary political deed is one for which he is exiled lends Hegel's position on Thucydides a certain irony. The surrender of Amphipolis, Thucydides tells us, causes "great fear" among the Athenians in part because of the material resources of Amphipolis, in part because of its strategic location, and in part because of the symbolic value of Brasidas's success in liberating such an important city from Athens's yoke. And, indeed, revolts of other cities from Athenian rule follow (4.108.1–3). Thucydides' failure to act facilitates Brasidas's blow for freedom. By the time Thucydides arrives with his fleet to protect Amphipolis, the city has already surrendered to Brasidas.[30] Thucydides' pace at sea is more reminiscent of the Athenian ship that carries the order to destroy Mytliene than of the ship sent to countermand that order (3.49.4).

Thucydides' exile from Athens after his command at Amphipolis allows him "to be present at the actions of both sides, especially of the Peloponnesians," and thus "to perceive more" about the events of the war than he otherwise would have done (5.26.5). His exile thus facilitates his gathering of materials for his history. Like Alcibiades, he is an exile who does not hesitate to go among the Peloponnesians when it suits his broader purpose. Like Brasidas he has a mission that leads him away from his city. His whereabouts in his travels he leaves mysterious, although he goes wherever he can discover the truth.[31] Unlike Brasidas, however, whose mission of liberation

---

29. Georg Wilhelm Friedrich Hegel, *Lectures on the Philosophy of History: Introduction*, trans. H. B. Nisbet, with an introduction by Duncan Forbes (Cambridge: Cambridge University Press, 1975), 12–14.

30. Not only does Thucydides arrive late for a battle (see Shakespeare, *Henry IV, Part I*, act 4, scene 2), but he arrives too late for there to be a battle.

31. Ronald S. Stroud argues that Thucydides was in Corinth for a considerable period during his twenty-year exile, detailing the specific information Thucydides has about the events of the war

contravenes the politics of his city, Thucydides' mission of liberation is one that grows out of being an Athenian and is consistent with identifying himself as one. Whether or not he returns to Athens after his exile, by writing about the war he is able to achieve Alcibiades' goal of repossessing his city, but in a way that preserves rather than destroys its identity. That is because the "possession" he acquires is not merely his city, as Alcibiades sought, but his work that as a "possession for all time" he shares with others, in whom his memory of Athens will endure.

---

in which Corinth was involved. "Thucydides and Corinth," *Chiron* 24 (1994): 267–304. This does not preclude other travels. After all, he claims to have been present with "both sides" during his exile. Inasmuch as he was exiled from Athens, he lets us suspect that he accompanied some of the Athenians on their military expeditions. Strauss too appears to be interested in Thucydides' travels, as when he observes that Thucydides has access to an oral tradition about Athens's past that is "not accessible to every Athenian," and indicates that there may be evidence for that tradition among the Persians. *City and Man*, 197.

❧ CHAPTER 1

Periclean Athens and an Image of Freedom

Pericles has impressed many readers of Thucydides as the greatest statesman of his history. After all, Thucydides describes him as "the first man among the Athenians at the time, ablest in both speaking and acting" (1.139.4). Pericles' preeminence in Athens is reflected in his preeminence in Thucydides' history. For example, Thucydides has Pericles deliver the most famous speech of his history, the funeral oration for the Athenians who fell in battle during the first year of the war. Thucydides here gives Pericles the privilege of describing Athens—its regime and way of life—for which it will be remembered, and for which he claims it is worthy of being remembered for all time. Pericles is also the only one whom Thucydides allows to speak uncontested in Athens. Cleon is paired with Diodotus in the Mytilene debate, for example, and Nicias with Alcibiades in the debate over the Sicilian expedition.[1] When Thucydides announces Pericles' death, moreover, he delivers a sort of eulogy to the Athenian leader. For example, he praises "the foresight" of Pericles' war policy—that Athens rely on sea power and not undertake, while at war, new conquests to extend

---

1. Hornblower notes that Cleon was active in Athenian politics before Pericles' death, but that Thucydides does not give Cleon a speech while Pericles is still alive. *Thucydides*, 55. See also Gribble, *Alcibiades and Athens*, 173.

its rule. Pericles' foresight is appreciated all the more, Thucydides claims, when Athens later suffers the consequences of deviating from his advice (2.65.6). Had Pericles lived, Athens might have won the war.

Others argue that Thucydides is critical of Pericles. Pericles' very pre-eminence in fact appears at odds with democratic politics. S. Sara Monoson and Michael Loriaux, for example, argue that Pericles' support for Athenian imperialism undermines both the ideal of Athenian citizenship as reciprocal exchange and also the norms of moral conduct necessary in international affairs as a support for prudent action.[2] Gerald M. Mara argues that the thrust of Pericles' rhetoric is toward creating a political identity that lasts forever rather than toward developing judgment "as a democratic good."[3] So too Arlene W. Saxonhouse questions Pericles' vision of a unified city, which is hostile, she argues, to the diversity characteristic of communal delibera-tion and decision making.[4] These scholars understand Thucydides' Pericles to be in tension with Thucydides' own political thought, which is, as Mara for example argues, "less directive and more discursive; indeed, one that is potentially more democratic."[5]

Whereas this strand of scholarship understands Thucydides to criticize Pericles in the name of democratic freedom, others who offer a realist inter-pretation of Thucydides argue that he is skeptical of Pericles' "idealistic rhet-oric" and "high moral tone."[6] In praising Athens's politics and way of life and arguing that the city deserves to rule others, Pericles in this view dangerously misleads Athenians about themselves and their limits. Thus, according to Orwin, Pericles' presentation of the Athenian empire "as freely-chosen proj-ect" dresses it "in its Sunday best." From Thucydides' perspective, in contrast to Pericles', Athens's expansion due to the necessities of its situation would "vindicate [its empire] more convincingly if not more loftily than Pericles' vision of it as freely-undertaken." Even Pericles, according to Orwin, finally admits that for the sake of its own survival, Athens is compelled to take the

2. Monoson and Loriaux, "Illusion of Power," 285–97, esp. 287, 292, and 295.

3. Gerald M. Mara, "Thucydides and Political Thought," in *The Cambridge Companion to Ancient Greek Thought*, ed. Stephen Salkever (Cambridge: Cambridge University Press, 2009), 96–97, 105–7, 112, 115–16. Also Gerald M. Mara, *The Civic Conversations of Thucydides and Plato* (Albany: State University of New York Press, 2008), 114–16.

4. Arlene W. Saxonhouse, *Athenian Democracy: Modern Mythmakers and Ancient Theorists* (Notre Dame: Notre Dame University Press, 1996), 60–61. See her discussion of Pericles, 59–71.

5. Mara, "Thucydides and Political Thought," 116.

6. Peter R. Pouncey, *The Necessities of War: A Study of Thucydides' Pessimism* (New York: Colum-bia University Press, 1980), 100.

harsh actions necessary to maintain the empire.[7] After all, Pericles concedes that the Athenian empire is like a tyranny, and therefore it is too dangerous for the Athenians to let go (2.63.2).

Contrary to both the democratic and realist critics of Pericles, Thucydides presents Pericles as a model of statesmanship, even of leadership within a democracy, and freedom is central to that leadership in a variety of related ways. Most obviously, Pericles explains the Athenian regime and way of life in his funeral oration in terms of freedom, and the actions that are appropriate to freedom. Pericles both fosters freedom through his rhetoric and practices it in his deeds. This includes first and foremost the distinctively human freedom to become a cause of actions. However much the actions of human beings respond to circumstances—and Thucydides does not deny that they do—they also come "from within," as Pericles claims of Athenian courage. They are not merely compelled from outside. Freedom is a potential, not a necessity, although it is necessary for full humanity. It must be claimed, taken, and exercised. Freedom requires rule, of oneself and therefore of the circumstances with which one is presented, and to some extent of other human beings. "To rule" (*archein*) in one of its forms in Greek (*archesthai*) also means to begin or to initiate. Ruling is therefore the manifestation of freedom, even democratic rule in the assembly.

When Thucydides claims that with Pericles Athens is in name a democracy, but in fact "rule by the first man" (2.65.9), he is not criticizing Pericles for subverting Athenian democracy. Rather, as Yunis argues, Thucydides' statement is "a rhetorically clever way of impressing on the reader the extraordinary effectiveness of Pericles' leadership." When Thucydides says that Pericles "controlled the people with freedom" (*eleutheros*) (2.65.8), he means that Pericles ruled not by force, but by speech—"the only appropriate means for controlling a free people," who obey "only because, as befits free citizens, they are freely persuaded."[8] Thucydides presents Pericles as a model of the rule that is necessary for political life, even a democratic one, warning us that the "name" of democracy should not obscure this truth. Not only do the realists who emphasize the limits on action slight freedom; so do those who favor discursive or deliberative democracy, insofar as democratic consensus either eliminates or hides rule.

---

7. Orwin, *Humanity of Thucydides*, 27–29; Pouncey, *Necessities of War*, 101.

8. Yunis presents a good case that "with freedom" refers to both speaker and audience. He contrasts Thucydides' description of Pericles with the Thebans' statement that tyrants control the people "by force" at 3.62.4. *Taming Democracy*, 68–69 and 69n24.

In this chapter, I explore how Thucydides' presentation of Pericles sheds light on Thucydides' own view of the possibilities and limits of human freedom. I begin with the Athenians blaming Pericles as the cause of the war, after they experience its hardships (2.59.2). The issue of the war's cause is prominent in book 1, and therewith the question of whether humans are controlled by necessity or are free to choose their courses of action. Pericles does not deny the people's charge, but in fact claims that they too are responsible for agreeing to go to war when he urged them to do so. To deny responsibility is to abdicate freedom, but freedom is the condition of human excellence. If one cannot be blamed, one cannot be praised (see Aristotle, *NE* 1109b30–33 and 1111a29–31). I explore the extent to which Thucydides presents Pericles as the cause of the war, and argue that Thucydides shows the truth in the people's reproach, although that showing entails praise as well as blame.

I then turn to Pericles' funeral oration, in which Pericles praises Athens for exercising the very freedom to rise above necessity that is implied in praise and blame. In the third section of this chapter, I discuss Thucydides' account of the plague that devastates Athens, and Pericles' response to Athenian suffering in his final speech in Thucydides' work. Scholars have long noted Thucydides' striking contrast between the noble Athens of the funeral oration and the slavish degradation to which many Athenians succumb during the plague. Thucydides' juxtaposition of the two, I argue, does not undermine the nobility of Pericles' speech, as many suggest, or indicate a tragic doom that follows Pericles' overreaching.[9] Rather, Athens's failure to live up to Pericles' vision highlights that vision, giving it a luster or splendor even as so many Athenians fall short. The sufferings of the plague, Thucydides observes, were more than human nature could endure (2.50.1). So too is the image of Athens in Pericles' speech more than the Athenians can sustain. Finally, I discuss Thucydides' own eulogy to Pericles and his portrayal of Pericles as a model of freedom, a portrayal that includes blame as well as praise, as Pericles' own view of human freedom allows. The possibility of such freedom runs counter to the view of those who emphasize the compulsions and necessities of political life, and who criticize Pericles in Thucydides' name for unrealistically and dangerously idealizing Athens and its rule of Hellas. Contrary as well to those who argue that Thucydides makes a political critique of Pericles' politics, in the name of an ideal of

---

9. Francis M. Cornford, *Thucydides Mythistoricus* (Philadelphia: University of Pennsylvania Press, 1971; first published 1907, by Edward Arnold), 50. Also Parry, "Thucydides' Historical Perspective," 47; David Bedford and Thom Workman, "The Tragic Reading of the Thucydidean Tragedy," *Review of International Studies* 27 (2001): 51–67; and Shanske, *Thucydides and the Philosophic Origins*, 142.

reciprocal citizenship or of democratic deliberation and discourse, I argue that Pericles' politics as Thucydides presents it demonstrates the very possibility of the freedom required for deliberation and choice.

"Blaming" Pericles

After the Athenians have suffered from the plague and other burdens of the war, they blame Pericles as the cause (*aitia*) of the war and even attempt to negotiate peace with the Spartans (2.59.2). In book 1 of his work, as we have seen, Thucydides traces the war to the growth of Athenian power and Spartan fear that made the war necessary or inevitable (1.23.6). However, if the growth of Athenian power—and the consequent Spartan fear—made the war necessary, was the growth of Athenian power necessary? To what extent were choices the Athenians made responsible for the growth of Athenian power? And what were those choices? The Athenians' criticism of Pericles as the "cause" of the war—albeit in a time of suffering and anger—reopens the question of the war's inevitability.

When the Corinthians urge Sparta to go to war, they appeal to Athens's alliance to Corcyra and its siege of Potidaea as acts of hostility (1.68.4). Thucydides, however, does not present either as necessary. Athens's alliance with Corcyra and the subsequent naval skirmish alongside Corcyrean forces against Corinth both proceed from a decision made at Athens after an Athenian assembly has heard representatives from both Corcyra and Corinth. After the Corcyreans propose an alliance with Athens, the Corinthians urge Athens to reject such an alliance on the ground that it would be detrimental to the peace. Thucydides emphasizes that the decision might have gone either way by reporting that the Athenian assembly at first inclined against the alliance, changed its mind (1.44.1), and, meeting a second time, accepted Corcyra's proposal. Thucydides thus gives us the impression that the Athenians might have rejected the alliance, as at first they did. He gives us the reasons for the Athenian decision—that war with the Peloponnesians seemed to them to be coming, that they did not want the Corcyrean fleet to be taken by Corinth, that they wanted both Corcyra and Corinth to wear each other down, and that Corcyra was a useful ally because it was located on route to Italy and Sicily. But he does not give the speeches of those who spoke on either side, or even indicate who they were (1.44).[10] In spite of

---

10. In similar circumstances in Sparta, after the Corinthians urge Sparta to go to war with Athens and Athenians warn Sparta against doing so, Thucydides gives us another set of speeches, those of two Spartans, Archidamus and Sthenelaidas, on different sides of the issue (1.68–86).

the fact that Pericles was active in Athenian affairs for over three decades, Thucydides does not introduce him in his account of Athenian politics until just before the outbreak of the war.[11] Lattimore thinks that Plutarch's statement that Pericles was responsible for the Athenians' support of Corcyra is "probably correct."[12] Even apart from Plutarch, however, the opinions about the advantages of the alliance with Corcyra are consistent with the policies Thucydides attributes to Pericles once he introduces him into his history, such as his practice of recommending war against Sparta (1.127.3).

"Immediately" after the naval battle in which Athens fights with Corcyra against Corinth, the Athenians undertake measures against Potidaea, which lead to further conflict between Athens and Corinth. The Athenians demand that Potidaea, a Corinthian colony but tributary of Athens, pull down its fortifications, send hostages to Athens, and expel Corinthian magistrates there. Resistance by Potidaea and Corinthian forces who come to help leads eventually to the Athenian siege of the city. It is at this point that Corinth sends representatives to Sparta to press for war against Athens. Who among the Athenians are responsible for these measures concerning Potidaea? Again, Thucydides is silent about any particular Athenians involved, just as he is about those who support the alliance with Corcyra. No Athenian leaders are mentioned by name during this period, but events do not indicate an absence of direction. To the contrary, Athens's actions provoke war. According to Pericles, Athenians "have *compelled* every sea and land to be the highway of [their] daring" (2.41.4; emphasis mine). Athenians are the source of compulsion (see also 1.99.1). Thucydides observes that the Spartans are slow to go to war unless they are compelled (1.118.2).

The Spartans themselves understand the pivotal role Pericles plays in support of the war effort in Athens. Once the Spartans have voted to go to war, they send a message to the Athenians insisting that Athens drive out the descendants of those involved in an ancient curse in which Pericles' relatives were implicated. The Spartans do not believe, Thucydides tells us, that Athens will actually exile its leader, but rather hope to discredit Pericles in Athens by making the war "appear in part due to his misfortune" (1.127.1–2).

---

11. Thucydides does mention Pericles briefly in his account of the growth of Athenian power between the Persian and the Peloponnesian Wars (the approximately fifty-year period scholars call the "pentecontaetia" [1.89–117]), as a commander of Athenian troops in the field, but does not refer to any role in the decisions of the city (1.111, 114, 116–17). Westlake finds it "remarkable" that Thucydides "postpones so long the entry of Pericles." *Individuals in Thucydides*, 24–29.

12. Lattimore, *Thucydides*, 24, note on line 1.44; Plutarch, *The Lives of the Noble Grecians and Romans*, trans. John Dryden (New York: Modern Library, 1932), 204; Westlake, *Individuals in Thucydides*, 25.

As Palmer points out, one of the ways that Thucydides establishes "the importance of Pericles' presence in Athens at the beginning of the war" is through recounting this move on the part of the Spartans.[13] The Spartans are correct in singling out Pericles, Thucydides tells us, because he was "the most powerful man of his time in Athens, the leader of his regime, opposed the Spartans in everything, would never yield, and pushed the Athenians toward war" (1.127.3). Once he appears in Thucydides' history, he dominates Athenian politics, and Thucydides lets us infer how great his role has been by seeing how great his role is once he comes forward. By keeping Pericles in the background of the events leading up to the war, he enhances our sense of Pericles' control rather than dilutes it.

Among their other demands, the Spartans inform the Athenians that they can avoid war by revoking the decree that excludes Megara from the ports and markets of Athens (1.139.1). It is at this point that Pericles delivers his first speech to the Athenians in Thucydides' work. He insists that Sparta's demand that they revoke the decree is no "trivial" matter, but a test of Athens itself. If Athens yields on Megara, it will appear "slavish" and other demands will surely follow (1.140.4–141.1).[14] Pericles thus presents the war as a fight on the part of the Athenians to preserve their freedom, just as their fathers did against the Persians (1.144.4). Because Sparta has already voted to go to war, and refused Athens's offers of arbitration, "war is necessary," Pericles says. He also says that "it is necessary that [the Athenians] know" that war is necessary. Their knowledge should influence how they act. Without such knowledge of the war's necessity, the Athenians might not go to war. War is necessary to preserve their freedom. Therefore the "more willingly" (*ekousioi*) they accept the war, the sooner they will ward off the greatest dangers and achieve the greatest honors (1.144.3). While the Athenian envoys at Sparta explain the growth of the Athenian empire with reference to the "compulsions" of fear, honor, and advantage (1.75.3), Pericles' emphasis here is on honor. But to be

---

13. Palmer, *Love of Glory*, 15.

14. Monoson and Loriaux argue that "one thing, among others, that Pericles might have done otherwise" was to devise an honorable way to revoke the Megarian decree, which may well have forestalled or even prevented war, conveyed Athens's commitment to the Greek norm of independence of cities and to its treaty with Sparta, and challenged Sparta to reciprocate, while not foreclosing further measures against Megara if necessary. They speculate that Pericles did not consider these advantages because of his principled rejection of negotiation with Sparta and his hubristic refusal to reverse himself. "Illusion of Power," 293–94. For further discussion of Thucydides' treatment of the Spartan demand that Athens revoke the Megarian decree, see Orwin, *Humanity of Thucydides*, appendix 3, 215–16.

compelled by honor is not the same as to be compelled by fear. The former may entail, for example, risking one's life in order to manifest one's virtue or patriotism. It requires acting in spite of one's fear for one's life, or overcoming "compulsions" to which human beings are vulnerable. This "necessary" war, as Pericles presents it, is for the sake of freedom, voluntarily chosen. Only as a result will it bring the greatest honor.

Pericles, moreover, tells the Athenians that if they accept his recommendation for war, they are responsible just as much as he is. Indeed, he "holds it just" (*dikaioun*) for those persuaded now to support their common resolution later even if they meet setbacks, or else it is not just that they lay claim to the plan if it meets with success (1.140.1). One cannot claim credit for success if one does not also accept responsibility for failure. What Pericles tells the Athenians—those who are persuaded—of course applies to himself as well, the one who persuades them. It is a "common" resolution, and the responsibility is shared. Although Thucydides presents only Pericles' speech, he tells us that others spoke on both sides of the issue of the war before Pericles spoke (1.139.4). After Pericles speaks, Thucydides reports no divided vote, as existed among the Spartans on the question of the war (1.87.3). In contrast, "the Athenians, thinking that Pericles advised them best, voted as he advised them, and answered the Spartans as Pericles was minded, both on particular points and overall" (1.145.1). It is a unified city, if only for a moment.

When the Peloponnesians undertake their first invasion of Attica during the war, the Spartan commander Archidamus tries once more to prevent hostilities. The Athenians, however, do not admit his herald into the city, in compliance with Pericles' advice that no embassy be admitted from an enemy once he is in the field (2.12.1–2). When the Peloponnesian forces proceed to ravage the countryside, many in the city want to go out to fight, contrary to Pericles' policy to fight the enemy at sea rather than on land. Pericles refuses to call an assembly lest the Athenians "err by coming together in anger rather than in judgment" (2.21.3–22.1). Although Pericles' actions may seem authoritarian or undemocratic, Pericles refuses to allow the Peloponnesian herald to be heard and to call an assembly to discuss how to respond to the Peloponnesian attack in order to preserve the people's deliberation in the face of passions that arise in the heat of the moment.

In these various ways, Thucydides leaves ample room in his account for human control of events leading to the war, and even reason to attribute responsibility to Pericles, even when that responsibility is shared by those whom he persuades. Whether he "blames" Pericles in the same way the people do is another question, which involves Thucydides' view of whether Athens should go to war with the Peloponnesians, as Pericles believes, and his view of Athenian imperialism more generally.[15] We now turn to Pericles' funeral oration, which provides the clearest statement in Thucydides' history of Athenian nobility and freedom. The nurturing and survival of the excellence that Athens represents is the justification for its rule of Hellas and for war with the Peloponnesians.

Pericles' Funeral Oration

Pericles' daring is apparent from the very outset of his funeral oration. He begins by distinguishing himself from most of those who have given funeral orations in the past: whereas they praise the one establishing the law (*nomos*) that requires that a speech be given to honor the fallen, he himself thinks it sufficient that deeds—the elaborate public funeral—honor deeds.[16] The most famous speech in Thucydides' history thus begins by pointing out how much Athens relies on the power of speech. By finding fault with those who have praised the law when they delivered funeral orations in the past, Pericles finds fault with the law. Indeed, the law puts "the virtues of many" at risk, dependent on whether "one man speaks well or badly" (2.35.1). In attributing the law to the one who established it, Pericles calls attention to the fact that laws are made by human beings, whether well or badly, just as speeches are, and he even refers to "the one" establishing the law, not the many who might seem to be legislators in a democracy.[17] At the same time he speaks in defense of the many whose virtue the law puts at risk. His opening remarks set the tone for his speech: he shows little deference to the past, either to the law governing the occasion or to his predecessors who complied with it.[18]

---

15. For further discussion of choices that led to war, see Monoson and Loriaux, "Illusion of Power," 293; Lebow, "Play It Again Pericles," esp. 232, 242–48; Johnson, *Thucydides, Hobbes,* 34, 214.

16. A. W. Gomme points out that Pericles himself had been called on to deliver the funeral oration in the past, in 440 and 439 BCE. Gomme, *Historical Commentary on Thucydides* (*HCT*), with A. Andrewes and K. J Dover (Oxford: Clarendon Press, 1945–1981), 2:102. If Pericles' criticism of past speeches applies to his own as well as those of others, he is improving on his own past. He is like Athens itself.

17. Pericles' move here is reminiscent of Socrates' in the *Apology* when he cross-examines Meletus concerning his charge that Socrates corrupts the young. If Socrates corrupts the young, he asks Meletus, who improves them? When Meletus answers "the laws," Socrates explains that he is asking "what human being" does so. Both Pericles and Socrates highlight the dependence of law on human beings. When Meletus proposes that the jurymen, the councilmen, and those who sit in the assembly all improve the young, Socrates points out that in most human endeavors it is the one rather than the many who is able to improve human beings (*Apology* 24d–25b).

18. For discussions of these aspects of Pericles' oration, see Strauss, *City and Man,* 152; Palmer, *Love of Glory,* 21–22; Orwin, *Humanity of Thucydides,* 16.

Appearing to criticize the overreliance on speech, as opposed to deed, he in effect elevates his own speech above the law.

Of course, circumstances—that the speaker is Pericles—preserve the virtue of the fallen and thus the intention of the law. He is the one on whom their virtue now depends. He may seem to have an easy task, for unlike the Athenians who come forth to praise their city in Sparta, his task is to praise Athenians to Athenians (see Plato, *Menexenus* 235d and Aristotle, *Rhetoric* 1367b8–9). But his task, he says, is "difficult," precisely because he faces an audience composed of individuals with opposing expectations. Those who know the dead will think anything he says falls short of their deeds, while those who don't know them will never believe that their deeds could live up to Pericles' words about them. "Goodwill," on the one hand, and "envy," on the other, will question his credibility. Pericles' dilemma, as he presents it, is like that of one who tries to tell the truth about his own city, to both those who think that no words can capture its greatness, and those who believe, out of envy, that he exaggerates its virtues. And, indeed, as Pericles' speech unfolds, he himself faces this deeper dilemma, for he praises not so much those who fell in battle as Athens itself. As he says, he will delay praising the fallen soldiers until he has set forth the characteristic ways (*tropoi*) and form of government (or regime, *politeia*) by which Athens has come to its present greatness (2.36.4).

Athens's greatness has more to do with the present generation than with past ones. Although Pericles "honors our ancestors through memory," his expression of filial piety is brief. Our ancestors, he says, handed down the land on which they lived "in freedom" through a succession of generations.[19] Still "more" are the fathers of the present generation of Athenians worthy of praise, who acquired the empire in addition to what they received. But it is "we ourselves who are here," he says, who have so increased the resources of the city as to make it as self-sufficient as possible (*autarkestatē*) for war and peace (2.36.3). The present generation accomplished more than their ancestors, just as Pericles stands distinguished from the eulogists of the past who themselves gave too much credit to the past. Moreover, Pericles turns not only to the glorious present in contrast to the past, but from the war dead to his living audience, as he holds before them an image of their own deeds. It may seem that Pericles is flattering his addressees.[20] But here Pericles does not merely call forth his listeners' pride; he makes great demands on them.

---

19. Their "virtue" thus lies in preservation rather than in acquisition. See Aristotle's *Politics* 1277b24–25.

20. According to Orwin, Pericles' speech, "exalted and exalting," is "also an elegant piece of flattery." *Humanity of Thucydides*, 24. Monoson and Loriaux claim that Pericles "panders to the population." "Illusion of Power," 286.

Flattery makes the flattered complacent, but there is no complacency here (see 2.65.8). Athenians have much to live up to. Their virtue, for which they rely on themselves rather than on the compulsion of law, allows them to best their enemies in the field, as Pericles will soon claim. And anyone inactive in politics is regarded as useless (2.39, 2.40.2). Athens can therefore serve as a model (*paradeigma*) for others (2.37.1).

Pericles traces Athens's lofty independence to its democratic principles, which favor the many rather than the few. While treating all equally before the law in private matters, in the city's public affairs equality looks beyond wealth and birth to recognize virtue and accords it preeminence (2.37.1). Pericles' own preeminence by implication is consistent with Athens's democratic principles, indeed is due to them, although he does not say so.[21] Once he distinguishes himself from past orators, his emphasis is all on Athens, not on himself. The city seems like his beloved, and Pericles speaks as if he were one with the object of his love. After the opening lines of his speech, when he speaks in the first person, he often speaks in the plural.

We Athenians conduct ourselves with freedom, Pericles continues, in both our public and private affairs (2.37.2). Thus we differ from our opponents in the current war by opening our city to all rather than driving out foreigners, preventing no one from seeing or learning about our practices, even though others may benefit at our expense (2.39.1). So too in private life, neighbor does not become angry with neighbor for doing what he pleases (2.37.2). Athens's freedom is thus based on its strength, or self-sufficiency, which carries over into the lives of its citizens (2.36.3, 2.41.1). Athenians do not have to hide, and it is the strong that do not have to hide. They are law-abiding and heed the rulers and the laws, Pericles insists, in spite of his having begun his oration by criticizing the law concerning funeral orations and the one who made the law. Perhaps the Athenians with Pericles' guidance are selective concerning their laws and customs. Pericles now emphasizes that they follow especially the ones that are for the benefit of those who suffer injustice and the unwritten laws whose violation brings shame (2.37.3). Athenians are moved less by the fear of punishment from violating laws than

---

21. Edmunds, *Chance and Intelligence,* 52; Palmer, *Love of Glory*, 23. Saxonhouse points out that Pericles' "new democratic hierarchy sets Pericles on top." *Athenian Democracy*, 63. While this is true, it is only in his last speech, when blamed by the Athenians for the war, that Pericles reminds the people of his own abilities: inasmuch as they recognized his abilities when they accepted his advice about going to war, they should recognize them when he advises continuing it (2.60.7). That is, his outstanding abilities depend on the people for their success.

by their own sense of the shameful—and hence of the noble.[22] Moreover, as Pericles presents them, the Athenians are the protectors of those who suffer injustice; they right wrongs done to others. Pericles' presentation of Athenian virtue develops that of the Athenian envoys who defend their empire at Sparta. Even though the envoys place greater emphasis on fear in defense of their empire than Pericles does, they claim that the strong are worthy of their rule when they rule with more justice than they are required to do (1.76.3–4; also 1.77.1–2).[23]

With a glance at their opponents in the war, Pericles points out that Athens's more relaxed way of life leads its citizens to accept dangers just as readily as more laborious occupations practiced since youth, and more because of their characteristic ways (*tropoi*) than because of their laws (*nomoi*). It is in this context that Pericles refers to the virtue of the Athenians as coming from within themselves (2.39.1–4). So too do "we love beauty with thrift, and love wisdom [or philosophize] without softness" (2.40.1). We also offer relaxation from labor, he says, by instituting games and festivals all year round, while private buildings give daily delight (2.38.1). And because of our city's greatness, we draw the fruits of every land, the goods of which we enjoy with as much familiarity as our own (2.38.1–2).

Pericles began his speech with reference to those who may envy the virtues of the fallen, if they hear from him anything "surpassing their own nature" (2.35.2). But in his descriptions of the Athenian character there seems to be no room for envy, suspicion, or pettiness. When Pericles claims that Athens acquires friends by conferring rather than by receiving benefits (2.40.4), he describes a way of acting that Aristotle was to attribute later to greatness of soul (*NE* 1124b10–11). Whereas Aristotle describes an outstanding individual who possesses the peak of virtue (*NE* 1124a1), Pericles is referring to the Athenians in general. It is the Athenians themselves whom Pericles distinguishes "from the many," for "we alone are benefactors, not calculating advantage, but confident in our freedom" (2.40.4–5). Thus Athens is, as Pericles says, "worthy of wonder" (2.39.4).

Pericles' image of Athens is of a city for which an Athenian may give his life, and in doing so justify his life, as he becomes, as Pericles urges,

---

22. Comparing Pericles' reference to unwritten laws to Antigone's, Edmunds observes that for Pericles they "are sanctioned not by the gods but rather by an inner sense of shame at breaking them." *Chance and Intelligence,* 59.

23. The envoys call this virtue of the Athenians "equity" (*epieikeia),* foreshadowing Aristotle's later use of the word. Equity is a kind of justice, he says in the *Nicomachean Ethics,* that exacts less than is due (*NE* 1137a30–b2; also *Rhetoric* 1374a25–b2).

"a lover of his city" (2.43.1).[24] And it is in light of this city that Pericles praises those fallen in battle. He turns to them only after "the greatest part of the eulogy has been spoken" (2.42.2): the glory of those who are being buried is a reflection of the glory of the Athens Pericles has described, in whose service they have fallen. In light of their city, their deeds and their lives lose any other significance. Pericles offers no account of any specific deeds they undertook, or battles in which they fell, or anything specific that their deaths accomplished. They simply gave their lives for Athens. The funeral oration might have been delivered after any battle, in any year of the war. Even if they otherwise gave no signs of any merit, Pericles says, their final act was sufficient to efface evil with good (2.42.3).[25] They were men who, "even if they failed in some other effort, did not think it worthy to deprive the city of their virtue but rather offered it as their noblest contribution" (2.43.1–2).[26] These will be remembered always, having "the whole earth" as their tomb. Rather than being remembered merely by an inscription in their own land, they will have an unwritten memory in thought (2.43.2–3).

The lives—and deaths—of the fallen are in effect forgotten, as the tombs that hold their remains fade in time and significance, in contrast to the memory of an Athens for which countless gave their lives. That Pericles' eulogy requires a forgetting rather than a remembering becomes explicit when he addresses the parents of the fallen. Those still of childbearing age, he advises, must hope for others in their place who will help them "forget those whom they lost" (2.44.3; see Aristotle, *Rhetoric* 1365a31–32, 1411a2–4). Just as those who fell for Athens in the midst of "strength and common hope," Pericles says, experienced "an unfelt death," grief for the fallen must be replaced by hope. This is the only time that Pericles uses the word for "death" in the funeral oration. Death thus appears only when it is "unfelt." The funeral

---

24. For an excellent analysis of Pericles' appeal to Athenians to become lovers of their city, see Ludwig, *Eros and Polis*, 327–51.

25. When in Shakespeare's *Macbeth* the traitorous thane of Cawdor dies asking for pardon and with "deep repentance," Malcolm observes that "nothing in his life / Became him like the leaving it" (*Macbeth*, act 1, scene 4, 7–8). The same may be said of Macbeth himself, although he dies not with repentance but in unyielding resistance to his foes (see *Macbeth*, 5.7.79–80).

26. The word I translate as "contribution" is *eranos*, which was used to mean a meal to which one contributed a share and, by extension, any contribution. There is no evidence that the word is derived from the verb "to love" (*eran*), but Pericles' use of it in this context echoes his urging Athenians to become lovers (*erastai*) of their city. Connor's translation captures this: they brought "their contribution to the fairest of love feasts." *Thucydides*, 69.

oration in effect calls for a forgetting of death.[27] Pericles describes the memory and praise of the fallen—and the memory of Athens's daring—as "everlasting" (*aieimnēstos*), "ageless" (*agēraos*), and "eternal" (*aidia*) (2.41.4, 2.43.2). He is very close to saying "deathless," *athanatos*.

Thucydides confirms that Pericles' advice requires forgetting the present in light of the eternal when he has Pericles speak briefly to the widows of the fallen, and only "as much as it is of use." He advises them that their reputation is greatest when they have the least fame among men, whether for virtue or blame (2.45.2). By not appealing to their hope for other husbands, as he had appealed to the hope of the parents of the fallen for other children, Pericles acknowledges the limits of his rhetoric. Pericles closes his speech by asking his hearers to depart "having finished their lamentations" (*apolophuromenoi*) (2.46.2). But it is the women relatives, Thucydides had told us, who on such occasions "are present at the grave as mourners" (*olophuromenai*) (2.34.4–5). Thucydides asks his readers to hear the lamentations that Pericles himself must have heard on the occasion of his speech. By referring to the lamentations as complete when he ends his speech, Pericles cannot but evoke the sorrow from which they sprang. In this way, Thucydides allows the lamentations of the women to continue to echo after Pericles stops speaking.

The Plague at Athens and Its Effects

Thucydides offers no comment about the funeral oration, nor does he mention any reactions to it in the city. He proceeds to describe the plague that visited Athens at the time. Its form (*eidos*) was "beyond all accounting" or "beyond speech" (literally, "stronger than speech," *kreisson logou*), and its terrors and sufferings were "harsher than human nature could bear" (2.50.1). In his funeral oration, Pericles distracts his hearers from the bodies of the dead by appealing to their everlasting memories, as if speech were "stronger than death." Thucydides in contrast focuses his readers on the bodies of those suffering from the disease, describing the movement of the disease from the head to the extremities: from the high fever in the head, the bloody throats and tongues, the coughing in the chest and empty retching, the convulsions, burning bodies, unceasing thirst, and in some cases blindness and loss of the extremities, including private parts (2.49). Theirs was no "unfelt death." The plague afflicts its victims with "the inability to rest" (*hē aporia tou mē*

---

27. See Palmer, *Love of Glory*, 26; Orwin, *Humanity of Thucydides*, 19.

hēsuchazein) (2.49.6). Their condition mimics the restlessness the Corinthians attributed to the Athenians, who "are born to take no rest [*hēsuchia*] and allow none to others" (1.70.8–9).

The plague attacks not only the bodies of the Athenians but their character. Scholars have often noted "the brutal juxtaposition" between "the idealized image of Athenian patterns of life articulated in the funeral oration with the actual behavior of the Athenians during the plague."[28] Connor observes the stark contrast between the orderly ceremonies of the state funeral at which Pericles speaks and the shameless neglect of burial customs during the plague.[29] "The funeral customs [*nomoi*] previously observed were thrown into confusion, and each was buried in any way possible." Even "the most shameful burial practices" are resorted to (2.52.4). When Pericles concludes his funeral oration, as we have seen, he asks the Athenians to depart inasmuch as their lamentations have been made. He himself, he says, offers not lamentation (*olophuresthai*), but comfort (*paramuthesthai*) (2.44.1). But no comforts stop the laments now. During the plague, the laments (*olophureis*) of the dying are so great that the relatives caring for them are finally worn down from them (2.51.5). The dying are mourning themselves.

As if in answer to Pericles' boast that Athens's democratic "equality" allowed the virtuous to rise to prominence, the plague treats all alike, whether strong or weak, regardless of whether or not they receive care (cf. 2.37, with 2.51.3). As the disease spreads, in place of the liberal confidence and trust in the future to which Pericles appeals and the "common hope" (*koinē elpis*) for Athens that soldiers have even while giving their lives, we find hopelessness (*to anelpiston*) (cf. 2.40.5, 2.43.6, with 2.51.4). Whereas Pericles urges Athenians to place both their bodies and possessions in the service of their city, during the plague "they live for immediate enjoyment, supposing their bodies and possessions equally ephemeral." Far from "loving the noble [or, the beautiful]," "no one pursued the noble" during the plague, Thucydides observes, in fear of "perishing before achieving it" (cf. 2.53.3, with 2.40.1) And even worse, Athenians were not deterred from crime, supposing that they would perish before they could be brought to trial for their wrongdoing

---

28. Monoson and Loriaux, "Illusion of Power," 289; Palmer, *Love of Glory*, 32.

29. Connor, *Thucydides*, 63–64; Monoson and Loriaux, "Illusion of Power," 289; Palmer, *Love of Glory*, 32. Of course, even when abiding by its requirements Pericles himself criticized the law concerning funeral orations. June W. Allison shows connections between Thucydides' description of the plague and Pericles' first speech in Thucydides' history: "Pericles' Policy and the Plague," *Historia* (1st qtr., 1983): 14–23.

(2.53.2–3). The noble and free Athenians whom Pericles describes become ugly and base, and even slavish (see 2.61.3).

Although Thucydides' account of the plague is filled with such disappointing generalizations about the conduct of Athenians, he does mention several exceptions. Especially those who made claims to virtue, he observes, were out of shame "unsparing of themselves" in going to their sick friends (2.51.5). Their deeds, at the risk and in some cases at the cost of their own lives, make true their claims to virtue. Moreover, those who recovered from the disease, having knowledge of its horrors, all the more pitied the sick and the dying. They could be confident that the disease would not attack them again, "at least not fatally" (2.51.6). Their service to those most needy, in the defiance of the plague's horrors, may not entail the noble loss of life in the city's wars that Pericles claimed would be remembered for all time. But Thucydides does not fail to mention their deeds in a work that he thought worthy of being possessed forever (1.22.4).

That the Athenians do not succumb entirely to the plague allows Pericles to succeed in part in defending himself when the suffering Athenians blame him for the war and want to negotiate peace with Sparta. Addressing the Athenian assembly, Pericles does not deny the charge that he is the cause of the war. Indeed, he implies the truth of the people's claim, when he points out to them that they are in fact the causes of the war along with him, because they supported it as well (2.64.1) As John G. Zumbrunnen notes, Pericles "envisions, and demands that the Athenians recognize, a collective responsibility that follows from the decision to take a speaker's advice." It does not follow from this, however, that Pericles is "attempt[ing] to evade blame for his advice in the past."[30] Pericles is part of the collective—indeed, the one who persuaded the people. Emphasizing the reasons Athens should remain at war, he takes credit, and shares that credit. By manifesting his own confidence, he tries to restore the people's confidence and thereby soothe their anger (2.59.1–3). Just as Pericles presents Athens as a model for others to imitate, so he now presents himself as a model for the Athenians. While the Athenians have changed and regretted their decision to go to war because of their sufferings, Pericles remains "the same" and has not changed (2.61.2). While the Athenians are confounded by domestic afflictions and neglect the common safety, Pericles is "a lover of his city" (*philopolis*) (2.60.5).

---

30. John G. Zumbrunnen, *Silence and Democracy: Athenian Politics in Thucydides' "History"* (University Park: Pennsylvania State University Press, 2008), 100, 102; Palmer, *Love of Glory*, 16.

Pericles admits that he is inferior to none in knowing what must be done and interpreting it, but he also claims that he is speaking to a city that is likewise inferior to none. Indeed, the Athenians do not comprehend their own greatness: by commanding the sea, they in effect also command the land, and are thus able—although Pericles leaves this to his audience to infer—to rule the whole world. Having placed this vision of Athens's might before them, Pericles encourages them to resist their sufferings. The Athenians should not continue to negotiate with the Spartans for peace nor give any indication to them that they are weighed down by their present sufferings, he tells them, for "whoever is least pained in mind by disasters and most resistant to them in deed, both private individuals and cities, are the most excellent" (*kratistoi*) (2.64.6). Indeed, Athens "has the greatest name among human beings because it has not yielded to disasters and has expended the most lives and labors in the war" (2.64.3). Thucydides tells us at the beginning of the history how great was the suffering of the Hellenes during the war (1.23.1–3), but here Pericles interprets Athens's great suffering as a sign of its achievement.

Only if they use Pericles as a model can the distraught and suffering Athenians show themselves worthy of the rule they have achieved, and maintain both their rule and their freedom. It is Pericles who has resisted disaster by leading Athenian forces to attack the Peloponnesus even during the plague (2.56.3–4), and whose mind is not overcome by personal suffering as he addresses a despondent and angry populace. Although other sources tell us that Pericles lost his son and other relatives to the plague,[31] Pericles does not mention any personal losses in his defense speech, nor does he recount anything about his family's experience of the plague. He does not, metaphorically speaking, bring his family into court, to appeal to his audience's pity. In this he is like Socrates in Plato's *Apology*, but unlike Socrates he does not mention that he has a family and might have brought them forth but chooses not to. He does not, like Socrates, claim that he is descended "from human beings, not from rock or oak" (*Apology* 34b–d). He stands before the assembly, as self-sufficient as the city he describes in the funeral oration (2.36.3; see also 2.41.1).[32]

---

31. Plutarch says that Pericles' son Xanthippus died of the plague, as well as his sister and "the greatest part of his relations and friends." He did not betray his spirit under the burden of his misfortunes, Plutarch recounts, until he lost his last surviving son, at whose funeral he "burst into exclamations, and shed copious tears, having never done any such thing in his life before." *Lives*, 210. We find none of these personal details about Pericles in Thucydides' work.

32. "Self-sufficient" (*autarkēs*) occurs only four times in Thucydides' work, and twice it is used by Pericles in praise of Athens and its citizens (2.36.3, 41.1). Thucydides does not put as positive a

Thucydides reports the results of Pericles' speech: "with respect to the public matter his words persuaded them," and the Athenians cease trying to negotiate with the Spartans. But "with respect to the private [*idiai*]," they remain pained by their suffering, and their anger at Pericles does not cease until they fine him (2.65.2–3). On the one hand, Pericles is only in part able to overcome the overwhelming sufferings that the plague brought to the Athenians; they cannot conform to the model of himself that Pericles presents and think only of the city. On the other hand, if the people cease negotiating with Sparta because they are persuaded that Pericles is right about the war, what ground do they have for fining Pericles? For a man who is "above money" (2.60.6), moreover, and has already donated land and houses to the city (2.13.1), a fine may not be very significant, especially in light of the decision to continue the war. With the latter, the people have given Pericles what he most urges. Once their anger ceases, they choose Pericles as general again and turn "all their affairs" over to him (2.65.4). Whereas Pericles asks them to turn themselves over to the city by becoming its lovers, the people are willing to turn themselves over to Pericles. Pericles mediates their love or devotion to the city. The ways of the city that Pericles recognizes as worthy of love become manifest in his own ways. He has indeed sacrificed himself for his city. His ways are its ways, as he represents Athens to the Athenians.[33] He presents himself to the Athenians as unaffected by adversity, as above not only money but also personal grief and suffering. In his bearing before his city, if not in fact, he does not succumb to the plague.

Praising Pericles

Although the Athenians again trust their affairs to Pericles, and he remains active in Athenian politics for at least another year until his death, Thucydides does not recount any more of his speeches or deeds. Instead, almost immediately after Pericles' speech to the distressed Athenians, Thucydides announces his death and the loss to Athens it signifies. Monoson and Loriaux observe that the suddenness of Thucydides' announcement, and his silence about any

---

spin on the word as Pericles does. He lets the Corinthians use the word disparagingly of Corcyra in their speech at Athens in book 1 when they claim that Corcyra's "self-sufficiency"—which makes it independent of other cities—allows it to commit wrongs without being observed (1.37.3). The fourth occurrence of the adjective—and the only use of it by Thucydides himself as opposed to his speakers—is found in his description of the plague: "no body, whether strong or weak, proved self-sufficient" against the plague, but all succumbed (2.51.3).

33. Edmunds, *Chance and Intelligence*, 90.

other events in which Pericles may have been involved, let us "experience vicariously the shock and confusion that the Athenians of the period must have felt [with the loss of Pericles]."[34] Thucydides removes Pericles from his history as quickly as chance deprives Athens of his advice and leadership.

After announcing Pericles' death, Thucydides gives in effect a eulogy of his own to Pericles and to his leadership in Athens. He praises both Pericles' policy and his character. Pericles was able to guide the city both in peace and in war. He foresaw the city's power at the outset of the war, claiming that it would prevail if it promoted its navy and did not attempt to extend its rule. His "foresight," Thucydides says, became recognized even more after his death, when Athens did not abide by his advice (2.65.5–7). With Pericles in charge Athens might have succeeded against Sparta. Thucydides appeals to Pericles as a standard by which to measure his successors: his successors sought private gain and honor, competed among themselves to be first, flattered the people, and turned affairs over to their pleasure. In contrast to Pericles, who led the people, they were led by them. When Pericles perceived the people were emboldened by hubris, Thucydides recounts, his speech would strike terror in them, and when the people were unreasonably afraid he restored them to confidence. He was even able to contradict the people when they were angry, because his "worth and judgment" were manifest (2.65.8–10). Pericles' rule is thus characterized by balance or measure (*metrion*), both in his policies (2.65.5) and in the effect of his rhetoric on the people. Balance or measure also characterizes the Athenians he describes: "we love beauty without extravagance, and we philosophize without softness" (2.40.1). Thucydides underscores the difficulty of the balance when he says that Pericles advises the people to remain still, or at peace (*hēsuchazein*), when they are at war (2.65.7; so too at 2.22.1).[35] It is not surprising that his successors cannot live up to the measure that Pericles represents.

Monoson and Loriaux make a strong case that Thucydides largely criticizes Pericles in his history. According to their analysis, Thucydides questions

---

34. Monoson and Loriaux, "Illusion of Power," 290.

35. It is Thucydides who uses this paradoxical expression to describe Pericles' advice to the Athenians for the war (at both 2.65.7 and 2.22.1), in contrast to Pericles himself, who simply advises the Athenians not to undertake new conquests while at war (1.144.1). It is therefore Thucydides who reveals the difficulty inherent in Pericles' advice, almost as if the city had to move and to be at rest at the same time. See Shanske's discussion in *Thucydides and the Philosophic Origins*, 48–49. (Thucydides uses two different words for peace, *eirēnē* as well as *hēsuchia*, the former as a time when formal treaties are in place, the latter referring more generally to rest, calm, or the absence of turmoil. He does, however, contrast *hēsuchia* with war, at 1.72.1.) See also Monoson and Loriaux "Illusion of Power," 291n16.

Athenian imperialism and therefore Pericles' promotion of it. On the issue of empire, Pericles caters to the desires of the many, and is "a consummate follower." When Thucydides shows the extent that Pericles' choices contribute to the war, he means only to blame. So too do they understand Thucydides' description of Athens during the time of the plague as undercutting Pericles' image of Athens in the funeral oration. They acknowledge that Thucydides seems to praise Pericles, but they argue that appearances cannot be trusted in an era of corrosive skepticism such as Thucydides'. Indeed, Thucydides "dresses [images] up rhetorically as unchanging, inevitable realities" in order to later reveal them "to be mere social and intellectual constructs." The reader is consequently led to doubt "anything and everything that [he] may have previously accepted as knowledge, wisdom, or truth." If we are "alert" to the historian's methods, we will expect him to undermine his "explicit glowing appraisal" of Pericles. Thucydides' praise of Pericles thus belongs to his method of nurturing expectations that he later dashes.[36]

Monoson and Loriaux argue that Thucydides nevertheless holds that humanity depends on moral norms for "the necessary support of prudent conduct." They appeal to Thucydides' portrayal of the Sicilian leader Hermocrates as evidence: in his speech to the Sicilian cities at Gela in book 4, Hermocrates proposes Sicilian unity on the basis of "a set of shared norms [that] has evolved to facilitate interaction, deliberation, and the settlement of grievances." Whereas Pericles refuses to make concessions and disdains Athens's adversaries, Hermocrates evokes fear of Athens so that the warring Sicilian cities will band together in "meaningful negotiation" among themselves for the defense of Sicily.[37] This opposition between the two statesmen, they conclude, "contains a prescriptive lesson." Both Pericles and Hermocrates are realists. But unlike Hermocrates, Pericles fails to appreciate that power must sustain "the normative conditions for its intelligent and prudent application," and that the statesman must defend and indeed "craft" those norms.[38] Morality demands a utilitarian construction and maintenance of norms of international action necessary for survival.

Such a critique of Pericles gives little weight to the nobility or beauty in the image of Athens that Thucydides' Pericles presents. The nobility or beauty that Pericles attributes to Athenian politics enriches both a realist

36. Monoson and Loriaux, "Illusion of Power," 286, and 289–90.

37. Ibid., 292 and 294.

38. Although Monoson and Loriaux admit that Thucydides values Pericles' mastery in acquiring and applying power, the mastery they attribute to him is limited, inasmuch as they argue that Pericles' politics undermines the conditions necessary for the exercise of power. Ibid., 294–95.

concern for survival and a constructivist's recognition of the need to craft the norms conducive to survival, inasmuch as it turns attention to the character of what survives. A political community has a character or integrity, and its support may merit prudential calculation as much as does mere survival. This is what Pericles means by Athens's regime and way of life, as he explains them. As J. Peter Euben observes, "What matters to [Pericles] is less the fact of [his city's] mortality than what Athens achieves during its life and how it is remembered after its physical demise."[39]

In some ways, Hermocrates himself serves as a foil that brings out even more sharply Pericles' nobility. Thucydides gives a major role in Syracusan and Sicilian politics to Hermocrates—and he is the only Syracusan to merit three speeches in Thucydides' work—but his appeal is primarily to interest and fear. Because Athens wants the goods of Sicily, he tells the Sicilian cities at Gela, they should unite in resistance (4.61.3). Since peace is agreed by everyone to be best, Hermocrates asks, how can we not make peace among ourselves? Peace holds "honors and splendors of a less dangerous kind" (4.62.2; cf. 6.33.4, 66.34.4), he claims, using the word with which Pericles describes Athens's splendor or brilliance (*lamprotēs*) (2.64.5). But he does not specify what they are. The "best thing" is peace. His listeners should not overlook his words, but look to them for "their own safety" (4.62.2).[40] For Pericles,

---

39. J. Peter Euben, *The Tragedy of Political Theory: The Road Not Taken* (Princeton: Princeton University Press, 1990), 195; Parry, "Thucydides' Historical Perspective," 61.

40. Hermocrates is a shadowy figure in Thucydides' work, and Thucydides leaves it unclear as to whether his goals are anything grander than security and safety. Unlike his introductions of major Athenian leaders, Thucydides tells us little about Hermocrates (see 4.58.4, 6.32.3). When Athenagoras accuses Hermocrates and his faction of seeking power in Syracuse, Thucydides offers no speculation concerning the validity of his charge, and allows it to stand unanswered (6.382–84), Thucydides later mentions almost in passing that Hermocrates was exiled from Syracuse, but does not tell us any of the circumstances (8.85.3; cf. Xenophon, *Hellenica* 1.1.27–28). As to Hermocrates' aspirations for Syracuse, when he tells the Sicilian cities that Athens seeks their goods, he refers to them as "common property" (6.41.3)—surely an ominous statement. Moreover, Hermocrates does not blame those who are strong enough to rule others, only those who allow themselves to be subject to them (4.61.4). Whereas he encourages the Sicilian cities to unite against Athenian subjection, he tells the members of his own city that by resisting Athens they will gain the preeminence that Athens itself once gained by opposing Persian aggression (6.33.6). Syracuse, he suggests, will be the new Athens, the new empire (see also 6.11.2–4, 6.85.3). As Thucydides presents him, Hermocrates has privileged information from Athens about Nicias's reluctance to undertake the expedition to Sicily (6.34.6), and he deceives Nicias into delaying his army's retreat by pretending to offer friendly advice (7.73.1–3). Could Hermocrates be among those, Thucydides almost forces us to ask, who insist on Nicias's execution lest Nicias reveal those in Syracuse with whom he was conspiring (7.86.4)? For more positive assessments of Hermocrates, see Orwin, *Humanity of Thucydides*, 171; Burns, "Virtue of Thucydides' Brasidas," 508, 519; Pangle and Ahrensdorf, "Classical Realism," 31; Mara, *Civic Conversations*, 118–19.

in contrast, it is Athens's splendor and nobility that justify his appeal to the Athenians to become lovers of their city, and that he believes make Athens a model or example for other cities to imitate. To be sure, that model of a noble or beautiful Athens lives more in Pericles' speech than in Athens's deeds, as Thucydides presents them, and it is expressed more in Thucydides' Pericles than in the city he purports to describe—and interpret—to itself. When portraying Pericles, Thucydides makes an effort to preserve his nobility, for otherwise we could not understand Pericles, neither his words nor his deeds.

Consider Thucydides' sudden report of Pericles' death. Not only does Thucydides announce Pericles' death prematurely—inasmuch as Pericles remains active at least another year in Athenian politics—he also gives no details about Pericles' death. In particular, whereas other historians tell us that Pericles dies from the plague, Thucydides does not. Thucydides' avoidance of any account of the circumstances of Pericles' death does not simply quicken his presentation of the loss of Pericles, it also supports the image that his Pericles presents to the city of his own nobility or self-sufficiency. Dying of the plague is not a noble death (see Aristotle, *NE* 1115a33–b6). Had Thucydides revealed the circumstances of Pericles' death, he would have called attention to Pericles' vulnerability. He would have made clear that his statement that no one was able to resist the plague (2.51.3) includes Pericles himself.[41] By his silence about Pericles' sufferings, Thucydides imitates Pericles' deeds, as when Pericles avoids mentioning in his last speech his own losses during the plague. So too Thucydides' choice not to recount the circumstances of Pericles' death serves as a silent tribute to what Pericles accomplishes.

The effect of Thucydides' keeping Pericles in the forefront of his account only during this brief but crucial period at the beginning of the war is not to minimize Pericles' contribution but to concentrate it.[42] By leaving Pericles offstage as much as possible, Thucydides lets his power appear greater for its operation behind the scenes (as in the Corcyra and Potidaea affairs), and makes his preeminence shine forth when he does appear. No report of either mundane or routine events of the last year of his life or of the details

---

41. Once again, as with his account of the deaths of Pericles' relatives from the plague, Plutarch provides explicit detail about how the disease attacks Pericles, almost (but not quite) as graphic as Thucydides' own description of the effects of the disease on whomever it attacked. *Lives*, 211. Cf. Thucydides 2.49.

42. Shanske also calls attention to how Pericles enters and exits Thucydides' history, but understands Thucydides' purpose as dissolving identity over time rather than concentrating it in the present: "there is no telling where Pericles begins and ends." *Thucydides and the Philosophic Origins*, 150.

of his death diminishes Thucydides' beautiful image of Pericles. Thucydides captures Pericles in the briefest but noblest moment of his political life, just as Pericles' funeral oration captures Athens in a single moment, in a timeless image of beauty.[43]

In his last speech, as we have seen, Pericles tells the Athenians that they have complete control (or sovereignty, *kuriōtatoi*) over the sea, and can therefore go wherever they wish (2.62.1–2). The implication is clear: those who control the sea control the land as well. Future acquisitions can add nothing—at least nothing essential.[44] The city at the acme has nowhere higher to go. It is therefore not surprising that Pericles acknowledges that Athens may give way, for "all things naturally diminish," but if Athens does fall, the memory of its great power will remain for eternity, for those generations who come after (*epigignomenoi*) (2.64.3).[45] Later generations may remain at the peak, or they may fall from it, but they will always be generations that come after the present generation, epigones. At best they can reach a height that others have reached. It is therefore not surprising that in the last speech of Pericles that Thucydides records, which is in effect his "defense" speech to the Athenian people, Pericles urges his addressees to prove themselves equal to their fathers, and is silent about their superiority to them. He even tells them it is more shameful for them to be deprived of what they have than to be frustrated in acquiring (2.62.3).

Pericles has been criticized for neglecting the future, insofar as he leaves the good of Athens dependent on chance. For example, did Pericles expect that Athens without his leadership could maintain the difficult balance between refraining from foreign conquests and engaging in war?[46] Thucydides indicates his concern for the future in the context of praising Pericles himself, as we have seen, by describing his successors and the ways in which they fall short of Pericles. Thucydides' writing, like Pericles' memory of Athens, will be an eternal possession, but it is one that looks forward to its utility over time, for the events of the future will resemble those of the past. They

---

43. Consider too Pericles' reference to the last deed of those who fell in war: "in the briefest moment" (*di' elachistou kairou*), "at the acme of their reputation" (2.42.4).

44. Pericles' allusion to absolute Athenian dominion therefore is not a deviation from his cautious advice against expanding the empire while Athens is at war.

45. Connor suggests that with these words, Pericles "writes Athens's epitaph." *Thucydides*, 71.

46. Palmer, *Love of Glory*, 39; Forde, *Ambition to Rule*, 8; Strauss, *City and Man*, 153. Thucydides has Pericles himself suggest an awareness of the difficulty, when he criticizes the law that establishes a funeral oration for those who fall in war: the law makes too much depend on one man, the man who is called on to deliver the speech.

will not necessarily be inferior to those he narrates. That the preparations of Athens and Sparta for war were at their peak at the outset of the war (1.1.1) does not mean that human history has achieved a peak.

Pericles and Thucydides

Thucydides' greatest tribute to Pericles may be the extent to which he presents him as his own model in writing his history. Just as Pericles claims that he is inferior to no one in being able to know what is required (*ta deonta*) and to explain or interpret it (*hermeneuein*) (2.60.5), so does Thucydides claim that he composes the speeches of his history according to what is required (*ta deonta*) by the circumstances (1.22.1). He allows Pericles to declare that explaining something is as great an ability as knowing it. Pericles' rhetoric about the past in his funeral oration resembles Thucydides' explanation of his own work. Just as Pericles boasts of the accomplishments of the present generation in contrast to those of his "ancestors" and "fathers," Thucydides describes the Hellenes who undertook the expedition to Troy, as well as the generation closer in time who resisted the Persians. Both of these generations fall short of the living generation, Thucydides claims, those who have brought the preparations for war to their height. And just as Pericles distinguishes himself from past speakers, who praised the custom they were following, Thucydides distinguishes himself from others in the past who praise the Hellenes and their exploits, such as Homer and Herodotus. Like Pericles, he criticizes the fabrications of poets (2.41.4, 1.21.1), and also offers the truth as "an everlasting memory" (2.43.2, 1.22.4). Both offer proofs and evidence for the greatness they describe (*sēmeia*, 2.41.4, 2.42.1, 1.21.1; and *tekmēria*, 2.39.2, 1.21.1). In offering an approach that differs from that of the poets and chroniclers of the past, and that will have greater credibility than theirs, Thucydides too is characterized by judgment and daring. He also follows Pericles in offering the world a lasting memory of Athens.[47]

Lowell Edmunds argues that "of all the speakers and actors in his History, it is really only Pericles whose views resemble Thucydides' own." Pericles, representative of a "new humanism and secularism" in Athens, is the spokesman for intelligence and art in Thucydides' history, which "bears the stamp

---

47. For further parallels between Pericles and Thucydides, see Leo Strauss, "Thucydides: The Meaning of Political History," in *The Rebirth of Classical Political Rationalism*, ed. Thomas L. Pangle (Chicago: University of Chicago Press, 1989), 88; *City and Man*, 158–59; Euben, *Tragedy of Political Theory*, 193; Parry, "Thucydides' Historical Perspective," 61; Edmunds, *Chance and Intelligence*, 201–4; also 67; Gribble, *Alcibiades and Athens*, 205.

of these principles." Consistent with his secularism and humanism, according to Edmunds, Pericles "never mentions a god or the gods." The apparent exception proves the rule: when Pericles details the city's financial resources as it faces war, he refers not to Athena but to her gold-covered statue. Indeed, as Pericles says of the statue, the "forty talents of refined gold" with which it is plated are "all removable" (2.13.5). Moreover, the only time Pericles refers to "*ta daimonia*" he speaks, according to Edmunds, "with doubtful piety."[48] Perhaps this is because Pericles' reference to "daimonic things" alludes to the plague (2.64.2). As Strauss observes, Thucydides leaves it open whether the word signifies "happenings of non-human or superhuman origin" or whether the word "is best understood as synonymous with 'natural.'"[49]

If Thucydides leaves it open, however, Pericles may as well. Pericles is, after all, the one who commissioned the statue of Athena and had it adorned with gold. He consoled the Athenians with the thought that if their resources ever made it necessary, they could use Athena's gold, but he is quick to assert that if they do so they must restore it later (2.13.5). Pericles thus reminds the Athenians of the limits of their resources, of the "divine" help they hold in reserve, and their obligation to return what they deplete. Even if Thucydides' Pericles rejects the gods, Strauss holds back from ascribing Pericles' treatment of the gods to Thucydides himself, even contrasting Pericles with Thucydides, who says "quite a few things about gods and sacred matters in his narrative of the plague, which immediately follows on Perikles' Funeral Speech," as well as elsewhere.[50] Thucydides describes the erosion of piety in Athens during the plague (2.53.4). It is when he observes that the plague did not enter the Peloponnesus to any extent worth noting that he mentions the oracle that promises the Spartans that the god will assist them in their war

---

48. Edmunds, *Chance and Intelligence*, 209–10, 76. Orwin argues that Pericles "presents Athens as the first 'atheistic' society." According to Orwin, Pericles' Athens "can dispense with the gods," for "the empire renders them superfluous, by satisfying, without reference to the divine, the deepest longings," conferring "ageless life on each whose radiant virtue shines through." *Humanity of Thucydides*, 20. Of course, Pericles' Athens is not identical to the Athens Thucydides portrays throughout his history.

49. Leo Strauss, "Preliminary Observations on the Gods in Thucydides' Work," *Interpretation* 4, no. 1 (1974): 1.

50. Ibid., 2. In this later work, Strauss corrects an earlier lecture he gave on Thucydides, in which he says that "Pericles observes, just as Thucydides himself, icy silence about the gods." "Thucydides," 88. In Pangle's introduction to the volume of Strauss's work in which this essay appears, he warns the reader that Strauss's lecture on Thucydides, which presents him as "the greatest pre-Socratic political theorist," "must be supplemented, and even corrected, in light of Strauss's later, mature, published comparisons between Thucydides and Socratic political rationalism." Introduction, xxxi–xxxii.

with Athens (2.54.4–5). Thucydides nevertheless does not blame the gods for the plague, but claims not to know its causes. He must leave it to others "to say if they know where the plague came from," and "what causes" could bring about "so great a disturbance" (2.48.3). Thucydides can describe only what the plague is "like." He does not know its causes, and in his experience of the plague he has encountered what is "beyond speech" or "beyond reason" (2.50.1).

By showing that Athens at the time of the plague falls far below the beautiful city that Pericles describes, Thucydides suggests that the beautiful is an abstraction from the deeds of life. Human life becomes manifest only in time, and is consequently always incomplete or imperfect. The beautiful cannot be simply identical with the true. Palmer observes that Pericles is correct that Athens needs no poets to beautify her, inasmuch as his own "paean to Athenian daring" in his funeral oration "does the job."[51] In this, Pericles performs the task of a poet, "delighting for the moment" (2.41.4), even if it is a moment that he imagines enduring for eternity. Thucydides' Pericles replaces the poet he criticizes. The historian Thucydides, in contrast, records what happens, and thereby reveals both Pericles' idealization of Athens in his funeral oration as well as the plague that follows.[52] In demanding the beautiful, Pericles demands too much of his city—and also of himself. In contrast to Thucydides, however, he demands too little, for Thucydides shows the human without undermining the beautiful. That is why he does not explicitly criticize Pericles.

Pericles is therefore wrong when he says that he is inferior to no one in knowing what is required and interpreting it (2.60.5). Unlike Pericles, who leaves the individuals who fell in the war anonymous, and praises them only in light of the city for which they gave their lives, Thucydides refers to many individuals—on both sides—by name, and allows us to judge cities by their leading men. Unlike Pericles, who neglects to provide for Athenian leadership after his death, Thucydides tells us immediately about Pericles' successors, who not only fail to live up to the standard that Pericles sets but also do great damage to the city. Thucydides does not end his writing about the war with the death of Pericles. He does not present a simply noble or beautiful city in describing Athens, but a city that fails, and even defeats itself. He calls himself an Athenian, but his view of Athens does not abstract his city from time and failure.

---

51. Palmer, *Love of Glory*, 24–25.
52. Mara, "Thucydides and Political Thought," 104.

Thucydides captures his superiority to Pericles by one small fact, which emerges during his account of the plague, and which is consistent with their different attitudes toward the lamentations of the women for their dead at the time of the funeral oration (that is, Pericles dismisses all lamentations as complete and Thucydides refers to those of the women in particular). Unlike Pericles, who is silent about his own suffering from the plague, Thucydides tells his readers that he can describe its course because not only did he see others suffering from it but he himself had the disease (2.48.3). Like a true Athenian, as Pericles presents him, Thucydides does not have to hide. He does not have to hide his own weakness. Pericles conceals his. That is, in presenting an image of Athens. Thucydides demonstrates a freedom even greater than Pericles', for he speaks without any pretense of self-sufficiency.

❧ CHAPTER 2

Athenian Freedom in the Balance

Mytilene and Plataea

Mytilene, a city on the island of Lesbos, off the coast of Asia Minor, long chafed under Athenian rule. With Athens weakened from the plague and the ongoing war, the Mytileneans revolt. Although Athens allowed Mytilene greater scope than its subjected allies—in fact, the revolting Mytileneans admit that they are "in name autonomous and free" (3.10.5, 3.36.2, 3.39.2)[1]—Mytilene seeks greater freedom from Athens and rule over the island of Lesbos (3.2.3). Although the Spartans promise aid, the city falls to Athens before help arrives. Sending the Mytileneans whom he holds most responsible for the revolt to Athens as prisoners, the Athenian commander Paches requests instruction about how to proceed with the captured city (3.1–19, 3.25–35). The angry Athenians decide to execute not only the prisoners but all the men of Mytilene, and to enslave their women and children. They immediately dispatch a ship to Mytilene carrying these orders. At least some of the Athenians soon experience "regret," concerning their "savage" decision "to destroy a whole city" (3.36.4). When the question

---

1. Cleon, who speaks for harsh punishment of Mytilene in the Athenian assembly, mentions that unlike subjected cities, the Mytileneans kept their own fortifications and their own ships, lived "under their own laws [*autonomoi*]," and were honored by the Athenians (3.39.2). Of course, he is attempting to present the circumstances of their rebellion in a way that justifies the harsh punishment he recommends.

of the treatment of Mytilene is reopened in the assembly, Cleon and Diodotus come forward to speak on different sides of the issue, the former in support of the harsh expedient, the latter in favor of leniency.

By recording the speeches delivered after the initial decision was made,
Thucydides indicates that the vote could go either way: the Athenians have
already taken one vote, and now they are reconsidering. He thereby suggests
that speech matters, that at least some of the Athenians are listening to what is
said, and that it will influence their vote. Although Thucydides has included
opposing speeches in his history previously, and mentioned cases in which
Athenians debated in the assembly (1.44.1 1.139.4), this is the first time he
records two Athenian speeches on opposite sides of an issue. In this way,
Thucydides highlights the importance of the Mytilenean debate. Deliberation allows choice. It frees human beings from compulsion, whether coming
from their passions and interests, or from the circumstances to which they
react. Minds have changed, and minds are changed. This happens in Athens,
and it proceeds from Athenians themselves. As we have seen, Thucydides
claims that Pericles ruled the people "with freedom" (2.65.8); that is, they
were persuaded to follow his advice rather than forced into action. Now we
glimpse another, perhaps greater, expression of freedom in the reflection and
deliberation that occur in the Athenians' treatment of Mytilene. Thucydides
not only shows us this potential but also suggests the problems that militate
against its development, including the power and appeal of men like Cleon.
Cleon, the first speaker in the Mytilenean debate, who is "the most persuasive among the people," is also "the most violent [or forceful, *biaiotatos*] of
the citizens" (3.36.6).

Cleon uses his speech as an opportunity not only to support punishing
Mytilene but also to denounce the defects of democracy, specifically, the
endless speech and indecisiveness endemic to democratic government
(3.38.7–39.1). The Athenians, after all, are reconsidering their decision against
Mytilene. Diodotus answers Cleon by defending the role of speech in a
democracy, for great matters require deliberation many times over. Haste and
anger impede good counsel (3.42.1). Accordingly, Mara understands Diodotus's speech as a "contribution to the democratic good of critical *logos*."[2]

Against Cleon's appeal to the justice of retaliation, Diodotus argues that
the Athenians should consider what treatment of Mytilene will be to their
advantage in dealing with future revolts. He argues, in effect, that leniency

---

2. Mara, "Thucydides and Political Thought," 118. Saxonhouse suggests that "Diodotus is the
true democratic theorist from antiquity." *Athenian Democracy*, 75.

is the best policy. In the first place, the prospect of harsh punishments will not deter rebellion when the greatest things—freedom and rule—are at stake, and when human beings are ruled by *erōs* and hope. In the second place, if rebellious cities know that their destruction follows their failure, they will fight until the end. Lenient treatment, in contrast, will make friends of the ones spared, and teach other rebellious cities that surrendering can lead, if not to reconciliation, at least to survival. Diodotus's account of the power of the passions, I argue, far from excusing the excesses they might provoke, aims at moderating the passions of the Athenians in order to make space for thought and deliberation. Whatever compulsions moved the Mytileneans to act, the Athenians must take time to deliberate, and even to rethink, rather than act out of anger. Deliberation gains distance from the compulsion of passion. The Athenians are responsible for their treatment of Mytilene.

Diodotus is an advocate of democratic politics and discourse, but he insists that the people require the guidance of leaders, who see further than others, and who accept accountability, even when it is dangerous to do so (3.42.3–43.4). The Athenian virtues of daring and judgment that Pericles praises remain at work in Diodotus's politics. Diodotus, like Pericles himself, intervenes in the affairs of his city to remind his addressees of their better selves and therefore to offer them appropriate reasons for action.

After discussing the debate in Athens concerning Mytilene, I turn to events surrounding the fall of Plataea to the Spartans and their allies, with which Thucydides intersperses his account of Mytilene's fall to Athens. By this juxtaposition, Thucydides gives us the opportunity to compare the actions of the antagonists in the war. How Sparta treats the fallen city of Plataea leads us to appreciate all the more how Athens treats Mytilene. There is also a debate at Plataea over how a city should be treated when it surrenders. That debate occurs before Spartan judges who listen to the case the Plataeans make for lenient treatment for themselves and the case that the Thebans make for their punishment. Thucydides agrees with the Plataeans that the debate between them and the Thebans does not affect what the Spartans do: the Spartans have already decided to gratify the Thebans, whose support they need against Athens (3.68.4). The real issue is advantage, not justice, an advantage already determined by Sparta's need of the Thebans. There is no deliberation. Speech makes a greater difference for Athens than for Sparta in determining actions. Whereas Thucydides records several further speeches at Athens, and reports even more instances of differences of opinion, there are no speeches of Spartans at Sparta once the war begins. Indeed, the only speech Thucydides lets us hear at Sparta after book 1 is that of the Athenian Alcibiades, who comes there to betray his city.

Thucydides juxtaposes not only the debate over Mytilene with that over Plataea, but Sparta's failure to help Mytilene with Athens's failure to aid Plataea. There are differences in the responses of the two more powerful cities. Athens's failure to aid Plataea follows from the military strategy Pericles thought necessary to win the war. In spite of the freedom of which Athens boasts, Thucydides thus reminds us of the extent to which Athens, like other cities, is constrained by external circumstances. Thucydides presents Sparta's failure to aid Mytilene, in contrast, as one of daring and judgment. Spartans do not exercise the freedom that they have to act even when it is in their own interest to do so. Because Athens's virtue is limited by necessity, it is not entirely responsible for Plataea's fall. Sparta's lack of virtue, in contrast, contributes to Mytilene's fall to Athens. Had there been a Diodotus in Athens who wanted to save Plataea, like the one in Thucydides' work who did save Mytilene, he would have found it more difficult to urge the Athenians toward action. But a Diodotus among the Spartans at Plataea would be out of place, for the Spartan judges are there not to deliberate, or even to judge, but to condemn. Diodotus is an Athenian, whose intervention in Athenian politics, like Pericles' funeral oration, presents the Athenians with an image of freedom. His appearance in Athens, and in Thucydides' history, is only momentary. Athenian freedom hangs in the balance. But freedom always does.

Cleon's Speech against Mytilene—and against Athens

In the "Mytilenean debate," as scholars refer to it, Thucydides gives us the first speeches by Athenian leaders after the death of Pericles. Thucydides prepares us to see a decline in Athenian politics when he contrasts Pericles with his successors (2.65.10). Cleon is the Athenian politician who becomes predominant from the third through the fifth books of Thucydides' history. Cleon, it seems, represents that decline: Thucydides introduces him as "the most violent of the citizens" and "the most persuasive among the people" (3.36.6; also at 4.21.3).[3] A man may be violent in his actions and persuasive in his speech, and politics may require both. But the very speech that

---

3. The only other man Thucydides calls "violent" is the Spartan Pausanias, who betrays his city to the Persians in an earlier period (1.93.1). Pausanias has such a harsh disposition, Thucydides says, that "no one was able to go near him" (1.130.2). The Corinthians call the Corcyreans "violent" (1.40.1), a judgment borne out by the civil war that takes place among them. Other usages of "violent" in Thucydides' history refer to specific deeds (e.g., 6.54.4, 8.48.6, 8.66.2), and even to war itself (3.82.2), rather than to an individual or a people.

Thucydides has Cleon give undermines the legitimate role for speech in democratic government. In attacking speech itself, Cleon subverts the very distinction between persuasion and violence or force.[4]

The "violent" Cleon advocates the violent destruction of the Mytileneans. He urges violence, while telling his addressees that their "pity" shows them soft and incapable of the actions required to rule. So too does their "change of heart," he claims, for ruling requires standing firm by what has been decided. Democratic assemblies tend toward speaking endlessly (*authis legein*, literally, "speaking again"), which wastes time (*diatribē chronou*) and blunts the urge to act. This inability to remain steadfast, Cleon says, is the greatest weakness to which democracy is prone (3.37–38). At first glance, Cleon appears to echo Pericles, who also reproached the people for shifting their position and attempted to restrain them from their characteristic vices (cf. 3.38.1, with 1.140.1, 2.61.2).

Cleon, however, blames not only the people in a democracy, but also the speakers in the assembly who influence them. The people are at fault for listening to clever speakers, who manipulate them with their beautiful and pleasant words, as they wage contests in intelligence and wish to appear wiser than the laws. If the people are prone to errors, their unscrupulous leaders take advantage of them. Although Cleon echoes Thucydides' criticism of Pericles' successors for being led by the people's pleasure and competing among themselves to be first, Thucydides described such "leaders" in order to contrast them with Pericles, who truly led. Cleon's criticism attacks leadership itself, and flatters the people, when he goes on to claim that "the common [or the vulgar] are better able to manage their cities than are the more intelligent."[5] Those who "distrust their own intelligence," he continues, and

---

4. Scholars have noted Thucydides' hostility to Cleon, and some speculate that Thucydides had a personal bias against him because Cleon was instrumental in securing Thucydides' exile from Athens. See discussion in Westlake, *Individuals in Thucydides*, 60. Connor defends Thucydides' harsh words concerning Cleon by suggesting that they are provisional, and "evoke reactions already likely to be present in Thucydides' audience." They are "initial assumptions" that can be "modified as new situations are investigated." *Thucydides*, 85–86, with 86n15. It is possible, however, that Thucydides' animosity to Cleon is in fact deserved. Thucydides is not the only contemporary critical of Cleon. In his comedy the *Knights*, Aristophanes presents Cleon as a demagogue, the head slave and overseer of other slaves such as Demosthenes and Nicias, who all serve Demos (or the People). Although Donald Kagan warns against supporting Thucydides' judgment of Cleon by appeal to that of another enemy of Cleon, one may ask why Aristophanes too is his enemy. Kagan, *The Archidamian War* (Ithaca, NY: Cornell University Press, 1974), 324n67. Strauss explains what may have been a cause of animosity against Cleon when he observes, "Cleon betrays the soul of Athens." *City and Man*, 213.

5. Here Cleon criticizes intelligence (*xunesis*), the very virtue for which Thucydides earlier praised the Athenian statesman Themistocles (1.138.2).

hence do not suppose that they are wiser than the laws, should therefore not look to the more capable for guidance but rather distrust those who try to influence them (3.37.4–5). Cleon by implication is one of the people, or, as Orwin puts it, his speech is "a masterpiece of populism," appealing to both the people's distrust of elites and their distrust of themselves for listening to elites.[6]

Cleon's position on Mytilene is straightforward: the Mytileneans have done Athens the greatest harm, and Athens should respond in kind before its anger is dulled (3.38.1, 3.39.2, 3.40.5, 3.40.7). The punishment of Mytilene should be as its injustice merits, with no distinction made between the few who led the revolt and the people who joined them (3.39.6–7). Pardon (or forgiveness, *suggnōmē*) is only for those who act unwillingly. There are three mistakes to which those who rule should not succumb, he continues. Those mistakes are pity, being seduced by the pleasures of speech, and "equity."[7] Pity and equity, he claims, should be extended only to those from whom we can expect them in return, not to those such as the Mytileneans, who will of necessity be our enemies forever (3.40.1–3). Cleon teaches his audience that the pity for the Mytileneans that moved them to reconsider their decision is a sign of an incapacity to rule, as is the very virtue—equity—that the Athenian envoys suggest is the virtue of the Athenian empire, when Athens exacts less justice from its subjects than it is due (1.76.3–4). By warning his listeners to expect and guard against seductive speeches, he speaks with an eye to any who speak after him, whose position he tries to undermine. Cleon speaks frequently of enemies, but he never uses the word "friend." Among the enemies of Athens are not only the Mytileneans, but by implication anyone who offers advice contrary to his, inasmuch as they would endanger Athens and its empire (3.40.7).

Although Cleon refers to justice when he speaks of what the Mytileneans deserve (3.40.4), he is speaking only of revenge. While inveighing against yielding to the "momentary pleasure" of his opponents' entertaining rhetoric (3.40.2–3), Cleon himself offers the momentary pleasure of revenge. He appeals to the people's fear as well: if we do not pay the Mytileneans back for what they did, others will be tempted to revolt (3.39.8, 3.40.7). Athens's self-interest thus supports exacting the punishment that the Mytileneans deserve.

---

6. Clifford Orwin, "The Just and Advantageous in Thucydides: The Case of the Mytilenaian Debate," *American Political Science Review* 78 (1984): 486.

7. For discussion, see Jacqueline de Romilly, "Fairness and Kindness in Thucydides," *Phoenix* 28 (1974): 95–100; Shanske, *Thucydides and the Philosophic Origins*, 110–14.

Whereas Pericles tried to moderate the passions of the people, risking their anger at him by contradicting them, arousing their fear when they were overtaken by hubris, and encouraging them when they lost hope (2.65.8–9), Cleon renders those who offer the people moderate advice suspect, arouses their fear in support of their anger, and encourages them to carry out what some of them have come to see as a "savage" decision.[8]

Anyone who speaks after Cleon must overcome the suspicion against speech that Cleon creates. Should he seem to have the better argument, he should not be trusted because he is a clever speaker. His dilemma is similar to the one Socrates claims to face when he rises to defend himself in Plato's *Apology*: because his accusers have argued that he is a clever speaker who makes the weaker argument the stronger, if he persuades his jurors he will only confirm what his accusers said (*Apology* 17a–b). Like Cleon's opponent, Socrates must either fail to persuade—and therefore lose—or get the better of the argument and create suspicion against himself as a clever speaker—and thereby lose. And just as Cleon associates the arguments of anyone who opposes him with sophists, Socrates claims that he runs the risk of being confused with sophists (3.38.2, 3.38.7; *Apology* 19d–20a). Both Socrates and Diodotus, the man who dares to speak against Cleon, are in dangerous positions, Socrates because he has been accused of a crime for which he could be executed, Diodotus because Cleon has suggested that anyone who favors leniency is a traitor to Athens with personal motives for deceiving the people (3.38.1–3).[9] Diodotus himself acknowledges his precarious position when he claims that good citizens should not frighten those who speak against them, nor should a moderate city dishonor or punish speakers whose position does not prevail (3.42.4–5). Socrates thinks that he will fail to persuade and thus prove his accusers wrong, inasmuch as he is not clever at speaking (*Apology* 17a–b). Socrates' speech does fail, by a surprisingly close vote (*Apology* 36a). Although the vote concerning Mytilene is also close (3.49.1), Diodotus's speech succeeds.[10]

---

8. Connor, *Thucydides*, 79n1; Thomas F. Scanlon, "Thucydides and Tyranny," *Classical Antiquity* (October 1987): 288–89; Yunis, *Taming Democracy*, 89; Macleod, "Reason and Necessity," *Journal of Hellenic Studies* 96 (1978): 69–70.

9. As Orwin observes, because Cleon makes it appear that any who dare to speak for Mytilene "are manifest enemies of the people," his speech "can be dismissed by no opponent who values either his name or his skin." "Just and Advantageous," 486.

10. Just as Diodotus's name means, literally, "gift from the god" (specifically, Zeus), in Plato's *Apology* Socrates presents himself as "a gift from the god" to Athens—a gadfly able to sting the city to reflect on itself, and to strive for virtue (*Apology* 29d–e, 30d–31a). It is possible that Thucydides was in Athens during Socrates' trial in 399 BCE—he tells us that he was an exile from his city for

Cleon "wonder[s]" at those who reopened the question about Mytilene, and thereby caused a delay that favors wrongdoers. He wonders as well (repeating his use of the verb) at any who would come forward and speak in favor of Mytilene, who must persuade his addressees that what was decided remains undecided, and thereby mislead them for the sake of profit (3.38.1–2). Thucydides uses "wonder" in a more positive sense, describing Themistocles as "worthy of wonder" (1.138.3). And Pericles uses the same phrase of Athens in his funeral oration (2.39.4). Whereas Thucydides and his Pericles look up or admire, Cleon has contempt. The language of wonder that Thucydides attributes to Cleon further reveals Cleon's character, and the difference between him and Pericles. So also does Cleon's "wonder," with the rhetorical repetition, prepare us to wonder at Diodotus, when he comes forward to speak.

Diodotus's Answer to Cleon

Before speaking in favor of leniency toward Mytilene, Diodotus responds to Cleon's warnings about clever speaking in democratic assemblies. Although the question of Mytilene may be more pressing, inasmuch as the ship with the order to destroy Mytilene has already set sail, Diodotus would have no chance of success without allaying the suspicion of clever speaking that Cleon attempted to evoke. He also may need time to calm the anger and fear to which Cleon appealed before he brings up Mytilene. He needs to slow things down before he can speed them up. He needs to control the time, rather than being sucked into quick action as the Athenians were in their anger, or wasting time as Cleon claimed that further speech would do. He begins by asking his addressees to think about themselves, their form of government, and the proper place of speech and deliberation in ruling. In this, he follows Pericles' move in his funeral oration, when he delays speaking about the fallen in order to explain the regime and way of life for which

---

twenty years after his command at Amphipolis (5.26.5). Since this happened in 424 BCE, his exile ended around 404. Of course, we do not know what Socrates actually says at his defense, and therefore what Thucydides would have heard had he been present, or what others might have reported to him if he relied on hearsay. Given Thucydides' interest in Athenian politics, however, it seems likely that he was aware of the historical Socrates and of his trial and execution, if indeed Thucydides were still alive at the time. For speculation that Thucydides was writing his work as late as 395 BCE, on the eve of the Corinthian war—and therefore four years after Socrates' trial—see Mark Munn, *The School of History: Athens in the Age of Socrates* (Berkeley: University of California Press, 2000), 318–21. Even if no reflections on Socrates influenced Thucydides' writing up of the war, parallels exist, and highlight aspects of Thucydides' history.

they sacrificed their lives. Because he too urges his addressees to consider who they are and to act accordingly, the memory of Athens is also at stake. And because he argues that intelligent advice should guide deliberation, his speech escapes the contradiction of Cleon's, which advises its addressees not to listen to advice. Diodotus leaves room for himself, for his own speaking and advising, in the speech that he delivers.

Diodotus argued strongly against killing the Mytileneans on the previous day (3.41.1), but when he comes forward to speak against Cleon's position, he adopts the impartial stance of the judge, who must weigh the arguments. He presents himself as a model for his addressees. Their job is not to hear and delight in speeches, as Cleon claimed they do, nor to suspect whatever they hear, as Cleon urged them to do, but to listen and to judge what is said (see *Apology* 18d). Diodotus does not blame those who have reopened the debate, he says, nor does he "praise those who find fault with frequent deliberation" about important matters (3.42.1). While he clearly distinguishes himself from Cleon—for Cleon has indeed blamed and found fault where Diodotus does not—his holding off from blame and praise gains for himself and his audience the distance they need for deliberation. Whereas Cleon criticizes speaking as a waste of time, Diodotus responds that "speed and anger" are hostile to "good counsel," the one accompanying folly, the other a lack of education and stupidity (literally, "density in judgment"). And whoever "contends [*diamachetai*] that speech does not teach how to act" is either lacking in intelligence (*axunetos*) or afraid of his own inability to speak (3.42.1–2). Diodotus does not wonder at the man who spoke before him; he knows him well, and he knows that he reduces speech to contention or fighting.

Thucydides gives Diodotus language that echoes Pericles, language that by way of contrast highlights not only the anti-intellectualism of Cleon's speech but its anti-Athenian character. Diodotus's criticism of "the lack of education" (*apaideusia*), for example, recalls Pericles' praise of Athens as a school (*paideia*) for Hellas (2.41.1). His reference to "judgment" (*gnōmē*) recalls how Pericles attributed this virtue to Athens, along with daring (e.g., 1.144.3). His insistence that good counsel requires that speech become "the teachers of deeds" resembles Pericles' observation that Athenians believe in being instructed before they act (2.40.2–3). Diodotus begins, in other words, by reminding the Athenians of who they have been, at least as their character is reflected in Pericles' rhetoric, and therefore of who they might be. And by reminding his audience of Pericles, who was, according to Thucydides, the ablest of his time in *both* speaking and acting (1.139.4), he reminds them of leadership at odds with Cleon's description of how policy should be decided.[11]

Diodotus clarifies the effect of the suspicion of intelligence and speech that Cleon fosters: if all speech is suspect, all who give advice must have ulterior motives. Good advice is then no less suspect than bad. If Cleon's perspective prevails, no one will believe that an adviser has goodwill for his city, and he must consequently explain himself in other terms. A good adviser must lie in order to be trusted (3.43.1–2). Words themselves cannot be trusted (see Plato *Phaedo* 89b).[12] The city will have no way of distinguishing benefactors from deceivers. Everyone deceives. Diodotus thus not only reminds Athenians of the free people that they appear in Pericles' funeral oration, but also hints at the suspicious and slavish people they might become, if Cleon and what he represents prevails (see also 1.68.2).

If we suspect everyone who speaks, as Cleon implies we must, we deprive the city of the benefit of advisers. And Diodotus is such an adviser. When the greatest matters are at stake, he says, those of us who see further than others must be expected to speak, especially since we can be held accountable. When accountable, he observes, human beings make better decisions (3.42.3–43.5).[13] However "democratic" Diodotus's vision may be, he, like Thucydides in his praise of Pericles, affirms the necessity of leadership for good government (2.65.8). It is a leadership that must be held to account, and the people must therefore be able to do so for democracy to succeed. Unlike Pericles in his funeral oration (see 2.37.1), he even makes his own leadership explicit. And in contrast to Diodotus, Cleon says nothing of his own responsibility, while urging that all the Mytileneans should be held responsible for the revolt.

---

11. Yunis also finds in Diodotus's speech "a Periclean orientation." He suggests that Thucydides chose a speaker who otherwise plays no major role in Athenian politics—and no other role in Thucydides' history—so that the speaker would escape the taint that Thucydides attributes to post-Periclean politics. *Taming Democracy*, 93. See also Jacqueline de Romilly, *Thucydides and Athenian Imperialism*, trans. Philip Thody (Oxford: Basil Blackwell, 1963), 158. Others argue, on the contrary, that Thucydides emphasizes the differences between Pericles and Diodotus in favor of the latter. Saxonhouse, *Athenian Democracy*, 60, 75; Mara, "Thucydides and Political Thought," 106, 115–16.

12. As Macleod observes of Cleon's position, "Facts are preferred to words," but "words are not merely set against deeds but linked with falsehood." "Reason and Necessity," 70.

13. Martin Ostwald speculates that Diodotus's reference to his accountability refers to his holding an official position in Athens, at the end of which he would be held accountable. "Diodotus, Son of Eucrates," *Greek, Roman, and Byzantine Studies* 20 (1979): 5–13, esp. 8–9. Connor does not think this is necessary, inasmuch as Diodotus may simply be alluding to his responsibility in introducing the proposal into the assembly for reconsidering the decision. *Thucydides*, 87n19. In either case, however, he is acknowledging that he is accountable.

Only after referring to his work of advising and his accountability does Diodotus turn to Mytilene. Whereas Cleon had advised a hasty revenge before anger dulled, Diodotus tells his listeners to consider "the future rather than the present." The issue is not guilt or innocence, or justice, but what is advantageous to the city. Contrary to Cleon's argument that only harsh punishment will deter the revolts of other cities from Athens's rule, Diodotus argues that when the stakes are the greatest, no threatened punishment will deter actions. And this is the case when men fight for freedom and rule. *Erōs* and hope lead human beings to irrational risks. The penalty of death has not worked even in lesser matters. Prosperity leads to hubris and insolence, and poverty to the daring of necessity. Fear yields to *erōs* and hope. Reason yields to the irrational. Not only will deterrence not work, Diodotus argues, it will be counterproductive: if rebels know that there is no hope from surrender, they will fight to the death. On the other hand, if we are lenient, we will give rebel cities cause to capitulate, saving us lives and expense. It would therefore be expedient to blame as few of the Mytileneans as possible, so that in the case of future rebellions the majority in revolting cities will trust to Athenian leniency. It is especially expedient not to blame the people as opposed to the leaders of rebel cities, even if all supported rebellion, for the people are the ones most likely to have goodwill toward us, he says (3.44–47). Even when people are accountable, accountable leadership such as Diodotus's does not necessarily hold them to account. By implication, goodwill finds goodwill in others and acts in order to promote it, all to the advantage of one's city in maintaining its rule of other cities.

Whereas Cleon refers to the rebels as "enemies forever," toward whom pity and equity are inappropriate (3.40.3), Diodotus implies that a city's actions toward rebel cities can make enemies of friends and friends of enemies. He refers to "human nature" and its compulsions, when he speaks of *erōs* and hope (3.45.5), but he proposes that actions will influence what happens in the future. He implies this as well when he claims that those who look further than others should be held accountable for their advice. Consistent with the advice he gives, he asserts in the end that the majority of the Mytileneans did not take part in the revolt, and that they "voluntarily surrendered" to Athens as soon as they were able. "Athenians would do injustice if they kill their benefactors" (3.47.3). Justice is a standard he holds up, his protestations to the contrary. Actions can be voluntary or involuntary, and one should respond in kind. Connor regards Diodotus's claim about the people of Mytilene as a flagrant misstatement of the facts—the commons were not nearly as opposed to the revolt or as favorable to Athens as

Diodotus says.[14] But Diodotus is only following his own clear advice to the Athenians—let us not blame the people even if they are responsible; let us "pretend" that they have more goodwill than they have as a way of cultivating their goodwill (3.47.4). Even if they are more responsible than Diodotus suggests, the Athenians should be more lenient to them than they deserve. Seeing further, both than the present and than others, Diodotus can see Athenian interest, and his rhetoric calls Athens to share that sight and act on it.

Diodotus attempts to turn his addressees away from their pain, their desire to exact revenge because of the harm Mytilene has inflicted on their city, and toward making decisions that demonstrate their freedom. Treating their enemy better than he deserves demonstrates that same spirit of liberality or generosity that the Athenian envoys describe at Sparta, when they argue that the stronger will ever rule the weaker, but the stronger are "worthy" of rule and of praise when they rule more justly than they are compelled to do (1.76.3–4; also 1.77.1–2). So now Diodotus urges the Athenians to exact less than justice allows them, albeit in the service of saving Athenian lives and expense in the future. It is better "to submit voluntarily to injustice [from Mytilene]" than "to justly destroy those whom it is not necessary to destroy" (3.47.5). The equity that the Athenian envoys attributed to Athens's rule toward its subjects resurfaces here in Diodotus's argument. In following Diodotus's advice, Athens will serve its interest in cultivating friends rather than enemies. Whereas Cleon urges Athens's self-gratification under the cloak of justice, Diodotus urges liberality and self-restraint, and connects the city's self-interest with leniency rather than revenge, and with the strength required for freedom and rule rather than with the weakness that would be its downfall.[15] If Diodotus deceives his addressees—as he hints that even the best advisers must do in the political climate created by Cleon—it is by

---

14. Connor, *Thucydides*, 87. Connor claims that Diodotus's account of the role of the people at Mytilene contradicts the one Thucydides himself gives earlier, and writes that "a reader who shares Thucydides' professed regard for exact detail is likely to recognize and deplore the distortion" (88). See also Daniel Gillis, "The Revolt at Mytilene," *American Journal of Philology* 92, no. 1 (1971): 38–47; H. D. Westlake, "The Commons at Mytilene," *Historia* 25, no. 4 (1976): 429–40. Kagan, in contrast, finds the evidence concerning the involvement of the people of Mytilene in the revolt inconclusive, and correctly points out that this is beside the point. "Speeches in Thucydides," 87–88. See also Orwin, "Just and Advantageous," 486.

15. Mara also connects Diodotus's argument with that of the Athenian envoys at Sparta. According to Mara, the position that the Athenians should be more just toward the Mytileneans than the latter's material power requires respects "the priorities of a democratic culture that measures equality on terms other than power." *Civic Conversations*, 248. Rahe calls the Athenian action toward Mytilene an act of generosity. "Thucydides' Critique of Realpolitik," 114.

concealing under the cloak of a narrow self-interest what is demanded of a powerful and a free people. Free and powerful is nevertheless precisely what he in the end asks the Athenians to be. Like Pericles, he asks Athenians to confer benefits. This is how one secures friends (2.40.4). As would Pericles, he claims that the greatest things are freedom and rule (e.g., 2.36.1–2, 2.43.4).

Athens as well, although Diodotus does not say it explicitly, is moved by *erōs* and hope when it comes to freedom and ruling, as when it fought for freedom against the Persians and then acquired its empire over its allies. By appealing to *erōs* and hope to explain rebellion, Diodotus reminds the Athenians that the Mytileneans are like themselves. They share that daring in which Athens takes pride.[16] He thereby makes the friendship with the people in Mytilene that he claims leniency will produce more plausible. If he implicitly warns Athens against its own *erōs* and hope, which lead human beings to suppose they can do more than they can (3.45.6), his doing so implies the possibility of resisting and overcoming the irrational passions that lead to doom. Moreover, although Diodotus claims not to appeal to pity and equity (3.48.1), so discredited by Cleon, he does not deny their goodness.[17] It is, after all, the "change of heart" over their brutal decision that allows a reopening of the debate (3.36.4). Diodotus does not explicitly ask the Athenians to pardon or to forgive the Mytileneans, for that too has been the object of Cleon's disdain. But to the extent that the Athenians see their similarity to the rebels, they are more likely to see the revolt from the perspective of the rebels and to be able to pardon them. The literal meaning of "pardon" in Greek (*suggnōmē*) is "to know with," that is, to understand what the other did when he acted.

Once the vote is taken, and Diodotus prevails, a second ship is sent to Mytilene and arrives just in time to countermand the order carried by the first ship. This outcome requires that the second ship hasten, and the first ship tarry. Why do the men on the second ship hurry, and those on the first

16. See F. M. Wassermann, "Post-Periclean Democracy in Action: The Mytilenean Debate (Thuc. III 37–48)," *Transactions of the American Philological Association* 87 (1956): 38; Forde, *Ambition to Rule*, 42. Orwin observes that "Diodotus reminds the Athenians that the rebels are their mirror image," for "in revolting from servitude . . ., they have done only what the Athenians would themselves have done." Orwin understands Diodotus to reinforce the view that all human beings are subject to the compulsions of nature, however, rather than appealing to the desire for freedom and rule that they share. "Just and Advantageous," 492.

17. Strauss observes that Cleon "ruled out of court the consideration of compassion and mildness as wholly incompatible with empire," in contrast to Diodotus, who "refuses to appeal [to either] without saying that [they] have no place whatever in an empire." *City and Man*, 234.

ship proceed slowly? The Mytilenean ambassadors aboard the second ship, we learn, promise the sailors rewards if the ship arrives in time. But the sailors on the first ship are promised no rewards for delay; nor do they know that a second ship follows with a countermand. Those sailors, Thucydides tells us, "were sailing without urgency for their monstrous [*allokoton*] business" (3.49.4). No self-interest, whether in preventing future rebellions or in rewards for their delay, slows them down, only their simple horror of what is to come. And what moves the Athenians who vote on Diodotus's side? Thucydides does not speculate. Perhaps it is not simply Diodotus's arguments about the prospects for deterrence that move his audience, but the vision of themselves to which he is able to appeal, and hence to their disgust at what they might become. As Forde says, Diodotus "succeeds in delivering [both] the Mytilenaeans from slaughter and the Athenians from the kind of barbarism they later succumb to at Melos."[18] It is not only the fate of Mytilene but the character of Athens that hangs in the balance, its freedom from compulsion, liberality toward others, and the very "forgiveness" or "pardon" in which that freedom is manifest.

Thucydides does not resolve the issue about Athenian freedom, inasmuch as Diodotus carries the day only in part. Near the end of his speech, Diodotus reminds his addressees of the second question before them—the fate not only of those left in Mytilene but that of the Mytilenean prisoners whom Paches sent to Athens "on the grounds that they did injustice." He advises the Athenians to "judge" them "at their leisure" (or, "when at peace," *kath' hēsuchian*), while deciding now to allow the others in Mytilene to keep their homes (3.48.1–2). By raising the issue of the justice of the prisoners from Mytilene, as well as by his urging the Athenians "to judge" them "at leisure," Diodotus seems to have a trial in mind, or least a decision based on justice as well as advantage. The Athenian envoys at Sparta praise their city inasmuch as it allows its subject cities to take their complaints to Athenian courts, although it has the power to decide any conflict between them at will (1.77). But Thucydides recounts no trial of the prisoners. Immediately after his account of the dramatic arrival of the second ship in time to save Mytilene, Thucydides reports that the Athenians, according to Cleon's judgment (*gnōmē*), kill the prisoners, there being slightly more than a thousand of them.[19] The Athenians find no "leisure" or "peace," as Diodotus urges,

---

18. Forde, *Ambition to Rule*, 40n34; see also Mara, *Civic Conversations*, 114–16, 251.

19. Scholars have found the large number of Mytilenean prisoners executed to be unlikely. Gomme, *HCT*, 2:325. Connor notes that there is no textual reason to change the number Thucydides gives, and suggests that the number is meant to shock. *Thucydides*, 86n18.

for consideration of this issue. Thucydides mentions no further discussion about the Mytilenean prisoners; nor does he mention Diodotus, either here or anywhere else in his history of the war.

Moreover, the Athenians tear down the walls of Mytilene, seize its ships, divide most of the land on the island, and give lots or shares to their own citizens, while forcing the inhabitants to pay them to cultivate the land. The original plan had been to kill the men and enslave the women and children. Now it seems all who survive are more or less enslaved. This may be to the advantage of the Athenians, at least of those among whom the Mytilenean land is divided, but it is not the "advantage" that Diodotus mentions when he argues that lenient treatment of the Mytileneans will have a good effect on others who might revolt in the future.[20] Cleon's "*gnōmē*" is a sad reflection of the "judgment" for which Pericles praises Athens and for which Thucydides praises Pericles. His brutal policy is ineffective in preventing cities from revolting as later events prove (4.122.6–123.1), and it is completely without *suggnōmē,* or "likemindedness," with its implications of pardon or forgiveness.

Diodotus and Thucydides

Diodotus is known to us only through Thucydides' history, and only from this one appearance in it. As far as we know from the historical record, he exists only in speech—in Thucydides' work—and not in fact. Not surprisingly, Diodotus has attracted considerable attention from scholars, both because of his dramatic appearance in the history and the remarkable speech he gives. While some, like Mara and Saxonhouse, argue that Diodotus's view of democratic deliberation reflects Thucydides' own,[21] others, who focus on Diodotus's recommendation of leniency as advantageous rather than just, criticize Diodotus and his rhetoric for contributing to the increasing amorality that characterizes Athens in the course of the war.[22] Orwin defends

---

20. Connor understands this treatment of the Mytileneans to be exactly what Diodotus intended as the alternative to killing the males and enslaving the women and children. He refers to Diodotus's advice that the Mytileneans should be allowed "to keep their homes," as support. In other words, they keep their homes, while working for the Athenians among whom their land is divided. Connor does, however, express surprise that Diodotus is not clearer about this result in his speech, inasmuch as it held "the prospect of profit for several thousand Athenian voters." *Thucydides,* 87n19. That this is Diodotus's intention concerning the people in Mytilene seems less obvious to me, inasmuch as Diodotus makes a clear argument for profit in a larger sense that requires leniency.

21. Saxonhouse, *Athenian Democracy,* 75–79; Mara, "Thucydides and Political Thought," 116–19.

22. Euben, *Tragedy of Political Theory,* 180; Monoson and Loriaux, "Illusion of Power," 292. See also White, *When Words Lose Their Meaning,* 76.

Diodotus by pointing to the concern for justice underlying his arguments for advantage. Because human beings inevitably yield to irrational *erōs* and hope in matters of freedom and rule, the Mytileneans act "only as they could not have helped acting." Punishing them would be unjust.[23] Orwin in effect defends Diodotus's justice at the cost of the responsibility that makes justice praiseworthy.

If Diodotus's "plea constitutes as sweeping an exculpation of wrongdoing as has ever been heard," what, then, could Diodotus think of executing the oligarchic perpetrators of the revolt, Orwin asks. They too are prompted by the compulsions of nature. Just as Cleon insists on no distinctions in punishing Mytileneans, for all are similarly responsible, the logic of Diodotus's view, according to Orwin, is that all deserve pardon. But, Orwin argues, the harsh punishment of the few who instigate the revolt is as necessary to future deterrence as is leniency toward the common people of Mytilene. He therefore concludes that in the case of Mytilene, Diodotus finds "no reconciliation between justice and self-interest," and that advantage prevails.[24]

In this way, Orwin comes around to Monoson and Loriaux's position that Diodotus separates advantage from justice. Unlike Monoson and Loriaux, however, he is not critical of Diodotus for doing so, nor does he point to a more hopeful political alternative such as they find in Hermocrates' perspective. Diodotus's perspective, Orwin argues, is Thucydides' perspective. In this regard, Orwin's position is closer to that of Connor, who also emphasizes Diodotus's presentation of laws, conventions, and punishments as ineffective against the power of *erōs* and hope. Diodotus's speech breaks out of the rational limits of Thucydides' work "to reveal a world of shadowy powers, who, momentarily personified, swiftly retreat into darkness and gloom."[25] But whereas Connor leaves us with the bleakness of the prospect Diodotus

---

23. Orwin, "Just and Advantageous," 491. Orwin's emphasis on Diodotus's reference to the compulsions of nature is consistent with his interpretation of the Athenian empire. Like the Mytileneans, the Athenian empire is better defended by appeal to compulsion—one cannot be blamed for what one is forced to do—than as a freely chosen project. If all perpetrators deserve pardon, so do the Athenians. See my discussion in chapter 2. In contrast to Orwin, Strauss argues that Diodotus's "vague" suggestion that all injustice is involuntary when arguing that deterrence is ineffective serves his rhetorical strategy. That strategy is to "put his audience in a mood in which it is willing to listen to a plea of innocence," and his suggestion that injustice is involuntary "prepares that mood." *City and Man*, 234. Also Mara, *Civic Conversations*, 246–47.

24. Orwin, "Just and Advantageous," 490–93.

25. Connor, *Thucydides*, 85–91, esp. 90–91. See also Macleod, who concludes his analysis of the Mytilene debate with the observation that given the impulses that drive human beings, the "tragedy is that to see the truth is sometimes to see that all advice is futile." "Reason and Necessity," 77–78.

presents, Orwin argues that Diodotus's very understanding of the "incurable folly" to which human nature is subject constitutes a certain wisdom that "lifts" Diodotus "far above the city's perspective on its own good," indeed to "an Olympian height" from which he can "gaze down on Athens."[26] For Diodotus, Orwin writes, "*tout comprehendre est tout pardonner*," since transgression is error and hence "vice is ignorance and virtue wisdom." This represents "Thucydidean wisdom."[27] Whereas Connor's argument leaves us with despair, Orwin's leaves us with resignation.

Connor acknowledges Diodotus's action in saving Mytilene, but finds it outweighed by the bleakness of his argument about the power and irrationality of human passion.[28] Mara, in contrast, argues that Diodotus's deeds offer a corrective to his speech: Diodotus's "pessimistic conclusion" is "softened by Diodotus's own practice."[29] Thucydides himself of course asks us to judge the speeches in light of the deeds or the facts (1.21.2). The fact as Thucydides presents it is that Diodotus does intervene in order to save lives, and to argue for the goods of political deliberation, foresight, and leadership. Neither despair nor resignation about politics is consistent with Diodotus's intervention in Athenian politics to help the Mytileneans, even his effort to speak a second time rather than acquiesce in his losing the debate on the previous day. Nor is either despair or resignation consistent with Diodotus's defense of deliberation or the need for speech to inform action. He comes forward to risk speaking against Cleon and to warn Athens against what Cleon represents.

Diodotus's very call for deliberation about the justice of the prisoners' actions indicates that he thinks that their justice is a question that must be decided (3.48.1–2). That is, he does not suppose that justice demands pardoning the prisoners because they were compelled by their passions, or that Athens's advantage trumps justice in demanding their execution. He refers to an opposition between advantage and justice, to be sure, but it is in the context of his recommending the advantage for Athens in being more lenient than justice requires (3.47.5). For him justice yields not to the compulsions of passion or interest but to a calculation of self-interest that produces liberal actions. By implication, justice must be understood in terms of what is good for the one who is just. When Diodotus argues that it is better voluntarily to

---

26. Orwin, "Just and Advantageous," 494; *Humanity of Thucydides*, 162.

27. "Diodotus announces a more terrible truth than that human beings are evil; namely, that they are not." Orwin, *Humanity of Thucydides*, 203. Also Palmer, *Love of Glory*, 116.

28. Connor, *Thucydides*, 91.

29. Mara, "Thucydides and Political Thought," 118.

suffer injustice (from Mytilene) than to destroy, however justly, those whom it is not necessary to destroy (3.47.4), he comes closer to the Socratic teaching that doing injustice is worse than suffering it (*Gorgias* 469b–480e) than to the view that vice is ignorance and wisdom virtue.

If Diodotus were invented by Thucydides, he would not be a "gift from Zeus," as his name suggests,[30] but Thucydides' gift to Athens. Diodotus offers his city a principle that would prevent the Athenians from fluctuating between pity and cruelty, as events and speakers happened to move them, namely, the Periclean principle of freedom and liberality. If he resembles Thucydides, as many have argued, it is because he attempts to save the soul of Athens. As in other speeches in his history, Thucydides attributes to Diodotus's speech what is required in the circumstances (1.22.1–3). Perhaps also required was an Athenian leader to deliver it.

Insofar as Athens is characterized by reflection and speech as well as deeds informed by them, as Pericles asserts, Cleon's attack on speech is an attack on Athens. A successful attack on speech would lead to silence, paralleling the silencing of the Mytileneans that Cleon urges. Cleon is defeated not simply by Diodotus, but by the author who records his speech as a response to Cleon's. Whereas Diodotus's restraining Athenian anger and revenge preserves Athens for a moment, Thucydides' writing up the war preserves Athens for the future, at least Athens as it was or as it might have been. Even if the man who answers Cleon in the Athenian assembly is a fictional character, inserted by Thucydides into history, the man who answers Cleon by creating Diodotus is an actual person who lived in time, whose existence is attested to by his deeds, his writing up the war between the Peloponnesians and the Athenians.

This is not to deny that Diodotus's and Thucydides' perspectives transcend that of their city or their political community. But that transcendence does not simply look down from above in resignation: theirs is a transcendence that allows them to produce representations of their city that give Athenians standards for action, including daring, liberality, and pardon, and even judgment itself.

The Trial of the Plataeans

Shortly after he concludes the story of Mytilene, Thucydides turns to developments at Plataea. Plataea is besieged by the Peloponnesian forces, suffers

---

30. Thucydides also designates Diodotus as "the son of Eucrates," literally, the offspring of "good rule" (3.41.1). That the name of his father has a meaning as well offers supporting evidence that Diodotus was invented by Thucydides.

from want of provisions, and sees no sign of the promised help from Athens. Plataea "surrenders voluntarily" to the Spartans, accepting the offer of the Spartan commander "that the Spartans would serve as judges to punish the unjust, and to punish no one contrary to *dikē*" (judicial procedure, trial) (3.52.2). It is important to the Plataeans that they surrender to the Spartans, and not to the Spartan ally Thebes, with whom they have long had hostile relations (3.59.4). The Spartans do not specify exactly what they mean by a "trial," and the distressed Plataeans are in no position to ask. They "trust" the Spartans, as they themselves admit later (3.53.1). The word *dikē*, related to the adjective for just, *dikaios*, can refer to a trial, where justice is determined. Whatever may be customary with regard to prisoners of war,[31] however, the Spartans have promised a trial and justice, not simply a consideration of advantage (cf. 3.44.4; Aristotle *Rhetoric* 1258b). Accordingly, they wait for judges (*dikastaí*) to arrive from Sparta in order to conduct the trial. This event occurs, Thucydides reports, "around the same time" as the fall of Mytilene to Athens (3.52.1–3).[32] Whether or not Thucydides invented Diodotus, he invents no Spartan to speak for leniency for the Plataeans when they have their day in court. It is more fitting—if futile—for the Plataeans to speak for themselves.

Their trial, to the Plataeans' surprise, consists in the judges' posing only one question to them: Did the Plataeans in the present war do anything to benefit the Spartans and their allies? What sort of trial is this, the Plataeans ask. They expected "a more lawful trial," with charges brought forth for them to answer, and judges who act fairly. Instead, they hear no charges, and they are asked an inappropriate question, they claim, for it assumes what is not the case—that the Plataeans were friends of Sparta during the present war, not enemies. If they were enemies, they did no wrong in not benefiting the Spartans; if they were friends, the Spartans should not have attacked them. If they say in response to the Spartans' question that they have not benefited the Spartans, they will condemn themselves; if they say that they have,

---

31. Connor states that the Greeks did not accept killing prisoners who surrendered, and refers to P. Ducrey, *Le traitement des prisonniers de guerre* (Paris, 1968), chap. 9.

32. Scholars point out the similarity between the situations of the two weaker cities, who are at the mercy of larger, more powerful ones. C. W. Macleod, "Thucydides' Plataean Debate," *Greek, Roman, and Byzantine Studies* 18, no. 3 (1977): 243. Connor argues that the similarities between the plights of Plataea and Mytilene lead the reader to an "increasing awareness that in the world Thucydides describes advantage and not right decides the outcome of discussions." *Thucydides*, 91–93. In contrast, I emphasize the differences between Athens and Sparta that Thucydides' juxtaposition reveals. See also Strauss, *City and Man*, 190, 215; Rahe, "Thucydides' Critique of Realpolitik," 114.

they will condemn themselves as liars. They fear that their trial is a sham, and that the judges have already made a decision to gratify others. They allude to the Thebans. (3.53–54). Once the Plataeans have spoken, the Thebans request to speak as well (3.60). Because these speeches were not part of the plan for the "trial," the defense comes before the accusation; but if it were simply up to the Spartans, there would be neither. It is thus only because of the Plataeans' request that these opposed speeches are delivered.

The Plataeans make an eloquent speech. Instead of focusing entirely on events of the present war, to which the question posed by Spartan judges is directed, they speak as well of the days when the Hellenes joined together against the Persians. The Plataeans contributed to that struggle. They fought side by side with the Spartans on Plataean land (3.54.4). In annual ceremonies, they honor Sparta's fallen soldiers who are buried in their territory (3.58.4). And they even helped Sparta when it was threatened by an uprising from its subjugated population, the Helots. These are things that should not be forgotten (3.54.5). As to Plataea's alliance with Athens, Plataea first went to Sparta for help against Thebes, and Sparta turned it away, recommending Athens, a city located closer to Plataea. The Spartans are therefore responsible (*aitioi*) for that alliance (3.55.1; see 1.118.2). The Plataeans of course did not consider the Peloponnesus too faraway to go to the aid of the Spartans against their revolting Helots, as the Plataeans' reference to the help they extended to Sparta makes clear. Moreover, the Plataeans continue, it was the Spartan ally Thebes who made an unprovoked attack on their city (3.56.1). Sparta's reputation in the Hellenic world will suffer if it destroys Plataea, for it will appear to sacrifice lawfulness to expedience, in its subservience to Thebes and that city's long-standing hatred of Plataea (3.56.3 3.57.1–2). The Plataeans deserve pity for their plight, considering the terrible character of their destruction and the fact that misfortune may come to those who do not deserve it (3.59.1). Finally, they call on the gods and the Spartan ancestors with whom Plataeans fought and died not to betray them to their worst enemies (3.59.2).

When the Plataeans remind the Spartans of the good deeds the Plataeans did for them in the past, they remind them of Sparta's weakness rather than its strength, of its need rather than its power. Those who think themselves worthy of great things, Aristotle says in the *Nicomachean Ethics*, want to remember the good deeds they have done for others and to forget the good deeds others have done for them. Thus when Thetis asks Zeus for a favor, Aristotle illustrates, she does not mention the good deeds she did in the past for him (*NE* 1124b10–16). The Plataeans, in contrast, dwell on their own good deeds toward the Spartans, whom they present as their beneficiaries. So too do they claim that they are worthy, and hence do not deserve their misfortune. When they claim pity for their plight, it is only a moderate (*sōphrōn*) pity (3.59.1). They do not grovel. Their claim that misfortune can come even to those who do not deserve it, such as themselves, moreover, means that it might come to the Spartans as well. They remind their addressees that they too are vulnerable. By implication, if Sparta helps Thebes now in its unjust attack on Plataea, Sparta may indeed deserve whatever misfortune comes. As to the Plataeans' holding the Spartans responsible for their alliance with Athens, Macleod observes that it "nullifies their attempts at tact or flattery."[33] Had Plataea made attempts at tact or flattery, he would be correct that this would nullify them. The Plataeans' references to the sham trial the Spartan judges are conducting, to Sparta's subservience to Theban interests, and Plataea's past efforts to benefit Sparta hardly fall in this category. Macleod proceeds to observe that the Plataeans' blame of Sparta for its alliance with Athens reveals how Plataea "is, and always has been, at the mercy of greater powers."[34] This of course is true, but it also highlights Plataean boldness in its dealing with those powers, which Thucydides has shown us as well in his account of the actions of the Plataeans in defending their city (e.g., 2.3.1–4, 3.20–24).

The Plataeans mention the Spartan commander Pausanias, with whom they fought alongside in the war against the Persians (3.58.5). We heard about Pausanias's troubles from Thucydides in a digression in book 1, both his attraction to Persian customs and his intrigues with the Persians against Spartan interests. In fact, after recalling Pausanias from his command, the Spartans decided not to send out further Spartan commanders "in fear of their corruption" when away from home. The leadership of the combined Hellenic forces was thus left to Athens, and this facilitated its growing ascendance and power in the Hellenic world (1.94–95). To remind Sparta of this past is to remind Sparta of its weakness. So too do the Plataeans remind the Spartans that they were unable to control their own subjugated population, the Helots, when they mention the help Plataea rendered them at the time of the Helot revolt. Throughout their speech, the Plataeans remind the Spartans of what they might prefer to forget. Thebes's invasion of Plataea, which the Plataeans also mention, so troubled Sparta throughout the first phase of the war, Thucydides later tells us, that the Spartans did not prosecute the war with vigor, feeling justice was on the side of their opponents (7.18.2).

---

33. Macleod, "Thucydides' Plataean Debate," 230.
34. Ibid.

The Plataeans conclude their speech by pleading that the Spartans become their "saviors," and not destroy them while "freeing other Hellenes" (3.59.4). They mention only briefly and in passing that for which the Spartans might feel pride—their purpose of liberating Hellas from Athenian rule—and mention nothing about the goodwill they would gain from other Athenian allies who might welcome them as liberators. They do not stoop to the rhetoric whereby Thetis manipulates Zeus, but then they do not expect they have a chance to sway the Spartans. Nobility is all on their side, both in their deeds, which they recount, and in their speech as they do so. They are Athens's true ally, even though Athens abandons them to their enemies. They did surrender, but now they have made a last stand. Their praise of themselves is not lost on the Thebans (3.61.1; cf. 1.86.1).

After the Plataeans speak, the Thebans request to speak as well. They would not have done so, they say, if Sparta had not allowed the Plataeans to speak (3.61.1). Their purpose in speaking is to prevent the Plataean speech from having any effect. They begin with an account of a more distant past—their own founding of Plataea, and the Plataeans' refusal to recognize their leadership. The Plataeans betrayed their own ancestry (3.61.2). Just as Corinth, another of Sparta's allies, claimed against its colony Corcyra, the mother country did not receive the respect and deference due to it, but only hostility (see 1.38.1–2). Thebes, like Corinth, appeals to filial piety. And their nighttime invasion of Plataea was merely an offer to Plataea to join the ancestral government of all the Boeotians—and they came by the voluntary summons of the first men of Plataea in family and wealth, who let them into the city. For this Thebans were violently attacked and killed by the Plataeans, to whom they came in an attempt in fact to free them from a "foreign" alliance (3.65.2, 3.66.1). The Thebans thus claim to serve the liberation of Hellas from Athenian domination, at least when it comes to those cities that should be subordinate instead to Thebes. The Thebans are nevertheless not so overcome with this noble goal as to forget to tell the Spartan judges that Thebes supplies more horses for the war effort than does any other ally (3.64.4).

Hatred and anger mark the Theban speech, so much that it is reminiscent of the one Cleon gives in favor of punishing Mytilene. The Thebans too want revenge against their enemy, although they hide their passion behind the appearance of a trial and behind their ally's reputation for law–abidingness (3.67.5; see 1.84.3). They even rejoice over the prospect of the punishment of Plataea: those who suffer justly, they say, do not deserve pity. Rather their suffering should be "rejoiced over" (*epichartoi*) (3.67.4). The word, used only here by Thucydides, connotes a sort of malicious joy in the suffering of others (e.g., Aeschylus, *Prometheus Bound* 159). Like Cleon, they claim that pity is appropriate for friends, not for enemies. They want the Spartans to believe that the enemies of one's friends are also one's enemies. They object to the Plataean appeal to its past friendship with Sparta, insisting that the Plataeans are inconsistent in claiming credit for their good deeds in defense of Hellas during the Persian War while denying that they are responsible for their complicity in Athenian domination of Hellas after that war (3.62.1, 3.63.1–2, 3.54.3, 3.55.1; but cf. 3.55.2). They make the point that Pericles tried to teach the Athenian people—one cannot take credit for one's successes while denying responsibility for one's failures. But while they reproach Plataea for doing this very thing, they proceed to do it themselves, evading responsibility for their own alliance with the Persians against Hellas, while claiming credit for their fight against Athenian tyranny (3.62.2–4).[35] They inconsistently blame Plataea and exonerate themselves. All the more hypocritical, then, is their conclusion, in which they denounce the "clever rhetoric" and "fine" or "beautiful" words with which the Plataeans cover unjust deeds (3.67.6–7), warning against a rhetoric that makes the weaker argument the stronger. As Cleon warned the Athenians, the Thebans warn the Spartans—they should not listen to speech, which will seduce and deceive them. Of course, the Spartans are prepared from the outset of the "trial" not to listen to speeches that weigh complex issues, as demonstrated when they pose a single question, and demand a simple answer.

After the Thebans' speech, the Spartan judges resume questioning each Plataean whether he did anything to benefit the Spartans and their allies during the present war. They ask the question, Thucydides tells us, of each captive Plataean one by one. The five Spartan judges—who remain anonymous—speak with one voice, and they ask the same question at least two hundred times, for it is "not fewer than two hundred men" whom they execute. They are like the written word that Socrates criticizes in the *Phaedrus* for always repeating the same thing, and with which he contrasts the living words of someone who engages in the back and forth of discussion (275d–276a).

This outcome, as the Plataeans thought, appears preordained. Sparta acts, Thucydides agrees, "for the sake of the Thebans, whom they believed useful in the war" (3.68.4). While the Spartans act wholly out of self-interest, they conduct a trial and thus pretend to act out of justice. But the speeches do not matter. Unlike the Mytileneans, the Plataeans never have a chance.

---

35. See discussion ibid., 239.

The Spartans not only put all the men in Plataea to death, they enslave the women, eventually destroy the whole city to its foundations, and rent out the land to the Thebans (3.68.3). They treat Plataea in the way Athens refuses to treat Mytilene. As far as we are told, the vote of the Spartan judges is undivided. No Spartan shows sympathy for the Plataeans, as Athenians do for the Mytileneans. No Spartan engages in debate over Plataea.[36] By juxtaposing the deeds of these two cities in comparable circumstances, including the different influence of speeches on those deeds, Thucydides shows the superiority of Athens.

Sparta's and Athens's Failures to Act

We have thus far considered how Athens treats Mytilene in contrast to how Sparta treats Plataea. Mytilene falls, however, when Sparta fails to send help in time. Shortly before the events leading to the surrender of Mytilene, those in the city stop expecting the Spartan fleet to arrive (3.27.2). So too do the Plataeans give up hope of aid from their ally Athens (3.20.1). Thucydides' juxtaposition lets us judge not merely how Athens and Sparta treat captive cities, but how they treat cities to whom they have made commitments.

After agreeing to aid Mytilene, the Spartans send word to the Mytileneans that help is on the way—forty ships under the command of the Spartan general Alcidas (3.25–26). But Alcidas does not hasten to save Mytilene. To the contrary, the Spartan fleet under Alcidas "took its time" (*egchronizein*) on its expedition (3.27.1). Thucydides' choice of a verb to describe the Spartans' tardiness underlines their inability to act: *egchronizein*, which Thucydides uses to mean to "delay," or to "take time" about something, looks as if it means, literally, to be "in time."[37] The Spartans take too much time to sail toward Mytilene, because they are in a deeper sense caught "in time." Soon Thucydides repeats the thought: whereas "it was necessary for them to come with speed to Mytilene, they wasted time and sailed at leisure [*scholaioi*]" (3.29.1). But a fleet on a mission has no time for leisure. The Spartans do not use time well, and others suffer for it. Thucydides contrasts the tardiness of the Spartans in sailing toward Mytilene with the speed of the Athenian reaction to the news of the Mytilenean revolt. They "suddenly" send off forty

---

36. Strauss, *City and Man*, 190.

37. The verb is rare in extant Greek literature, used by Thucydides only here, and found only four other times in use by other authors. Plato, for example, uses the verb in reference to a disease's "being chronic" or incurable (*Gorgias* 480b). See also Aeschylus, *Libation Bearers* 946.

ships—the same number as are sent with Alcidas—so that "by making haste they would take the Mytileneans by surprise" (3.3.2–3).[38] It is the Athenians who act in time.

When Alcidas hears about the fall of Mytilene, several allies offer advice. It is proposed that a sudden attack on Mytilene would catch the Athenians there off guard, since they will not expect to have their capture of the city contested by the Peloponnesians.[39] Others urge Alcidas to seize one of the Ionian cities as a base of operation, and to work from there to aid other cities in their revolts from Athens. Both proposals would serve the goal of liberating Hellas from the rule of Athens. But Alcidas, Thucydides reports, wants to return to the Peloponnesus "as quickly as possible" (3.30–31.2). He does, however, plunder along the way home, slaughtering most of the prisoners taken until Samian envoys point out that killing those who are allies of Athens only "by necessity" is not a "noble way to liberate Hellas" (3.32.2). Thucydides attributes irony at Sparta's expense even to the anonymous Samians who must instruct a Spartan general about their noble "aim" in the war. Their advice to Alcidas sounds like Diodotus speaking to the Athenians: unless Alcidas stops the slaughter, he will convert few enemies to friends and make enemies of potential friends (3.32.2). The liberation of Hellas, which Sparta had proclaimed as the aim of its war with Athens and which had inclined the Hellenic world to its side in the conflict, is thus far in Thucydides' history mentioned more by others—by both the Plataeans and the Thebans in their opposing speeches at Plataea, for example, by the Mytileneans themselves when they request Spartan help (3.13.7), and now by the Samians—than by Spartans themselves. Sparta's support of revolting Mytilene is not only a dismal failure. The Spartan promise of support encourages Mytilene to hold out against Athens; their persistence no doubt increased Athenian anger toward the city (3.25.2).

What, then, is the Athenian role in the fall of Plataea? When the Plataeans are attacked by the Thebans, Athens promises help (2.73.3). By the following year, with the Spartans blockading their city, the Plataeans see "no hope of aid from Athens" (3.20.1). Thucydides refers us to no discussion in Athens

---

38. Although the Mytileneans are in fact warned of the Athenian approach and so are not taken by surprise, the Athenians do arrive in time to lay siege to the city before the Spartans arrive, which eventually leads to Mytilene's downfall (3.3.5, 3.27).

39. This advice comes from an Elean, Teutiaplus, who proposes to Alcidas that they proceed "suddenly" and by night, using the same word Thucydides uses to describe the Athenians' approach to Mytilene (*aphnō*) (3.30.3, 3.3.3).

about the issue. Kagan argues that the fall of Plataea and its abandonment by Athens were inevitable, for the city was "strategically untenable." An attempt to relieve Plataea would lead to "the great battle of hoplite armies that Pericles was determined to avoid."[40] If this is why Athens did not go to the defense of Plataea—and it seems plausible, given Pericles' emphasis on naval strength (e.g., 1.143.5)—Athens made a prudent decision, and the fate of Plataea was sealed by the necessities of the military situation. There are times during war when one must hold back for the sake of victory (see also 2.20.1–4). As to Athens's insistence that the city would come to Plataea's help, Kagan speculates that the message must have been sent when Pericles was momentarily out of power, "for the Periclean strategy permitted no way to rescue the city."[41] While this too is plausible, Thucydides makes no reference to divisions in Athens when he reports its promise of aid to Plataea that exaggerates its power at the cost of misleading and endangering its ally. Moreover, if Spartan forces were occupied in the siege of Plataea, they would be distracted from ravaging Attica. Earlier, Athens sent Plataea provisions and brought its women, children, and least able men to Athens (2.6.3). Was Athens's action a generous one of rescue? Or did the city take hostages as leverage to force Plataea to resist Sparta and its allies?

Although Thucydides does not explicitly implicate Athens in the destruction of Plataea, he concludes his description of the city's destruction by observing that matters ended for Plataea "in the ninety-third year after it became the ally of Athens" (3.68.4).[42] Given the short-lived character of alliances and treaties throughout Thucydides' history, especially during the "peace" of Nicias after 423 BCE, this may be the longest-lasting alliance Thucydides knows. For Thucydides, there is no "rejoicing" in the destruction of Plataea, as there is for Thebes. Indeed, his concluding remark about Plataea's long-lived alliance with Athens serves as a tribute to Plataea. By remembering in great detail the story of Plataea's resistance before its fall, he

---

40. Kagan, *Archidamian War*, 104–5, 174. See the balanced discussion of Athens and Plataea by Zumbrunnen, *Silence and Democracy*, 157–80.

41. Kagan, *Archidamian War*, 104–5, 174.

42. Connor points out that Thucydides typically includes such a "'rounding-off' formula" when he concludes his account of various events, although this one is unusual. He would expect Thucydides to recall the number of years Plataea had existed as an independent city or the number of years since the great Plataean victory against the Persians. Instead, according to Connor, Thucydides calls attention to Athens's ineffectiveness or unwillingness to aid Plataea. *Thucydides*, 91–93.

does not, like Athens, abandon Plataea,[43] even if his de-emphasis of Athens's role in Plataea's end suggests pardon of his own city rather than blame.

Necessity may have prevented the Athenians from going to the aid of Plataea, but Thucydides gives the Spartans no excuse in the case of Mytilene. Whereas success in the war against Sparta requires Athens to hold back from helping Plataea, success against Athens requires that Sparta venture at sea, far from home, for the relief of Mytilene. Sparta in effect acknowledges this when it sends the fleet that does not arrive in time to prevent Mytilene's fall to Athens. The Athenian ship carrying the command to destroy the captured city also wastes enough time on the way to Mytilene—just enough time, as we have seen, for a second ship to arrive to save the city. If Thucydides can forgive Athens for Plataea, perhaps this is why. But Thucydides shows no sympathy toward Sparta in its treatment of that city. For him, to understand all is not to forgive all.

In the next chapter, we will take a closer look at Sparta and at the great Spartan military leader Brasidas, with whom Thucydides does show considerable sympathy. Brasidas is a man who transcends his city, precisely because his aim becomes the very liberation of Hellas from Athenian domination that Sparta proclaimed as its goal in the war against Athens. Thucydides' admiring portrayal of Brasidas, a Spartan whose deeds did great harm to the Athenian cause, indicates that Thucydides' perspective transcends that of his city as well.

---

43. See Johnson on Plataea's virtue of "steadfast loyalty" toward both Athens and Hellas during the Persian War. *Thucydides, Hobbes,* 115, 123. Johnson demonstrates that the methods used by Thucydides in his account of Plataea's defense against attack foster "the conviction that the Plataeans are in the right" (122).

✵ Chapter 3

Sparta, Brasidas, and the Liberation of Hellas

In the previous chapter, I argued that Thucydides illustrates in his portrayal of Diodotus a politics cognizant of both the advantageous and the just, ennobled by the generosity or liberality that Pericles presented as a defining feature of Athens's excellence. Thucydides highlights this potential of politics by his implicit contrast between Athens and Sparta in the episodes involving Mytilene and Plataea. I also pointed out the ambiguities in Athens's treatment of Mytilene and Plataea. The politics of Pericles does not last—and perhaps cannot last—and in light of Athens's later excesses in Sicily, a case can be made for Sparta's virtues. The view that Sparta is superior to other cities because of its "prudent moderation" is expressed by the Spartan king Archidamus, when he urges his city against a hasty war with Athens.[1] Like Pericles in his funeral oration, Archidamus alludes to his city's superiority to its antagonist: "we are educated with too little learning to look down on the laws, and with such severity that we are too moderate to disobey them. Nor are we overly intelligent in useless

---

1. For discussion of Thucydides' sympathy for Sparta, see Orwin, *Humanity of Thucydides,* 183–84, 195, 199, 204; Strauss, *City and Man,* 212, 226, 271; Thomas Heilke, "Realism, Narrative, and Happenstance: Thucydides' Tale of Brasidas," *American Political Science Review* 98, no. 1 (2004): 130–31, 135.

matters." Consequently, "we alone do not become arrogant when success-ful." As such a city, Sparta has been "always free and most highly regarded" (1.84.1–3). Thucydides agrees: the Spartans, more than any he has known, "were moderate in their prosperity, and ordered their city more securely the greater it became" (8.24.4). Moderation, it seems, supports a free regime, by protecting it from the excesses that could lead to its downfall.

When the Corinthians urge Sparta to join them in war against Athens, they contrast the Athenian character, with its spirit of innovation and activ-ity, with Spartan caution and moderation. They nevertheless suggest that Sparta must overcome its characteristic moderation in order to protect its freedom—and indeed promote it in the Hellenic world—against Athenian expansion. Sparta must become, they suggest, more like Athens, or at least combine moderation with daring, even going beyond its old ways of fight-ing. Through the Corinthians' advice to their ally, Thucydides raises the question of whether the combination of stability and change required for freedom is possible. In its distinctive way, the more traditional Sparta also faces the difficulty of finding the balance or measure that Thucydides attri-butes to Pericles' politics and that made Athens under his guidance a city worthy of wonder—and that was so hard for Athens to maintain.

Thucydides sheds light on Sparta by his account of Brasidas, Sparta's greatest military hero, who spearheads the liberation of subjected cities from Athens in the name of his city. After discussing Thucydides' introduction of Sparta through the Corinthians' attempt to move Sparta to war and the Spar-tan response, in the remaining sections of this chapter I turn to Thucydides' account of Brasidas's exploits, and the relation between him and his city. Those who understand Thucydides as sympathetic toward Sparta—for its moderation, stability, and obedience to law—do not base their view on Bra-sidas. Indeed, Brasidas has been called "the Athenian among the Spartans." Thus his surprising success in Thrace is not Sparta's success.[2] Brasidas's very freedom from Sparta, which makes his war of liberation possible, makes him distrusted by his city. His success does allow Sparta to succeed in negotiat-ing the peace with Athens that it desires, inasmuch as Athens wants to stop

---

2. Strauss, *City and Man*, 213, 222; Connor, *Thucydides*, 134n67, 129; Edmunds, *Chance and Intel-ligence*, 90; Rahe, "Thucydides' Critique of Realpolitik," 138. Hornblower argues that Thucydides' presentation of Brasidas as isolated and alienated from Sparta is historically implausible, and suggests that Thucydides saw in one of the war's few military heroes the opportunity to write a heroic and epic *aristeia*, or "perhaps he was seduced by his own romantic picture of Brasidas as a loner or outcast, a Spartan not made like other Spartans." *A Commentary on Thucydides*, 3 vols. (Oxford: Clarendon Press, 1991–2008), 2.38–61, esp. 39, 60–61.

Brasidas and to have the cities he liberated restored to it. That Sparta succeeds in negotiating peace is a sign of its failure in a deeper sense, for it does not aim at the liberation of Hellas, and even betrays its allies in its separate peace with Athens. Sparta's failure, however, is Brasidas's failure. It is a failure that comes at great cost to those whom he "deceives" about their prospects for freedom. He needs the support of his city to make good on his promises in Thrace.

Because Brasidas's deeds of liberation cannot stand without Sparta's support, those deeds become as questionable as Sparta's. By representing his city, both in his words that describe its intentions and in his deeds that are understood to represent Sparta itself in the larger world, Brasidas is "a liar" (4.108.5, 4.81.2–3). This does not mean, however, that Brasidas is a sort of Machiavellian figure who deceives the cities in Thrace about his city's nobility in order to promote its interest in security, as well as his own reputation for serving his city (see 5.16.1).[3] Nor does it mean that Brasidas idealistically—and naively—accepts a noble view of his city that he tries to promote. Heilke criticizes Brasidas on this ground: whether because of a miscalculation of Spartan interests, stupidity, or deliberate or foolish disregard, Brasidas's actions were ultimately futile.[4] From this perspective, Brasidas is insufficiently a realist concerning politics. I argue, rather, that Brasidas attempts to liberate cities from Athenian rule in spite of his city's interests, aware of the risks he runs, for both the cities he liberates and of course for himself. Brasidas's "crusade" for freedom attempts to force Sparta to live up to its noble reputation. From this perspective, Brasidas is neither a realist who serves Sparta's self-interested goals, nor an idealist who misjudges his city's nobility, even if there is a kind of idealism in his effort to force Sparta to serve liberation.

Spartans want peace in part because the war has made them more vulnerable at home to revolts of their slave population, their Helots, an ancient population of the Peloponnesus whom they subjected (1.101.2). Thucydides indicates the centrality of the Helots to Sparta's politics and way of life. He refers to Sparta's "fear of the intransigence and numbers [of their Helots]," and says "that Sparta's affairs for the most part were always arranged with

---

3. Westlake raises this possibility, but claims that in the end Thucydides leaves Brasidas's attitude toward his own mission obscure. *Individuals in Thucydides*, 164.

4. Heilke, "Realism, Narrative, and Happenstance," 133, 136. In an interesting twist on this thesis, Timothy Burns argues that Brasidas did understand his city's intentions toward the liberated cities, but he turned away from this knowledge, "lacking the strength of soul to accept it." Thus Brasidas lies to himself. Burns, "Virtue of Thucydides' Brasidas," 518.

a view to protection against the Helots" (4.80.3).[5] The Spartan regime is supported by the Helots, insofar as their labor freed the Spartans for their famed military training and way of life. This, however, results in the problem that the Spartans cannot go faraway on foreign ventures because they must guard against the ever-present danger from the Helots at home (see 1.118.2).[6] Sparta's own tyranny at home over its subject population is in tension with its noble goal proclaimed at the outset of the war—freeing Hellas from Athenian tyranny (2.8.4).

Brasidas's army in Thrace includes a substantial number of Helots, whom Sparta was eager to send away so as to avoid slave revolts (4.79–81). The Helots therefore contribute to the liberation of the Thracian cities, which Sparta returns to Athens as part of the peace negotiations. Thucydides lets us see this irony. His sympathy is less with Sparta than with Brasidas, in spite of his reservations about Brasidas's actions in Thrace. Thucydides' considerable appreciation of Brasidas demonstrates his freedom from the perspective of his own city, even as it demonstrates his ultimate loyalty to the freedom that Athens at its best represents.

Introducing Sparta

Early in book 1, Thucydides gives an account of Sparta's claim to fame, not simply its power over the Peloponnesus and the formidable allies it leads, but its stability, freedom from tyranny, and laws. Sparta's very stability has made it a model for free government, and given it the power to defend freedom in the Hellenic world. Sparta has been able to arrange matters in other cities, including putting down tyrants in Athens and elsewhere. And it was Sparta, Thucydides says, who took the lead in the struggle of the Hellenic cities against the Persians (1.18.1–2). Hellas thus looks to Sparta to continue to oppose tyranny, now that it is exercised by the Hellenic city of Athens. In the first event Thucydides describes taking place at Sparta in his history, Corinth sends representatives to ask the Spartans for aid and indeed to join them in war against Athens. The Corinthians appeal to Sparta's reputation as a liberator.

---

5. Other Hellenic cities had slaves, but Sparta had more slaves (*oiketoi*) than any single city, Thucydides observes (8.40.2). Sparta's Helots, at least as reported by Herodotus, outnumbered the Spartans by seven to one in the army at Plataea (Herodotus 9.28–29).

6. According to Strauss, "Sparta was moderate because she had grave troubles with her Helots; the Helots made her moderate." *City and Man*, 191–92. As Strauss points out, this pattern is repeated in Thucydides' description of Chios, whom he names second to Sparta in moderation, as well as in the size of its slave population (8.24.4, 8.40.2). Also Orwin, *Humanity of Thucydides*, 84.

Sparta has not lived up to its reputation, the Corinthians claim, for by remaining inactive, Sparta has allowed Athenian power to double. "It is not the one who enslaves who more truly does the deed," they say, but rather "the one able to stop it who looks on, even if it has the reputation for virtue as the liberator of Hellas" (1.69). Moreover, Sparta's very virtues, they claim, contribute to the desperate state of affairs they face. Spartans' trust of their own regime, for example, makes them less trusting of what others tell them. This leads to caution and moderation, but also to "ignorance of external matters" (1.68.1). The Spartans do not understand how "completely different" they are from their antagonists. The contrast the Corinthians draw between Athens and Sparta is stark. The Athenians are innovators, quick both to conceive and to execute, whereas the Spartans are quick to preserve (*sōzein*) what they have, to decide nothing, and to act only when necessary. The Athenians never shrink from action, and are always away from home. The Spartans delay, and stay at home. Least of all do the Athenians enjoy what they have because they are always acquiring (*ktasthai*). Whereas the Athenians are born to have no peace, nor to allow any to others, the Corinthians say, the Spartans have "old-fashioned ways" (*archaiotropa*). Whereas "unvarying customs" (*akineta nomima*) serve a city at peace, cities compelled to act require artful invention (*epitechnēsis*). As in the arts, improvements prevail (1.70.2–71.3; see Aristotle, *Politics* 1269a20–24). The Corinthians attribute to the Spartans what Aristotle was later to designate the work of women—that of preserving—while they attribute to the Athenians the work of acquiring that Aristotle attributed to men (*Politics* 1277b24–25).

The Corinthians' appeal to Sparta requires, of course, that their description of the city not be perfectly accurate, for they are asking the Spartans to go to war against Athens, which requires their leaving home. It is the very thing the Spartans decide to do when they vote for war. The description the Corinthians give of Athens, moreover, facilitates their purpose: an Athens whose nature is never to be at peace is not one with whom Sparta might easily negotiate a compromise that preserves the peace. For Athens, they imply, there is no peace. As a consequence, there is none for anyone else. Like the Spartans themselves, the Corinthians speak in terms of necessity. They tell the Spartans that there is no choice, or that there are no options, just when they are asking them to make a choice, and to follow the option they set before them.[7]

---

7. Similarly, if the Corinthians have "rightly" described Athens as never at peace, their attempt to prevent its alliance with Corcyra would have been futile. And yet they make that attempt, an attempt that almost succeeds (1.44.1). In this instance as well, the Corinthians act as if there is more flexibility than their contrast between the two cities suggests.

The Corinthians do not merely know antagonists who are so completely different from each other, they themselves are not "completely" different from either of them. Earlier in the first book, when the Corinthians spoke at Athens in an attempt to urge the Athenians against the alliance the Corcyreans propose, they appeal to Corcyra's obligations as their colony toward its mother city. Corcyra has not paid Corinth the respect it is due (1.38). Unlike the Corcyreans, whose first word in their speech at Athens refers to "what is just," the first word of the Corinthians' speech refers to "what is necessary" (1.32.1, 1.37.1). The latter give advice to the Athenians as "the elder" to "the younger" (1.42.1). To the Athenians Corinth must seem like Sparta, who is Corinth's close ally and neighbor on the Peloponnesus.

In Sparta, in contrast, the Corinthians appeal to the arts over the law. Their statement that change prevails in both cases reveals their city's affinity with the innovative Athens rather than with law-abiding Sparta. Their reproach of Sparta's ways as "old-fashioned" is similar to the complaint of the Unjust Speech in Aristophanes' *Clouds* that the Just Speech is out of date (e.g., *archaios, Clouds* 889). Corinth is progressive. Like Athens and unlike Sparta, Corinth is a city of commerce, conveniently located for trade both by land and by sea (1.13.2–5). Corinth is the city in which it is said the first triremes were built, and it has one of the largest navies in the Hellenic world (1.13.2, 1.36.3). In book 1, we keep meeting the Corinthians "away from home," speaking first at Athens in response to Corcyra, then at Sparta in order to urge war, and at Sparta again at a meeting of the Peloponnesian league (1.120–24). The conflicts with Athens that bring Corinth to Sparta to ask for aid involve Corcyra, Corinth's colony to the west, and Potidaea, its colony to the east. Corinth has colonized all over the map. The Corinthians give more speeches in direct discourse in book 1 than the representatives of any city in all of Thucydides' history. And if Sparta does not decide to speedily invade Athens, the Corinthians threaten, Corinth will acquire new allies (1.71.4–6).[8] Corinth is flexible. To the Spartans, Corinth must seem like Athens. Perhaps they are too flexible to be trustworthy.

The Corinthians themselves recognize that the Spartans have difficulty trusting them when they try to allay that mistrust by tracing it to the Spartans' trust in their own regime—which they claim makes them distrust advice from others. When the Corinthians threaten to find new allies, they

---

8. A number of years later, after Sparta signs a peace treaty with Athens, Thucydides recounts negotiations between Corinth and Argos, an old rival of Sparta for ascendancy in the Peloponnesus (e.g., 5.37.1–2, 5.38.1, 5.48.1–3). Sparta finally forces Corinth to seek other allies.

also insist that they have "affinity" with Sparta (*sunēthēs*) (literally, share the same habits). They conclude their speech by appealing to the gods, to the oaths of alliance they have sworn, and to their ancestors (1.71.4–7). Do the Corinthians, then, integrate Athenian openness to change with Spartan stability, or do they merely appear one way in contrast to Athens, another in contrast to Sparta, and one way at Athens, another at Sparta?

Thucydides' presentation of events and speeches in book 1 that lead to the war suggests that both stability and change, rest and motion, are necessary to freedom. Athenians who happen to be there speak next to caution Sparta against war with such a formidable antagonist as Athens. The Spartan king, Archidamus, urges against immediate war by defending the Spartan character of moderation, and the freedom that Sparta has maintained for so many years by acting in accord with it. Sparta's acting in conformity to its character and ways frees it from the compulsions of time and events, such as those that the Corinthians urge upon it. Indeed, doing so, Archidamus implies, allows for action rather than reaction, inasmuch as one's actions proceed from who one is. The Corinthians, however, have reproached Sparta for allowing the power of Athens to grow. To refuse to react to circumstances is ultimately slavish, for it is to refuse to act. Freedom is manifest and realized in action, and its loss is threatened by inaction just as much as it is by constant change in response to circumstances. From this perspective, Sparta's inaction does not manifest its freedom. It endangers it. It is not surprising that the vote in the assembly is a divided one.

In speaking against an immediate declaration of war, Archidamus appeals to his experience in many wars, which cautions him against believing that war is either safe or advantageous. He asks the Spartans who are of a similar age and experience to remember war's dangers (1.80.1). He defends the old-fashioned ways in which Spartans are raised. Although his advice seems to confirm Corinth's reproach of Sparta for delay and caution, he is not cowed from giving it; he advises his city to strengthen its material preparations, acquire further allies, and gain time—even two or three years—by asking the Athenians to arbitrate the differences between themselves and the Corinthians (1.82.1–3). Archidamus favors not inaction, but sufficient preparation for action. Sparta's "slowness and hesitation" are not shameful, he claims, for haste in fighting now will only delay the end of the war if Sparta is not prepared (1.84.1). Such care demonstrates the moderation, respect for the laws, and discipline that Spartans have inherited from their ancestors and that have made them a "free and famous city." It is these qualities that distinguish Spartans from others, for they prevent them from becoming hubristic in success, and help them endure in misfortune (1.84.1–85.1). He knows the force that Sparta must face in Athens's wealth, resources, allies, ships, and naval capacity.

The Spartan strategy of invading Attica and devastating the Attic country-side, he warns, may not produce an easy end to the war. Perhaps he suspects Pericles's plan to move the Athenians to safety within the walls of the city, and to rely on its sea power. Athens's indomitable spirit, he points out, will keep it from becoming slaves of its land (1.80.2–81.6). He at least is not as ill informed about Athens as Corinth accuses Spartans of being.

Archidamus thus appeals to the stability, law-abidingness, and good government that Thucydides attributes to Sparta from early times (1.18.1–2). Thucydides also mentions in this same place, however, Sparta's long-standing reputation for resisting tyranny, and serving freedom. And the Corinthians have just appealed to Sparta to liberate Hellas from Athenian tyranny when they asked Sparta to join them in war against Athens. Archidamus, however, refers to the war Corinth proposes as one "carried on for the sake of private interests" (1.82.6). Does he ignore the Corinthians' noble purpose, or does he simply recognize Corinth's interest in maintaining its status and power in the Hellenic world? Is he wary about risking Sparta's freedom to pursue freedom for others?

The Spartan ephor Sthenelaidas responds, and urges immediate war. Whereas Archidamus combines moderation with intelligence, one of the virtues Pericles attributes to Athens, the daring that Pericles also attributes to Athens exists in Sthenelaidas with neither of Archidamus's virtues (cf. 1.79.2 with 1.144.3). Athens is doing injustice to the Peloponnesians and their allies, he proclaims, and it is no time for deliberation. Deeds must answer deeds. It is possible that by helping Corinth in the matter of Potidaea, the Spartans would be striking a blow for freedom from Athenian rule, but Sthenelaidas's concern is to strike a blow against Athens, who has wronged them. In the two Spartans who speak, Thucydides shows us cautious understanding versus unreflective action. Sthenelaidas claims not to understand the "long speech" the Athenians delivered after the Corinthians spoke, because it praised Athens without denying the Corinthians' charges. His claim not to understand the Athenians' speech calls into question whether he understands the subtleties of the Corinthians' similarly long speech. It is Archidamus who understands it, and attempts to answer it when he opposes following their advice.

After Sthenelaidas concludes his short speech, the Spartans choose between Archidamus's and Sthenelaidas's advice "by shouting rather than by voting," for this is how Spartans "make judgments," Thucydides tells us.[9] Sthenelaidas

---

9. The Spartans nevertheless understand their shouting as "voting," for in concluding his speech Sthenelaidas asks his addressees "to vote" for the war, and Thucydides describes him as "calling for a vote" (1.86.5–1.87.1). In Thucydides' history, "shouting" (*boē*) more typically refers to the noise troops make during battle (e.g., 4.34.2, 4.34.3, 4.35.2, 4.125.5, 4.127.1, 7.70.7).

claims that the "shouting" is so loud on both sides that he must ask those who support him to move to one side, and those who support Archidamus to the other, for he wants them to declare their position openly. The majority is on his side in favor of war (1.87.1–3). Sthenelaidas's is the last speech of a Spartan at Sparta in Thucydides' work. Spartans do not typically reflect on themselves as part of their public discourse, as the Athenians do—not only Pericles, but also Cleon and Diodotus, Nicias and Alcibiades. Archidamus does so only when his city is criticized by its allies. His is a defensive speech, prompted by others, even though it aims at preserving Sparta's freedom.

War nevertheless does not come at once. The Spartans assemble their allies to discuss the matter, the Corinthians speak again, and a vote is taken in favor of war. Although Sparta does not ask for the arbitration that Archidamus proposes, it does send delegations to Athens making a number of demands that Athens resists. It is not until the Peloponnesian ally Thebes invades Plataea that the war actually breaks out. Although Archidamus's proposal to delay the war lost in the assembly, Sparta proceeds in the cautious manner he advises. In the meantime, Sparta resolves to make overtures to Persia for an alliance against Athens (2.7.1). Soon after Thucydides recounts this fact, he observes that the Hellenic world had greater goodwill for Sparta than for Athens, inasmuch as Sparta proclaimed itself the liberator of Hellas (2.8.4). Thucydides does not say what form this "proclamation" takes, or who makes it on behalf of the city. When soon thereafter Archidamus encourages his troops in the field, he speaks to them of the widespread goodwill for Sparta, which he attributes only to the hatred of Athens (2.11.2).

Introducing Brasidas

Thucydides centers events of the first few years of the war on Athens, Pericles' funeral oration, the plague, and Pericles' death. Each spring, the Spartans lead a force against Attica, and ravage the countryside. In the third year, however, the Peloponnesians move instead against Plataea, and in the war's fourth year, Mytilene revolts, as I discuss in the previous chapter. While these are the major events in these early years, we do briefly meet Brasidas, a Spartiate,[10] in command of a small force, who comes to the aid of Methone on the southern Peloponnesian coast against an Athenian assault. As the Athenians are besieging the walls of the city, Brasidas with his hundred hoplites "runs

---

10. A Spartiate was a full citizen of Sparta, and a member of its highest military class.

through" their ranks, enters the city, and saves it (2.25.2).[11] For his "daring" at Methone, Brasidas is "the first" to be commended at Sparta during the war (2.25.1–2). Although Thucydides says that Brasidas is the "first" to be commended by the Spartans, he is the only one ever mentioned by Thucydides to be so commended. The military action, however, is only the first of Brasidas's daring exploits that Thucydides goes on to describe.

After serving as an adviser for several Spartan generals and having no decisive influence on events (2.87, 2.93–94, 3.79.3),[12] Brasidas commands his own ship in a Peloponnesian fleet sent to rescue Pylos on the southern coast of the Peloponnesus from Athenian occupation. The Spartan fleet faces the Athenians ensconced in their own territory, and attacks the Peloponnesus from the sea, as the Athenians are wont to do. Thucydides observes the strange reversal of customary tactics, with the land power proceeding to make a naval attack, and the naval power defending itself on its enemy's own soil (4.12.3). When the Peloponnesians hesitate to land in fear of wrecking their ships, Brasidas shouts out to them to run their ships aground rather than allow Athens a foothold on the Peloponnesus for the sake of "saving timber" (4.11.4). Brasidas "compels" his own steersman to do so (4.12.1)—words do not seem sufficient—until he himself faints from the many wounds he receives in the attempt, and falls back in the bow of his ship. Presumably he meant to be among the first to step on shore had a landing taken place. Whether any of the commanders of the other ships are persuaded to follow Brasidas's example, Thucydides does not say, observing only that the rest were unable to land (4.12.1–2).

Although Brasidas plays no further role at Pylos, Thucydides' brief account of his dramatic exploit stands in the background of Spartan misadventures there. The Peloponnesians place four hundred of their hoplites on the island of Sphacteria, opposite Pylos, in an attempt to prevent Athenian ships from entering the narrow straits to relieve the Athenians who are holding Pylos. But when the Spartans fail to block the Athenian ships that arrive,

---

11. Connor points out that Thucydides describes Brasidas as "running" "in a surprising number of passages," a "characterization all the more striking when the reader remembers the repeated criticism of the Spartans for their slowness." Connor cites Brasidas's running through Thessaly (4.78.5, 4.79.1), "overrunning" the country outside of Amphipolis (4.104.3), running with his troops into Torone (4.112.1), and running at top speed against the Athenians led by Cleon at Amphipolis (5.10.6). *Thucydides*, 128n45.

12. As Westlake says of Brasidas's early assignment in the war as adviser to Spartan commanders, he "did his best to infuse into his superiors something of his own enterprising spirit." And it "must have been a frustrating experience." *Individuals in Thucydides*, 149.

the Spartans on the island are trapped without sufficient food or provisions. So great is the Spartan sense of the disaster that they negotiate a truce in the field and send representatives to Athens to try to bring an end to the war. Just as Brasidas's deeds at Pylos stand in contrast with the deeds of the other Spartans there, so too does his brief but daring speech to his men contrast with the cowering speech that the Spartans give in Athens. With the exception of Brasidas's stirring and persuasive speeches in Thrace that Thucydides later records, this is the last Spartan speech in his work. The Spartan speech at Athens highlights Brasidas's very different speeches as well as his deeds.

The Spartans minimize their own failure at Pylos as much as possible—and therewith Athenian success—by attributing both success and failure in war to chance.[13] To save themselves from blame, they deprive the Athenians—and thereby human beings in general—of praise. They have come to their present predicament, they say, not because of their lack of power, nor because they have arrogantly overreached, but because they failed in judgment (*gnōmē*), a failure "to which all alike are susceptible" (4.17.5–18.2). Not only are all subject to fortune, but judgment does not distinguish one human being from another, for all are subject to its mistakes. Pericles, in contrast, earlier praised Athens for relying "more on judgment than on chance, more on daring than on power" (1.144.3). The Spartans do not only depreciate virtue, but they depreciate the very virtue in which Athens takes pride and which Pericles couples with daring itself.

So too, the Spartans continue, Athenians should not suppose from their present strength and resources that "chance will always be with [them]" (4.18.3). In other words, Athenians should grant peace out of recognition that they too could suffer disaster if the war continues. Should this happen, the Spartans warn them, they will be thought to have enjoyed what they now have because of chance, whereas if they end the war now they will have "a reputation for strength and intelligence that cannot be endangered" (4.18.5). The Spartans thus offer the Athenians the opportunity to secure a reputation that must by their own reckoning be a false one, inasmuch as reputation depends on chance. They warn the Athenians not to trust to *eupraxia*, a word that means both acting well and doing well or prospering, as if it were interchangeable with good fortune (*eutuchia*). So too they use "experience," which Thucydides earlier used to refer to the source of Athens's greater skill

---

13. As Rood observes, "Disparagement of the enemy's success is apt in an exhortation to the defeated troops, not in an appeal to peace." *Thucydides: Narrative and Explanation*, 40. On the Spartan speech in Athens, see also Strauss, *City and Man*, 173.

at sea (e.g., 2.85.2; cf. 2.89.2) to refer to the experience that teaches Athens and Sparta alike not to trust to "prosperity" (4.17.5).

Finally, the Spartans ask the Athenians to demonstrate their "virtue" in the present circumstances by accepting the very proposal they offer (4.19.2). Virtue lies in not taking advantage of fortune. This will also be advantageous to the Athenians, as Sparta will exercise toward them such "virtue" in turn. Thus Athens and Sparta will become "firm friends" in not exploiting the opportunities chance presents. They should act now, before "something irreparable comes between [them]," and produces "eternal enmity." Indeed, if Athenians accept Sparta's proposal of peace, they will gain the gratitude of the Hellenic world now engaged in war, for they will effect a "cessation of evils" (4.19.3–20.3). Of course, Corinth might not be grateful for Sparta's capitulation, or suppose easily "reparable" Athens's treatment of the Corinthian colony Potidaea (2.67.4, 2.70). More generally, the Spartans claim the end of war means the "cessation of evils," as if unaware that the evil that prompts at least some of Sparta's allies is the domination, even tyranny, of Athens.[14] Those allies, such as Corinth and Thebes, are not present; nor has Sparta consulted the Peloponnesian League in proposing an end of war, as it is careful to do before going to war. If Athens and Sparta are in agreement (literally, "say the same things"), the Spartans say, the rest of Hellas will "honor" the agreement from its weaker position (4.20.4), using a word that can only highlight the lack of honor in their own proposal. Their suit for peace comes to nil when they are denied a request to negotiate the terms of a treaty in private, which is necessary so that they will not be slandered to their allies (4.22). The Spartans are well aware that had they been successful, theirs would have been a separate peace, and a betrayal of the Peloponnesians and those allied with them.

After the Athenians reject the Spartan proposition, for they "want more" (4.21.2),[15] the fighting continues on Sphacteria. Sphacteria finally falls

---

14. Johnson, *Thucydides, Hobbes*, 48; and P. A. Brunt, "Spartan Policy and Strategy in the Archidamian War," *Phoenix* 19, no. 4 (1965): 273.

15. Cleon leads the opposition to Sparta's offer, Thucydides reports, but he does not give Cleon a speech in response to the Spartans. Hornblower finds it "unfair" of Thucydides to deny him a speech and attributes it to Thucydides' "personal malice" against him. *Thucydides*, 56. He was consequently, Hornblower speculates, "unwilling to dwell on Kleon's victory in the debate." *Commentary on Thucydides,* 2.170. By giving no Athenian speech in response, however, Thucydides emphasizes Sparta's capitulation by letting the Spartans' speech stand alone. As Rood observes, by writing a repellent speech for Cleon, Thucydides might have made the Spartan proposals more attractive. *Thucydides: Narrative and Explanation*, 42.

because of the well-laid battle plans of the Athenian commander Demosthenes, who uses light-armed troops, archers, and javelin and stone throwers against the heavy-armed Peloponnesians (e.g., 4.32.3–4). After retreating to a fort on the tip of the island, the Spartan forces are surprised by the enemy from the rear. Thucydides is reminded of Thermopylae, for there too the enemy surprises the Spartans from the rear, and they cannot hold out. Thucydides admits that to compare Sphacteria with Thermopylae is "to compare small things with great" (4.36.3). Facing defeat, the forces on Sphacteria send a message to Sparta asking what they should do. After "two or three exchanges," Sparta sends word that "they should decide for themselves as long as they do nothing shameful" (*aischron*) (4.38.3). After consulting with one another, Thucydides recounts, the soldiers decide to surrender to the Athenians (4.38.3). The Spartans at Thermopylae died fighting (Herodotus 7.223–28), whereas those on Sphacteria agree to what seems a shameful surrender (see 4.40.2). At Thermopylae, the Spartans do what they are trained to do, and what the world expects of them. They do not have to ask anyone what to do. Had the Spartans on Thermopylae received a message like the one Sparta sent her soldiers on Sphacteria, it would have seemed a sufficiently clear statement about what they should do, and they would have died fighting, as in fact they did in the absence of such a message. Of course, they would not have asked for advice in the first place. The Spartans on Sphacteria, in contrast, who ask for advice about what to do, already suppose that there is more than one way of acting. They are able to imagine themselves surrendering. Their discipline and laws, from which Pericles claims that Spartan courage comes, do not determine their actions. If they can ask Sparta what to do, they can ask themselves. The Spartans who advise them to do nothing dishonorable should know that their advice is useless, just as for those at Thermopylae it would have been unnecessary. When the prisoners who surrender are finally returned to Sparta as a result of a peace agreement, Sparta has difficulty trusting them (5.34.2).

Given the Spartans' reputation for never surrendering, the Hellenes found their capitulation on Sphacteria to be the most surprising thing in the war. Thucydides reports the anecdote of the Spartan prisoner who is asked on his arrival in Athens whether those who died rather than surrender were noble men, and replies that arrows do not distinguish the noble from the base. He makes it clear, Thucydides says, that those who die when hit by stones and arrows die by chance (4.40.1–2). His appeal to chance echoes that of the Spartan embassy that recently sued for peace, and failed (e.g., 4.18.3). Neither he nor they are like Brasidas, who stops fighting only when he faints from his many wounds (4.12.1). Since Brasidas places himself in the forefront of the fighting, it is not merely from chance that he is wounded, although it may be chance that he survives, and lives to fight again. His speeches and deeds on the Thracian campaign, to which I turn next, constitute one of the most dramatic chapters in Thucydides' account of the war. The division in the Spartan assembly between Archidamus and Sthenelaidas before the onset of the war gives way to a deeper and more fatal one between Brasidas and Sparta itself. Brasidas's collision course with his city, I argue, calls into question Sparta's status as the free city that Archidamus praised, and ultimately Brasidas's own freedom as well.

Brasidas's Thracian Campaign

The capture of its men on Sphacteria leaves Sparta demoralized. When Athens sends its navy against Corinth, there is no mention of Sparta's helping its ally (4.42–45). Athenian forces proceed to threaten the nearby city of Megara. Because Brasidas "happens" to be around Corinth, he plays a major role in the defense of Peloponnesian interests there. By leading a large Corinthian contingent, other allies, and the men he himself had already assembled for an expedition to Thrace, he produces a standoff with the Athenian forces near Megara's port of Nisaea. Once again, as at Methone, Thucydides presents Brasidas's exploits as if they come from his own initiative (4.70–74.1).

Although it is chance that Brasidas's presence in Corinth coincides with Athens's ventures in the area, he is there for a purpose, raising a force for an expedition against Athenian interests in Thrace, an expedition that succeeds in liberating several cities there from their subjection to Athens. The mission begins with Brasidas "wishing it," and with the request of revolting Chalcidians for Spartan help. Perdiccas, the king of Macedonia, offers to contribute funds for the expedition, inasmuch as he would like the army's help in subduing the Lyncestians. Because the Athenians still hold Pylos, the Spartans want to divert them from operations in the Peloponnesus by threatening them elsewhere, and agree to the expedition. It is also the case, Thucydides tells us, that once Brasidas succeeds in liberating cities in Thrace, the Spartans are able to exchange the "liberated" cities in their peace negotiations with Athens (4.81.1–2).

Moreover, the expedition gives Sparta an excuse to send away some of its Helots as hoplites in the army, lest with Pylos captured the Helots might start an insurrection (4.79.3–81.1).[16] Sparta eagerly sends seven hundred of

---

16. The word for "starting an insurrection" that Thucydides uses here is *neōterizein*, meaning literally "to attempt something new," or to make a political change or revolution. The Spartans fear the new, just as they fear the class they enslave.

its Helots with Brasidas to Thrace (4.80.4–5). Chalcidice's "eagerness" for help to come is matched by Sparta's "eagerness" for the Helots to go—for its own safety at home. Inasmuch as Brasidas is reputed to be a force for action (*drastērion*)—this is why the Chalcidians request him in particular (4.81.1)—one may suspect that Sparta's sending Brasidas along with the Helots also serves its safety. In addition to the Helots, the rest of the force Brasidas himself must recruit for pay (4.80.5). From Thucydides' account, Helots and mercenaries and one Spartiate, Brasidas, are on their way to Thrace to become the liberators of Hellas.[17]

When describing Sparta's dispatch of the Helots with Brasidas, Thucydides relates an anecdote about Sparta's dealing with its subject population that took place at some undetermined date in the past.[18] Sparta announces that the Helots who have done best against Sparta's enemies should come forth to receive their freedom, in order to test them. Those who think themselves worthy of freedom would be most likely to revolt, the Spartans assume, on account of their proud thoughts. About two thousand are selected and crowned with garlands, and celebrate "in the belief that they are free." Soon thereafter, "the Spartans make them disappear, and no one perceives in what way each of them perished" (4.80.3–4). Because Thucydides describes this event in the course of telling us about the seven hundred Helots Sparta sent with Brasidas to Thrace, he lets us imagine that Brasidas's forces might have been almost three times their number, and might have included the bravest and the best of Sparta's subject peoples—the ones that Sparta "made disappear."

En route to Thrace, Brasidas and his forces meet opposition to their passage through Thessaly, where many are favorably disposed to Athens. Although Brasidas agrees that they will pass only if the Thessalians are willing, he does not wait to find out. At a run, he and the army proceed before a large enough force can be gathered to stop them (4.78.2–5). Thucydides' tale raises the question of whether the deceived Thessalians would allow Brasidas and his troops return passage through their country. We have seen Brasidas attempt at Pylos to wreck his ship in order to land, cutting himself and his men off from an easy retreat. Later, when Sparta finally sends reinforcements to Thrace, Thucydides tells us, the Thessalians do not allow their passage and

---

17. Graham Wylie notes that Brasidas was given no Spartiate troops apparently because those in control at Sparta at the time "chose to treat the expedition as a semi-private venture." "Brasidas: Great Commander or Whiz Kid?" *Quaderni Urbinati di Cultura Classica*, n.s. 41, no. 2 (1992): 78n7.

18. Connor, *Thucydides*, 131.

they return home (4.132.2). Brasidas cut off an obvious route between his forces and his city.

Tension soon occurs between Brasidas and the Macedonian king, Perdiccas, who is funding part of Brasidas's army. Perdiccas has in effect hired an army, and wants it to do his bidding against his own enemies. In particular, Perdiccas wants to subdue the Lyncestians, whereas Brasidas wants to arbitrate between them and gain Lyncestis as a Spartan ally. Perdiccas objects that he did not bring in Brasidas as a judge or arbitrator (*dikastēs*), but as a destroyer (*kathairetēs*) (4.83.4)—using language that could describe how the Spartan judges in fact act toward the Plataeans. When Brasidas refuses to play his part in Perdiccas's plan, Perdiccas trims the pay of his forces (4.83.6). Soon Brasidas gets reinforcements, not from Sparta, but from the cities he liberates from Athenian rule (4.124.1).

When Brasidas and his army arrive at Acanthus, Brasidas requests that he be admitted into the city alone to speak to the people. "For a Spartan," Thucydides comments, Brasidas is "not incompetent at speaking" (4.84.2). This is his first solo speech in direct discourse in Thucydides' work (see 2.86.6, 4.11.4). Brasidas repeats its drift, Thucydides tells us, with equal success at Torone (4.114.3). He explains that Sparta has sent him and the army to prove true (*epalētheunein*) its claim that it is fighting to liberate Hellas from the Athenians (4.85.1). Although we have heard this claim about Sparta before, this is the first time a Spartan has so clearly made it (1.139.3), as opposed to those who have an interest in its proving true, such as the Mytileneans, the Samians, and the Plataeans. The truth of Sparta's noble purpose will depend on what Brasidas accomplishes.

Although Sparta has been slow to send aid to Thrace because the city was pressed by Athens nearer home, Brasidas tells the Acanthians, he has now come with utmost enthusiasm in support of their freedom. If they offer resistance, however, he will not hesitate to ravage their fields, for they would stand in the way not only of their own freedom but also of that of other Hellenes. Moreover, if Brasidas is turned away by Acanthus, other cities to which he goes will be less inclined to trust him, suspecting that he is too weak to defend them against the Athenians if they attack, or that Sparta is not fully committed to their freedom (4.85.2–6).[19] Thucydides, however, gives us reason to share such suspicions. As evidence that the Acanthians need

---

19. In speaking to the Acanthians, Brasidas slips from speaking in the first person plural, whether in reference to the Spartans in general or to the assembled force that awaits outside the city walls, to the first person singular (4.85.2–6).

not fear Athenian retaliation, Brasidas claims that the Athenians withdrew at Nisaea, even though their force outnumbered his. Thucydides has already told us otherwise, for the Athenians there do not want to face "the superior numbers" that stand with Brasidas since they have already accomplished their goals (4.73.4).[20] Nor does Brasidas now have the army in Thrace that he commanded at Nisaea, as he claims to the Acanthians (4.85.6–7). In fact, after the Athenians depart from Nisaea, the combined Peloponnesian forces under his command "disperse and go home" (4.74.1; see also 4.108.5).

Sparta's commitment to freedom for cities liberated from Athens is also suspect. Brasidas claims that he has come only after "obtaining the greatest oaths from the Spartans" that the cities liberated from Athens will remain "autonomous" (4.86.1). But Thucydides reports no such oaths taken by Spartans about the liberated cities' autonomy.[21] Brasidas has come not to side with one faction or another in the city, he continues. Nor would he truly offer freedom if it would enslave the greater part in their city to the few, or a smaller part to everyone. Such would be harsher than foreign rule, and the Spartans would be to blame for the very thing for which they blame Athens (4.86.4–5). Of course, in enslaving the Helots Sparta has enslaved the greater part to the few, even if Brasidas understandably does not mention this now. Moreover, recent events in Megara call into question Spartan commitment to the autonomy of "oppressed" cities it liberates. Once the Athenians depart from Megara, the Peloponnesian faction within the city executes those most friendly to Athens, and proceeds to turn the city into "an extreme oligarchy" (4.74.3). Megara is therefore an ominous precedent for the cities in Thrace.[22] The freedom with which Brasidas tempts his addressees, Thucydides admits later, depends on "a thoroughly unexamined hope" (*aperiskeptos elpis*) to which they turn over their desires (4.108.4).

Should Sparta deceive in its promises of liberation, Brasidas concludes this line of argument, the charge of depriving others of freedom would be even "more hateful" against Sparta than against a city that makes no pretense to

---

20. Thucydides is very careful to list the forces Brasidas commands at Nisaea: twenty-seven hundred Corinthian hoplites, four hundred Phliasians, six hundred Sicyonians, as well as the troops he himself had assembled for the Thracian campaign (4.70.1). In addition, they are joined by twenty-two hundred hoplites and six hundred cavalrymen from Boeotia, numbering six thousand hoplites alone (4.72.1–2). See Connor, *Thucydides*, 132, 138.

21. Hornblower admits that Brasidas's claim that the Spartans took such oaths "would be hard to believe" without collaboration from the narrative, but finds it at 4.88.1, where Thucydides reports that the Acanthians made Brasidas pledge to stand by those oaths. *Commentary on Thucydides*, 2:47.

22. Gomme, *HCT*, 3:554; Connor, *Thucydides*, 133; Orwin, *Humanity of Thucydides*, 79n20.

virtue. So too would it be "even more shameful" for those with good reputations to pursue their own gain by deceiving others than it would be for those who openly use force to rule (4.85.6–86.6). To the extent that Sparta does not live up to its title of liberator, Brasidas by implication hates his own city, and he is ashamed of it. Sparta lets the world think it fights for freedom.

Seduced by Brasidas's words and fearing for its crop, which is ready to harvest, Acanthus yields (4.88.1). Unlike Alcidas in going to assist Mytilene's liberation, Brasidas has perfect timing. Like that of the Athenian rhetoricians whom Cleon criticizes (3.38.2, 3.38.7), Brasidas's rhetoric is "seductive" and offers what is "pleasant for the moment" (4.108.5–6; see also 4.88.1). After Acanthus is persuaded by Brasidas, Stagiros revolts (4.88.2). Amphipolis, an Athenian colony against which Brasidas next campaigns, also comes over to Brasidas when it hears his moderate terms: those in the city wishing to remain, Amphipolitan or Athenian, can do so, keeping their property and privileges of citizenship, while those who want to leave can do so with their property (4.105.2). The loss of Amphipolis in particular causes great alarm in Athens, given that city's strategic location and material resources, such as timber and other revenues it provides (4.108.1). Hearing of the "mildness" shown by Brasidas and his proclaiming "everywhere" that he was sent to liberate Hellas, other cities in the region become encouraged "to make a change" (*neōterizein*) (4.108.1–3). Brasidas is now able to induce in these other "subjects" what the Spartans fear from their own subject population (4.80.2). Among his successes is Torone, to whom he offers similarly mild terms, while making clear the consequences of not accepting them. Brasidas tells the Toroneans in good Diodotean fashion that he "pardons" them for their past opposition to Sparta, for they cannot be blamed for an alliance into which they were forced by a stronger power. As for the present and future, however, he will hold them responsible for their errors (4.114.5). Pardon is both an act of generosity and good policy, for the past is past, but Brasidas offers it only in the context of making clear that he will hold them responsible if they do not grasp their freedom now.[23]

Brasidas's message about Sparta is so powerful that it wins the goodwill of the Hellenic world for Sparta for years to come. Even after the Sicilian expedition, years after Brasidas's death, "his virtue and intelligence, experienced

---

23. Burns argues, in contrast, that Brasidas contradicts himself in recognizing the force of necessity (and hence the need to pardon) while appealing to freedom. Following Orwin's interpretation of Diodotus (as I discuss in chapter 2), Burns understands Diodotus to avoid this contradiction by appealing to the full force of necessity. "Virtue of Thucydides' Brasidas," 516, 520, 521.

by some and believed from hearsay by others," caused goodwill for the Spartans among the Athenian allies. He is the first Spartan who went out from the city who seems good in all respects, and he left a firm hope that other Spartans would be so as well (4.81.2–3). In book 1, Thucydides tells us of another Spartan who went out from his city, Pausanias, as commander of the Hellenic forces in their alliance against Persia. He became so corrupt and acted so violently—more like a tyrant than a general—that he turned the allies against Sparta toward Athens (1.94–96).[24] Brasidas is not the "first" Spartan to go out to represent his city in the eyes of the world, but the first who goes out and seems good to the larger world. He has replaced the memory of Pausanias, and replaced it with something "new."

Like Pericles, Brasidas depicts a noble view of his city to the world, but he never speaks before the Spartan people. When after several successes, he asks Sparta for reinforcements, his request is denied. This is due in part to the envy of Sparta's leading men (literally, its "first men"), and in part because Sparta is occupied with the return of its soldiers who surrendered on Sphacteria to Athens and with ending the war (4.108.7). Thucydides describes Pericles as "the first man" of Athens, but Sparta has several such men, and Brasidas is not among them. He is in no position to speak for Sparta. In contrast, Pericles is able to interpret Athens to herself as well as to the world. However much Athens's deeds fall short of Pericles' noble words, Pericles can present Athenians with a view of themselves that they can imagine may be true. They do not laugh at his boasts, as on another occasion they laugh at Cleon's (4.28.5). Like Pericles when he speaks to both Athenians and foreigners about the virtues of his city (2.34.4, 2.36.4), Brasidas occupies a world stage. His speeches may have a greater impact on the Hellenic world as a whole than Pericles' speeches, but unlike Pericles, who occupies a world stage by holding the stage in his home city of Athens, Brasidas's stage is never in Sparta.

Brasidas's success in Thrace causes sufficient alarm in Athens that Athens becomes willing to offer Sparta a one-year truce in the fighting to allow time for negotiating the terms of a peace (4.117). The truce demonstrates the extent to which Brasidas's representation of his city to the world falls short

---

24. Connor observes that Thucydides uses similar language in describing Brasidas and Pausanias, so that Brasidas serves as "an apparent refutation of the generalization that when Spartans go abroad they observe neither their own *nomina* nor those of the rest of Greece (1.77.6)." *Thucydides*, 130n52, 139n79. The irony of the contrast of the Spartan who impresses others as virtuous, and even mild (4.108.2), and the one who impresses others as violent (1.95.1), however, is that it is not clear which of the two acts more contrary to the *nomina* (laws or customs) of his city.

of the truth. Sparta is more interested in stopping Brasidas, lest his successes make ending the war more difficult, than in supporting his war of liberation (4.117).[25] The truce isolates Brasidas from his city even further, as he continues to receive cities that revolt, first Scione and then Mende, contrary to the terms of the truce.

When Brasidas arrives at Scione, he praises the revolting Scionians for their strides toward freedom, especially given their vulnerability due to their location on Pallene, cut off from the mainland by the Athenian occupation of Potidaea. After hearing what Brasidas has to say, the elated Scionians place a gold crown on his head as the liberator of Hellas and deck him with garlands (4.120.3–121.1). When Brasidas takes the place claimed by Sparta as the liberator of Hellas, he reaches his highest moment. But he has already cut himself off from his city, if only by violating its truce with Athens. He is acting as an independent agent. The garlands with which he is decked ominously recall the garlands of the two thousand Helots at Sparta who come forward to receive their freedom and instead meet their deaths.[26] And in spite of his message to the revolted cities that they are safe from Athenian retaliation, he plans, as Thucydides reports, to proceed with the help of the Scionians to Mende and Potidaea, cities north of Scione on the way to the mainland, "before the Athenians arrive" (4.121.2).

When commissioners from Sparta inform Brasidas about the truce, he refuses to surrender Scione. He claims that the city came over to Sparta before the agreement, although Thucydides thinks the truce preceded the revolt of Scione by two days (4.122.1–6). When Mende then revolts, encouraged by Brasidas's support of Scione, Brasidas receives the Mendians as well. Cleon incenses the Athenians against what seems like Brasidas's clear violation of the truce, and they make preparations against Scione and Mende (4.122.3–6). Although Brasidas recognizes the danger, removes the women and children from both cities to safety, and sends troops to fortify the cities, he nevertheless takes some of his forces to join Perdiccas in his expedition

---

25. Brunt speculates that Sparta had no expectation that Brasidas could succeed: given Perdiccas's "notorious infidelity," it was likely that he would cut off his support and even prevent reinforcements coming to Brasidas. Nor could it be foreseen that Brasidas "would have secured in the Greek cities new bases and sources of supply," inasmuch as only minorities in those cities supported revolt from Athens. Indeed, Brasidas's army was small, "an expendable force." "Spartan Policy," 275–77.

26. Connor is also reminded of the Helots at Sparta, but believes that Thucydides is foreshadowing the fate of the Scionians: "their enthusiasm at their freedom was as ill-founded as that of the Helots." *Thucydides*, 136. But it is Brasidas who is crowned—like those Helots. Thucydides suggests that Brasidas is as problematic for Sparta as its Helots are. Both threaten "change" or "revolution" (*neōterizein*), which Sparta fears.

against the Lyncestians (4.123.1–124.1). It seems an inopportune time for him to leave the protection of the revolted cities in the hands of others. Presumably he needs the pay that Perdiccas still provides for his mercenaries.[27] The gap between the noble purpose Brasidas proclaims and military and political conditions necessary for its success seems all the greater when Sparta's reluctance to provide that support compels him to turn to Perdiccas. Brasidas's dependence on what he cannot control makes the liberation of Hellas impossible. Because he cannot depend on Sparta, he must depend on Perdiccas. But of course he cannot depend on Perdiccas either. It is not surprising that the Athenians make gains in his absence in the very territory he has liberated. His Lyncestian campaign is the beginning of the end of his Thracian one.

Liberation Unravels

Things do not go well for Brasidas when he joins Perdiccas. Although they enjoy an initial victory, mercenaries whose help they expect side with the enemy, and Brasidas and Perdiccas decide to retreat. When Perdiccas's troops experience an inexplicable panic during the night and take off for home (4.125.1), Brasidas must lead his army in retreat, abandoned in enemy territory, and facing superior numbers of barbarian forces. Brasidas arranges his retreating hoplites in a hollow square, with light-armed troops in the center so that they can "run out" to reinforce the hoplites wherever the enemy attacks. Brasidas himself chooses three hundred of his men to accompany him at the rear of his army in order to ward off the approaching enemy (4.125.2–3). Once again he is in the ranks that first meet the enemy, even if now those ranks are in the rear. Brasidas's army may appear to be in retreat, but it is also poised to fight as it moves toward safety. Although the enemy is fast approaching, Brasidas takes the time to address his army before they retreat, offering them what he calls a "true teaching" about their opponents' weakness and their own strength. The enemy gives a terrifying appearance, he tells them, with their huge numbers of weapons waving and the almost unbearable din of shouting. Unlike the hoplites who protect one another by their battle formation, however, the barbarians do not form ranks. Their fighting on their own (*autokrator*) provides a ready pretext to flee. They therefore threaten only "from afar," and will not hold out if they meet resistance (4.126).

---

27. Gomme, *HCT,* 3:612.

Enemy forces become a threat only when they occupy a pass in Brasidas's path of retreat. Discovering the situation, Brasidas commands his own three hundred men at the rear to break order and "run as fast as they can" to take one of the hills that guard the pass (4.128). With this success, Brasidas leads his army to safety. In confronting superior numbers and enemy forces both front and rear, Brasidas's troops are like both the Spartans at Thermopylae and those on Sphacteria. Thucydides does not explicitly remind us of Thermopylae now, or compare another small thing to a great one (see 4.36.3). Comparisons are left to us. Neither does Brasidas lead his army to their deaths, as did the Spartan commander at Thermopylae; nor do Brasidas and his troops surrender, as did the Spartans on Sphacteria. This replay of Sphacteria, as it were, can hardly redeem "Spartan" honor, for Brasidas's is a Spartan army only in name—composed of the Helots he brought from Sparta, the mercenaries he can still afford, and the new allies he has assembled from the rebel cities (see 4.124.1). Because of his confidence-inspiring speech, his disciplined arrangement of his soldiers, and his quick and forceful action, Brasidas retreats with no loss of honor. His command represents a combination of daring and judgment that characterizes Thucydides' own city at its best.

Brasidas's success nevertheless occurs in retreat, his alliance with Perdiccas shattered, and his accomplishments in Thrace unraveling. His rupture with Perdiccas leads the latter to ally himself with Athens. While Brasidas is away, Athens takes back Mende, and makes preparations to retake Scione (4.129.1, 4.130). In capturing the hill that guards the pass in his retreat in Lyncestia, Brasidas may occupy the "heights" (*meteōra*) (4.128.3) in more senses than one. It seems that there is nothing left for him to do but to descend, unless it is to find a way to make one last run.

When Brasidas returns to Thrace, he stations himself at Torone, where he watches over the city and "is quiet," or "at rest." He cannot go to the relief of Mende or Scione, which lie on the Pallene peninsula, cut off from the mainland by Potidaea, which is under Athenian control, while the Athenian navy cuts off any approach by sea (4.129.1). The verb that Thucydides uses to describe Brasidas, *hesuchazein*, is the one he often uses for being "at peace," or "at rest," the same verb used by the Corinthians, for example, when they claim that the Athenians are never "at peace," and never allow others to be so (1.70.9). Although "remaining still" is associated with Sparta, the verb, Westlake notes, is not "naturally associated with Brasidas."[28] Brasidas's work is

---

28. Westlake, *Individuals in Thucydides*, 158n2; see also Burns, "Virtue of Thucydides' Brasidas," 517.

soon thwarted in another way: Sparta sends "rulers" for the cities of Torone and Amphipolis, so that command would not be left "to any chance person" (4.132.3). These men owed their positions and loyalty entirely to the Spartan government, Kagan observes, not to Brasidas, and unlike Brasidas "could be expected to follow orders."[29] Later in the war, another Spartan commander in the field, Agis, makes a decision on his own authority, and Sparta once again attempts to bring him under control.[30]

Thucydides mentions—very briefly—a futile effort by Brasidas to take Potidaea from the Athenians, arriving at night, and placing a ladder against the wall, but on being discovered he quickly leads away his troops (4.135).[31] As Westlake observes, the act, "a flagrant breach of the truce, seems to have been the outcome of desperation on the part of Brasidas, who had no other means of helping Scione, where the [Athenian] blockade was now complete."[32] When Brasidas is absent from Torone, Athenian forces, led by Cleon, take that city as well (5.3). Brasidas then returns to Amphipolis, whose surrender to him earlier had posed such a threat to Athens. There Brasidas wins a battle, but loses the war. His death in battle at Amphipolis opens the way for a peace treaty between Sparta and Athens, one that returns the cities he liberated to Athens.

The Athenian forces that attempt to take Amphipolis are commanded by Cleon. Cleon had already led his troops against Torone, but only after learning that Brasidas was not there (5.2.3). He has no plans to attack Amphipolis as long as Brasidas is present in the city, at least not before sufficient reinforcements arrive for them to surround the city. When he leads his impatient men toward the city, he goes only "to look around" (*kata thean*) (5.7.1–3). Because he does not see that Brasidas is in fact watching his movements from high ground (*meteōrou*) outside the city, Cleon does not suspect an imminent attack (5.6.3–8.3, esp. 6.3 and 8.3).

---

29. Kagan, *Archidamanian War*, 315–16. See also Connor, *Thucydides*, 138; Westlake, *Individuals in Thucydides*, 160–61, with 161n1.

30. When Agis accepted an Argive offer of a truce and withdrew his army from an imminent battle without the consent of the majority and without deliberating with anyone (5.60.1), the Spartans vehemently blamed him for not subduing Argos at what they thought was an opportune moment. They are inclined out of anger to demolish his home and to fine him ten thousand drachmas. Instead, however, they "made a law for the present that they had never had before—choosing ten Spartiates as Agis's advisers, without whose authority he could not lead an army from the city" (5.63). Spartan innovation in the law has the effect of constricting, rather than opening up, possibilities.

31. Thucydides speaks as if there were only one ladder for the assault on the city. Gomme finds no need to emend it to the plural, for "it hardly means one ladder only." *HCT*, 3:626.

32. Westlake, *Individuals in Thucydides*, 158.

Brasidas's plan for the battle depends on hiding from the Athenians how poorly trained his own troops are in comparison to theirs, and hiding their inferior numbers by holding back some of his troops, and then causing a panic when they surprise the Athenians (5.8.3–4, 5.9.8). He proves victorious, Thucydides says, because of his stratagem, or art (*technē*) (5.8.2). He explains his plan in an address to his men before battle. Once Brasidas and his forces have fallen on the Athenians, Clearidas, the Spartan sent to rule Amphipolis, must lead a second attack to cause panic. He exhorts Clearidas to show himself a brave man (*agathos anēr*), like (*eikos*) the Spartiate he is, and the allies to follow bravely, for on this day they will become either free allies of Sparta or slaves of Athens, suffering an even harsher slavery than before, and hindering "the liberation of Hellas" (5.9.4–9). For Brasidas, courage and art serve freedom, and even a Spartan is free, in that he may or may not act "like a Spartiate." In encouraging Clearidas to do so, Brasidas continues even to the last to construct an image of his city to which free men can ally themselves. And he himself "will demonstrate that what he advises others he can accomplish in deed" (5.9.10). In other words, he will lead the way. Brasidas is seen sacrificing near a temple just before the battle, Thucydides reports (5.10.2). Perhaps he suspects that this battle will be his last.

Cleon finally recognizes the danger into which he has led his troops, and orders retreat. The retreat not being fast enough for him, he turns his right wing back contrary to the order of retreat, leaving his men vulnerable (5.10.2–4). Seeing the Athenians "in motion," Brasidas speaks once again to his men, telling them that the Athenians will not stand their ground, as he knows "from the way in which their spears and heads are moving" (5.10.5). Brasidas has seen the much-reputed motion of the Athenians, but that motion, instead of causing fear in others, now reveals their own fear. Brasidas orders that the gates be opened "for me," he says, and that "with confidence we proceed out against them as swiftly as possible." After what turn out to be his last words in Thucydides' work, Brasidas "dashes out in a run" (Thucydides speaks here in the singular), and routs the center of the retreating army panic-struck from its own disorder and its astonishment at Brasidas's daring (5.10.6). Brasidas does not even need Clearidas and his men to create panic with a second attack, although they come according to plan. Six hundred Athenians die in the retreat, one of them Cleon. Only seven of their adversaries are killed, and one of them is Brasidas (5.10.7–11, 5.11.2). In dying "like a Spartiate," Brasidas once again represents his city. Presumably both Cleon and Brasidas die running, the one in retreat, the other in pursuit.

By his suicide, if it is indeed a suicide, Brasidas chooses to represent a noble or idealized Sparta to the very end.[33] Had he lived on, he could have hardly continued his almost one-man show in Sparta's name against Athenian tyranny. Athens had already sent its military might against him—Mende and Scione had already fallen, and Amphipolis was threatened. Sparta was negotiating peace. His one-man show would have appeared just that, and he would be seen as a traitor to his city. His misrepresentation of Sparta would be clear. He died as he lived—for the sake of a Spartan nobility of which he was the best, perhaps the only, representative in Thucydides' history.

Brasidas's last battle illustrates his intelligence and daring, just as it shows both lacking in the Athenian Cleon who commands the forces opposed to his. The virtues that were once the pride of Athens have passed to Brasidas. As Shanske observes, in Brasidas the Athenians "encounter their own best selves."[34] To this extent it is true that Brasidas is "the Athenian among the Spartans."[35] And it is "near" Athena's temple that Brasidas is seen sacrificing before the battle in which he dies (see also 4.116.2).[36] But Brasidas is not an Athenian, nor does he live "among the Spartans." Brasidas has no home, no people. Even if he dies in service to Sparta, he dies less like a Spartan than like himself.

The wounded Brasidas is carried into Amphipolis, and is informed of the victory before he dies (5.10.11). He is given a funeral at public expense in the marketplace, Thucydides tells us, reminding us of the only other public funeral in his work, in which Pericles delivered his famous oration. The Amphipolitans sacrifice to Brasidas "as a hero," honor him in the games and annual sacrifices, and consider him the founder of their colony. They also tear down all the memorials to their Athenian founder Hagnon, in effect erasing the past and starting anew (5.11.1). Brasidas has found a home, if only in death.

With the deaths of Cleon and Brasidas, the two men on each side of the struggle most opposed to peace, Athens and Sparta sign a peace treaty (5.16.1). The terms of the "Peace of Nicias"—as tradition calls it, after its

---

33. Burns also recognizes that Brasidas's noble death is "not altogether un-looked for." He understands it primarily as an effort "to flee or overcome a life that must be mixed with evils." According to Burns, Brasidas could not resign himself "to the need of his own city to attend to her own good"—such as bringing an end to the war to attend to matters closer to home—"nor face the prospect of being an accomplice to her treacherous ways." "Virtue of Thucydides' Brasidas," 521.

34. Shanske, *Thucydides and the Philosophic Origins,* 56.

35. Strauss, *City and Man,* 213.

36. Rahe, "Thucydides' Critique of Realpolitik," 138.

leading advocate at Athens—include the return to Sparta of the men taken on Sphacteria, as well as the return to Athens of Amphipolis and Acanthus. In the case of Scione, it is specified in the treaty that the Athenians can proceed however seems best to them (5.18.5, 5.18.8). Connor finds Athens's destruction of Scione—putting the men to death and enslaving their women and children (5.32.1)—"one of the most notorious events of the war."[37] Cleon dies, but his spirit lives on, for the very punishment that he proposes for the revolting Mytileneans and that is successfully opposed by Diodotus, Athens now inflicts on the Scionians.

One of the more lasting results of Brasidas's Thracian campaign involves the Helots who accompanied him in his army, for Sparta votes to give them their freedom (5.34.1). Thucydides does not tell us any self-interested motives Sparta's action might have had, thus leaving open the possibility that the Spartans award the Helots freedom as a reward for their service.[38] Brasidas's liberation of Hellas from Athens has shrunk into the liberation of his loyal soldiers from their servitude to Sparta. When these freed Helots later serve Sparta again in the battle of Mantinea, they bear the names of Brasideans (5.67.1, 5.71.3). Clearidas, whom the Spartans placed in command of Amphipolis, resists returning the city to the Athenians in compliance with the treaty (5.21.1–3). He has come to act not "like a Spartiate," but like Brasidas.

In his presentation of Brasidas, Thucydides illustrates the daring and intelligence that Pericles attributes to Athens itself. These virtues are obviously not dependent on a specific regime for their existence, inasmuch as they are possessed by Brasidas. But they are dependent on a regime for support—Brasidas needs military reinforcements and diplomatic engagements to protect the gains he makes. Without that support, the cities he encourages to revolt run the risk of destruction, as happens to Scione, the very city that crowned Brasidas as the liberator of Hellas. While Brasidas does not need Sparta in order to act with daring and intelligence, he needs Sparta for his daring and intelligence to be truly good. Thucydides surely admires Brasidas's virtues, but by showing the limited, even pernicious, results of their exercise, he questions their ultimate goodness. Brasidas transcends his city in trying to make true its noble purpose of liberation, but Thucydides shows

---

37. Connor, *Thucydides*, 136.

38. Andrewes speculates that the performance of the Helots with Brasidas may have encouraged the Spartans to create the neodamodeis, a class of freed Helots that served Spartan military purposes. Gomme, *HCT*, 4:35–46.

us how much his actions depend on the necessities that Sparta provides. In politics, no one can be a one-man show.

At the same time that Brasidas acts as if he were freer than he is, he may concede too much to necessity when it comes to Sparta. Although Brasidas encourages the cities that he liberates to revolt, or "to do a new thing," he never speaks at Sparta to Spartans. Brasidas could succeed in speaking for Sparta only if he could speak to Sparta as well. It might seem as if Sparta would have to do, in effect, a "new thing" if it were to support Brasidas's efforts to make true its claim to fight for the liberation of Hellas. The Corinthians nevertheless had some success in urging Sparta to war, to act in effect contrary to the character they attribute to it. Moreover, at the outset of the war, Sparta did commend Brasidas for his action in battle. It would not be simply a new thing, even if it goes against the grain, for Sparta to continue commending distinction, which in effect recognizes the freedom of its own citizens. Without freedom to act on Sparta's behalf, Brasidas could not have succeeded in leading its forces in the field. Sparta depends on Brasidas's ability to act independently. Sparta supposes that what is true in the case of Pausanias, and perhaps also in the case of Agis—that it cannot trust what it does not control—is true generally. Whereas Sparta acts as if it were freer than it is, and thereby allows Athens's power to grow, it is afraid to allow too much freedom to its own citizens. Trusting that the harsh necessities, as Archidamus says (1.84.4), will make good men, Sparta yields too much to necessity. While Brasidas gives a "true teaching" to his retreating soldiers about their strength and their enemies' weakness (4.126.4), this is the "true teaching" that Brasidas gives to Thucydides. It has more to do with his side's weakness and his enemy's strength. Both teachings are confirmed by the deeds Thucydides reports.

Brasidas and Thucydides

Although the signing of the treaty between Sparta and Athens in 421 BCE might seem like the end of the Peloponnesian War, Thucydides insists that there is only the appearance of peace. Several of Sparta's allies refuse to accept the treaty, including the Corinthians (5.17.2), and even those who sign on do not comply with all its provisions. Each side tries to injure the other as much as possible, the Thracian cities remain hostile, and Boeotia and Athens have a truce that is renewed for ten-day periods (5.25–26.2). The war does not really end until seventeen years later, when the Peloponnesians finally defeat Athens (5.26.1–4).

In arguing that the war lasted twenty-seven years, Thucydides mentions that he lived through the whole of it, having been exiled from Athens "after his command at Amphipolis" (5.26.5). When Brasidas first approached the city with his moderate terms of accommodation, Thucydides had charge of a small fleet on the nearby island of Thasos. He is sent for to prevent the fall of Amphipolis, but discovers that the city capitulated before his arrival. He never really commands *at Amphipolis* (4.104.5–106.4). Thucydides does not mention the grounds for his exile; nor does he claim that his sentence is an unjust one. He tells us that as a result of his exile he is at leisure, or at peace (*kath' hēsuchian*), that he is able to be present with both sides in the war, especially the Peloponnesian, and that he observes matters all the better (5.26.5). Denying that the Hellenic world is in truth at peace after the signing of the treaty by Sparta and Athens, Thucydides claims this description for himself.

It is possible that incompetence, or even timidity, explains Thucydides' failure to come to the relief of Amphipolis.[39] As a result of his delay, however, Amphipolis, a city in a region in which his family has business interests, remains for a time at peace, its inhabitants are allowed to keep their property, whether they decide to leave or to stay, and they are freed from Athenian rule (4.105.4–106.2). Thucydides arrives too late—not too late to save Amphipolis from capture, but to prevent Brasidas from saving Amphipolis. Whatever his intention, which we cannot know with any certainty, his late arrival serves the cause of freedom, at least as Brasidas presents it to the cities he approaches. It is also possible that Brasidas appears to Thucydides, as he does to scholars, as Athens's own best self. It is rather Cleon, in Thucydides' account, the man who comes to Amphipolis to undo the work that Brasidas has done there, who wants to avoid confronting Brasidas out of timidity (5.7). Like Cleon at Amphipolis, Thucydides travels in the Hellenic world in order "to look," but unlike Cleon he is able to see what he goes to see. Surely that includes Brasidas, who in opening the gates of Amphipolis for Athenians to leave the city if they so desire would have opened them for Athenians to enter as well.[40] As Thucydides says, he was present on both sides, especially that of the Peloponnesians.

---

39. For speculation, see Wylie, "Brasidas: Great Commander or Whiz Kid?" 84; John R. Grant, "Toward Knowing Thucydides," *Phoenix* 28 (1974): 91.

40. Westlake emphasizes the "abundant information" that Thucydides has about Brasidas's achievements: "at several points [his account] betrays knowledge of motives which can have been disclosed only to a few persons," and thus "may have well been derived largely from personal contacts with Brasidas himself, or at least with one of his subordinates, when Thucydides was in exile." *Individuals in Thucydides*, 148; see also 153.

Once the peace is signed, the intrigues and shifting alliances of the period bring Alcibiades to the forefront of Thucydides' history, for they seem to be his natural habitat. Alcibiades is an Athenian; indeed, Pericles was his uncle and guardian. But before the war is over his stage of operations reaches as far as Persia. His intrigues find no limit in law, and he seems free of all conventional political loyalties. At different times he offers his services to Athens, Sparta, and Persia. He seems to act like a free agent, but once he is exiled, he has difficulty finding a base of operations and obtaining his recall to Athens. Unlike other characters (e.g., Pericles, Diodotus, and Brasidas), Alcibiades rarely mentions freedom. Rather, he is thought to aim at tyranny (6.15.4). In the next chapters, I explore what place Alcibiades has in Thucydides' reflections on freedom, first in his advocacy of the Sicilian expedition, and then in his attempt to return home. Alcibiades' expansion of freedom—beyond the confines of any particular city—turns out to restrict its exercise.

CHAPTER 4

Sicily, Alcibiades, and the Liberation of *Erōs*

During the sixteenth year of the war, Athenians invade the island of Melos. Before attacking the city, the Athenians attempt to persuade the Melians to surrender. Many readers understand the Athenian position in their dialogue with the Melians to be Thucydides' most developed statement of his own realist position on power politics. Rejecting any appeal to justice or nobility, the Athenians warn the Melians, in Crawley's memorable translation, "the strong do what they can and the weak suffer what they must" (5.89).[1] When the Melians resist, the Athenians subdue and destroy the city. The Melians suffer what they must, it seems, because they fail to abide by the sensible political realism the Athenians propose.

Soon after the Athenian forces destroy Melos, the Athenian assembly votes to send an expedition to conquer a much larger island, Sicily (6.1.1), an expedition that proves to be an utter disaster for Athens and the beginning of the end of its empire. Thucydides' juxtaposition of his accounts of Melos and Sicily—like that of the funeral oration and the plague—suggests a tragic pattern of hubris (Melos), followed by disaster (Sicily). Like a protagonist in a Greek tragedy, Athens oversteps and suffers defeat. Insofar as Thucydides

---

1. Crawley, *Landmark Thucydides*, 352.

shows that uncontrollable human passions undermine a rational pursuit of self-interest, he may be called a tragic realist, one who is less optimistic about the prospects for self-interested restraint and cooperation among political actors than are "prudentialist" realists.[2]

There is nevertheless considerable disagreement about how Thucydides accounts for this Athenian tragedy. Peter J. Ahrensdorf argues that Athens's disaster in Sicily stems from its failure to apply the realist principles that had been the key to the success of its imperialism, rather than from a hubris based on those principles. Two major events lend credence to this view. The first is the ill-timed removal of Alcibiades from his command in Sicily in order for him to stand trial in Athens. The Athenians are overcome with religious dread at the secret mutilation of herms (statues of Hermes), and Alcibiades is alleged to have been involved in this act of impiety as well as in mocking the Eleusinian mysteries. Athens's recall of Alcibiades removes its apparently most capable general from command, and leads him to betray his city to Sparta. Second, when the pious Nicias is left in charge in Sicily, he yields to omens, and delays the retreat of his forces from Sicily when there is still time to reach safety. According to Ahrensdorf, "The pious fears and hopes not only of Nicias but of the Athenian people as a whole . . . lead to the disaster." From this perspective, Athens's ruin in Sicily follows not from its assertion of power, but from its failure to do so adequately. Even "the extraordinarily realistic Athenians prove unable to free themselves from what their own thesis on justice and self-interest tell them are unreasonable feelings of moral guilt, religious terror, and religious hope." Thus Thucydides shows that an amoral realism is unrealistic, human nature being what it is. He gives a realist critique of realism.[3] Strauss suggests a version of this position when he speculates that "not indeed the gods, but the human concern with the gods . . . took terrible revenge on the Athenians."[4]

---

2. See W. David Clinton for the distinction among realists between "prudentialists" and "trage-dians," as well as an explanation of how realists seek to balance the two positions in their understanding of international politics. "Conclusion: The Relevance of Realism in the Post-Cold War World," in *The Realist Tradition and Contemporary International Relations*, ed. W. David Clinton (Baton Rouge: Louisiana State University Press, 2007), esp. 239, 241.

3. Peter J. Ahrensdorf, "Thucydides' Realist Critique of Realism," *Polity* 30, no. 2 (1997): 258–59. By suggesting that Athens's amoral foreign policy provokes a "furious moral and religious backlash in Athens," Thucydides raises the question of whether the moralistic and hypocritical Spartans have the more sensible and realistic position. Pangle and Ahrensdorf, "Classical Realism," 28–29; Orwin, *Humanity of Thucydides*, 123.

4. Strauss, *City and Man*, 209.

The expedition is doomed from the start, then, if political life itself cannot maintain "Alcibidean resolve." And this is why the Athenians, according to Forde, are defeated in Sicily. Forde argues, "If there is not room for [Alcibiades] in the city, it is because politics does not do full justice to human nature."[5] By this calculation, tragedy turns more on the limits of the city than on its excesses. It is not so much that Alcibiades fails the city by tempting it to conquer Sicily, but that the city fails Alcibiades. And Alcibiades fails by expecting too much of his city, expecting it to follow where he leads.

My own reading comes closer to the more traditional view of Athenian hubris than the revision suggested by Ahrensdorf and others. While Nicias obviously contributes to the disaster in Sicily, the deepest problem as Thucydides presents it is Alcibiades and what he brings to Athenian politics. Underlying his hubris is a rejection of all limits, which Thucydides captures in the *paranomia* he ascribes to him, a word that means literally "aside from the law," or "outside of law" (6.15.4). When the Athenians follow Alcibiades' advice to send an expedition to Sicily, an *eros* for "sailing away falls on all alike" (6.24.3). Whereas Pericles asks Athenians to be "lovers" (*erastai*) of their city, and presents Athens as a beautiful object of longing, with Alcibidean politics *eros* becomes liberated from a particular goal or object. The city, to be sure, cannot maintain "Alcibidean resolve" in Sicily, but the problem is not politics as such, I argue, but the infinite character of Alcibidean resolve, as Thucydides presents it. Sailing away is not sailing anywhere in particular. Of course, they are sailing to Sicily. But the conquest of Sicily opens the imagination to one conquest after another (6.6.1, 6.15.2, 6.90.2–3). Thus Alcibiades argues that "the quickest way to ruin for an active city is a change [*metabolē*] to inactivity" (6.18.7). He characterizes Athens and its way of life as motion for its own sake—without any goal or purpose to which it might be directed. The liberation of *eros* that characterizes Thucydides' Alcibiades and against which Thucydides warns us is not a liberation from the restraints of law or politics in the pursuit of higher goods; rather it is a liberation from the goods that human beings pursue, and in light of which they understand themselves.

In this chapter, I first discuss Athenian politics in the years following the Peace of Nicias, especially the role of Alcibiades in undermining Athens's peace with Sparta. Near the end of this period we hear the Melian debate. Although Alcibiades is not present, his spirit, I argue, animates the exchange. The position of the Athenians at Melos reflects Alcibiades'

---

5. Forde, *Ambition to Rule*, 76, 209–10. Also Strauss, *City and Man*, 209.

politics. The Athenians appeal there to the eternal law to which they, like the gods themselves, must yield—that the stronger rule the weaker (5.105.1–2). Their appeal is less an acceptance of necessity, I argue, than a pretext for their imitation of the gods. Their "law" does not limit their actions but relieves them of all restraint. Human beings who can act like gods render the gods unnecessary. If realism teaches human limits in the pursuit of power, it is a teaching the Athenians at Melos reject.

After discussing the Melian dialogue, I turn to Thucydides' introduction of Sicily as an object of Athenian longing and then to the debate about the Sicilian expedition in the Athenian assembly between Nicias and Alcibiades. Nicias attempts to dissuade Athens from trying to conquer Sicily, by emphasizing the difficulty of fighting in such a faraway place, where allies are uncertain. He points out the more pressing problems the Spartans continue to pose, closer to home (6.10–11). Nicias's concerns serve as a foil for those of Alcibiades. Alcibiades accuses Nicias of a "do-nothing" policy (*apragmosune*) that will ruin an active city such as Athens (6.18.3, 6.18.6–7). He may sound like Pericles, who praises an active city and citizen (2.40.2, 2.63.2–3), but Pericles recommends that the city not undertake any new conquests while at war, and in this sense to "remain still" or "at peace" (2.65.7). Alcibiades, in contrast, advises that Athens extend its rule to Sicily, even though the city can still be considered at war. He shows contempt for "peace" as inconsistent with human excellence (6.18.6). The Corinthians' earlier claim that Athens has no peace nor allows any to others (1.70. 9) is realized in Alcibiades. Whether war with Sparta was inevitable or became so as a result of actions intentionally undertaken by Athens, renewing the war with Sparta seems inevitable now, at least as long as Alcibiades or his spirit defines Athens. This is true precisely because Alcibiades' gaze is directed not to Sparta but to points beyond.

Alcibiades proclaims that that there is no limit to how far Athenians might "wish to rule," (6.18.3). Desire directed to the infinite, without a specific object, has nowhere to go. Appropriately, Thucydides describes the Sicilian expedition as more like a display of brilliance than a force for the purpose of conquering an enemy (6.31.4–6). Its finest moment is just before it embarks, in the image of itself that it conveys rather than in the actions it will undertake. It belongs in Athens, not in Sicily, even if in Athens it would have nothing to do. Thucydides captures this in the spectacle he paints of the fleet as it assembles for its departure from the Piraeus, which I discuss in the concluding section of this chapter.

Thucydides traces the Sicilian expedition to a liberation of *eros* that leads to disaster. Even if Thucydides had not already told us that the expedition would fail (2.65.11), his description of the spirit of Alcibiades that animates it would prepare us for this result. To be sure, Nicias shares the blame, but it is not his piety that is at fault, for his "piety" masks his caution. He does not manifest genuine piety, any more than the impious Alcibiades does. Genuine piety does not lie in ceding the human capacity to deliberate, judge, and act to divine forces, as Nicias does when he yields to the seers. Nor is it found in imitating the power of the gods to rule over the weak, as the Athenians imply at Melos, and Alcibiades manifests in his deeds. Rather, it consists in accepting the limits of the human in relation to the divine, limits in both knowledge and control, which by circumscribing action make it possible. Paradoxically, it is that great humanist Pericles who recognizes those limits and is able to act, as when, for example, he traces the plague to "daimonic things" that are "beyond reason," while continuing to prosecute the war with Sparta, or when he cautions them that they must pay back whatever gold necessity requires them to take from Athena's statue to continue the war (2.61.3, 2.64.2, 2.13.5). In failing to maintain "Periclean resolve," the city sends an expedition against Sicily, but that resolve requires a statesman more like Pericles than either Nicias or Alcibiades is.

Introducing Alcibiades

Thucydides first introduces Alcibiades as a prominent member of a group of Athenians who wish to dissolve the treaty between Athens and Sparta. Although he is still young (*neos*) for political honors in any other city, Alcibiades is honored in Athens "due to the worthiness of his ancestors" (5.43.1–2). Athens and Alcibiades belong together, for in Athens Alcibiades can achieve preeminence without biding his time, and Athens can profit from his energy and vigor. He is honored in Athens in spite of his age, however, because of his ancestors. He depends on them rather than simply on himself for the honor he receives. His honors consequently come primarily from Athens rather than from other cities, since it is in Athens that his ancestors would be remembered and honored. He comes from a prominent *Athenian* family. Thucydides prepares us from the outset to see that Alcibiades acts as if he were freer than he is.

Hostilities are brewing between Sparta and Argos, Thucydides reports, and Alcibiades thinks that it is better to take the side of the latter (5.43.2). Argos is a Dorian city on the Peloponnesus whose treaty with Sparta kept it out of the conflict with Athens. That treaty is now expired. Argos is also a democracy. Thucydides does not give us any reasons why Alcibiades thinks it better for Athens to side with Argos than with Sparta. He does tell us that in negotiating the peace treaty with Athens, Sparta conferred with Nicias and Laches, overlooking Alcibiades because of his youth. Nor did Sparta, Thucydides reports, show Alcibiades the honor he thinks due him because of the *proxenia* relation of old (*palaios*) between Sparta and his family.[6] Although his grandfather renounced the relationship, Alcibiades himself intended to renew (*ananeousthai*) it by helping out the Spartan prisoners from Sphacteria (5.43.2). Once again, Alcibiades' relationship to the past is ambiguous: correcting his grandfather, he seeks to renew the "ancient" political relation between his family and Sparta. It is a situation, however, in which the new is a return to the old. The new is not simply new. In these first political efforts that Thucydides recounts, Alcibiades cannot seem to find a place. Having failed to serve as the link between Athens and Sparta (during the negotiations of the peace), he turns his attentions to Argos, Sparta's old antagonist (5.46.5).

After persuading the Spartan envoys that it is in their interest to lie in the assembly about their authority to negotiate for their city, he then denounces them for their duplicity, for their "false intentions" and "inconsistent speech" (5.45.3).[7] Thucydides lets us see what the Athenians do not—that Alcibiades' accusation of the Spartans that they, literally, "have nothing true in mind," and "never say the same things" more aptly describes himself in his dealings with the Spartans. As he discredits the Spartans in Athens, Alcibiades urges the Argives "in private" to come to Athens "as swiftly as possible" inasmuch as it is an opportune time (*kairos*) for them to negotiate an alliance with Athens (5.43.3, 5.45.1–4). Like a dramatist, Alcibiades introduces characters at the moment they are needed to play a part in his plot.[8] He does not even wait for an opportune time; he creates it. His "machinations" succeed in intensifying suspicions between Athens and Sparta and in bringing about an Athenian alliance with the Eleans and Mantineans as well as the Argives (5.46.5). He obviously manipulates both Athens and Sparta in order to bring about this result. And after Alcibiades deceives the Spartans, the Spartans in turn deceive Nicias, their most ardent supporter in Athens (5.46.1).

---

6. Similar to the relation of *xenos* ("guest-friend") between citizens of different cities, as existed between Pericles and Archidamos, the *proxenia* was a formal relation between an individual of one city and another city. Like the "guest-friendship," the *proxenia* was often hereditary.

7. Donald Kagan argues that Sparta's following of Alcibiades' advice is not as incredible as it might seem. Since Alcibiades favored Sparta previously, and then turned against it, why should he have not turned again? *The Peace of Nicias and the Sicilian Expedition* (Ithaca, NY: Cornell University Press, 1981), 67–69.

8. Forde, *Ambition to Rule*, 73.

Alcibiades deceives, and cultivates deception in others. As far as we know, only Thucydides knows what he is up to.

The agreement between Athens and its new allies that Alcibiades brings about is made to last one hundred years (5.47.2). Athen's new alliance makes "a mockery," in Connor's words, of its two-year-old alliance with Sparta and of its provisions for fifty years of mutual assistance (5.23.1).[9] Although Sparta's failure to comply with all the provisions of their peace treaty might justify Athens's seeking this new alliance with Argos, Alcibiades' politics clearly rejects received agreements or laws for better ones (see 1.71.3). But if past agreements do not bind, neither will new ones if better ones become available. A city would be naive to bind itself by an agreement with a city that does not consider its agreements binding. In a world of such flux, can Athens rely on its new allies, or its new allies on it? When Alcibiades binds his city to an alliance with Argos for a hundred years, it might just as well be two hundred, or a thousand. There need be no limit to promises that can be revoked.

Time after time in his account, Thucydides shows that Alcibiades' actions become undone in time. Argos's alliance with Athens, for example, begins to unravel after the defeat of the Athenian allies at Mantinea (6.16.6, 6.89.3, 5.76.3, 5.78–79). Alcibiades leads the Athenian expedition to Sicily only to abandon it to its destruction there. He becomes the adviser to Sparta, until that city issues an order for his apprehension and execution (8.45.1). Later he brings the Athenians to negotiate with the Persian satrap Tissaphernes but they go home empty-handed (8.56). He succeeds in encouraging the Athenian oligarchs to overthrow the democracy and then later encourages others to overthrow the oligarchy (8.47, 8.86.6). And the more moderate regime that he then encourages lasts only about four months. Nothing that he touches seems to last.

After the battle of Mantinea, Alcibiades continues to work against Spartan interests in Argos, when he removes an oligarchic and pro-Spartan faction from that city—a group of three hundred men—and relocates them to neighboring islands under Athenian control (5.84.1). Alcibiades does not merely bring diverse cities together (as in the Argive alliance); he separates peoples from their homes. One can imagine him looking at a map to see how he might redraw its boundaries (see Aristophanes, *Clouds* 213–17). After

---

9. Connor, *Thucydides*, 146. See also Kagan, *Peace of Nicias*, 74. It is curious that the agreement that Alcibiades brings about with Argos is written to last twice as long as the one that Nicias is instrumental in achieving with Sparta, although it turns out to be even more short-lived.

reporting this relocation, Thucydides turns abruptly to an Athenian invasion of Melos, a Spartan colony that remained neutral during the Peloponnesian War. It is Alcibiades' politics that animates the Athenians on Melos, just as it will Athens's sailing to Sicily. It is not only that Alcibiades shares with the Athenians at Melos a similar contempt for Sparta. Nor is it only that the argument of the Athenians at Melos justifies the attack on Sicily that Alcibiades favors. When W. Liebeschuetz observes that the Athenians' arguments at Melos reveal them as "bullying and arrogant toward the weak, boundlessly self-confident, [and] lacking humility even toward the gods," he could have been describing Alcibiades.[10] The Athenians at Melos are not primarily interested in advantage, or safety—that is what the Melians urge—but in something much greater, a kind of absolute rule, free of all constraints.

The Dialogue between the Athenians and the Melians

When the Athenians arrive at Melos, they ask to speak to the people of the city, but Melian officials insist that they present their case only to the officials themselves. The Athenians suggest a dialogue. This will be even safer than a speech to the people, they say, when lengthy and seductive speeches are difficult to refute (*anelengkta*) (5.85). The Athenians thus express preference for a way of communicating for which Socrates was famous (see, e.g., Plato, *Gorgias* 448a, 461a, 462a, 473e; *Symposium* 194c; *Protagoras* 336b–d). The Melians object, however, that the Athenians are seeking not a dialogue but a way to impose their will. There can be no fairness when an armed force arrayed against them comes as judges of whatever is said (5.86). They also claim that the Athenians are not giving them alternatives, for if the Melians make a successful case in debate and decide not to surrender, they will face war and conquest by superior force; if they are persuaded by the Athenians, they must surrender and face slavery (5.86). In either case, they lose their independence. The issue is whether they will be persuaded to yield without a fight, not whether the Athenians will be persuaded against subduing them. Dialogue may be conducive to refutation, as the Athenians say, but the Athenians are not open to refutation—something Socrates discovers as well (*Apology* 23a). The dialogue in which the Athenians try to persuade the Melians to surrender their city is as much a sham as the "trial" the Spartans conducted for the Plataeans.

---

10. W. Liebeschuetz, "The Structure and Function of the Melian Dialogue," *Journal of Hellenic Studies* 88 (1968): 76.

The Athenians confirm the Melians' claims when they dismiss considerations of justice from the dialogue. They will not use "noble names" to claim they rule justly because they overcame the Persians, they say. Nor will they refer to any injustice done against them by Melos to explain why they are attacking it. So too they do not want to hear that the Melians have been neutral in the war, or that they have done nothing to merit Athens's attack. Justice is an issue between equals, whereas the issue between their cities is only what is possible: the powerful do what they can, and the weak can only acquiesce (5.89). In ruling out considerations of nobility and justice, their statement, Connor says, indicates "its unsentimental clarity in the analysis of power."[11] The Athenians at Melos mention nothing about helping those who suffer injustice, as does Pericles (2.37.3), nor about Athens's ruling more justly than it is compelled to do (1.76.3; also 1.77.1–2).[12]

The Athenians' position reminds scholars of that of Diodotus in the Mytilenean debate, inasmuch as he also renounces appeals to justice in favor of advantage. Although Diodotus defends "the moderate human policy," Euben writes, he does so "in relentlessly realistic terms that anticipate the Athenian arguments at Melos."[13] The Athenians at Melos, however, are not defending a moderate human policy toward a city that revolted but subjecting a city that has remained neutral in the war. Like the Athenians who reject the Spartan offer of peace, they "want more" (4.21.2). They sound less like Diodotus than do the Melians. Once the Athenians at Melos rule out appeals to justice, the Melians present "the moderate human policy," perhaps even the just human policy, in terms of advantage, just as Diodotus does in the case of Mytilene. When the Athenians require the Melians to speak of the expedient apart from the just, the Melians claim that speaking in terms of justice is itself advantageous, for such appeals serve "the common good" of everyone. This is especially so for the Athenians, who may one day have to appeal to justice themselves. The fall of Athens would be the occasion for "the greatest revenge," the Melians point out, inasmuch as their foes would want to make them "an example for others" (5.90.1). When Connor paraphrases the Melians' argument on this point, "that self-restraint may be in the long-

---

11. Connor, *Thucydides*, 157.

12. Johnson, *Thucydides, Hobbes,* 130; Rahe, "Thucydides' Critique of Realpolitik," 125; Mara, *Civic Conversations*, 163.

13. Euben, *Tragedy of Political Theory*, 180, 198. See also Johnson, *Thucydides, Hobbes,* 128–131, 135; Monoson and Loriaux, "Illusion of Power," 292; Orwin, *Humanity of Thucydides*, 111–13. Whereas Euben, Johnson, and Monoson and Loriaux connect Diodotus with the Athenians at Melos by the harshness of their principles, Orwin finds a more "moderate" realism in both.

term interest of the more powerful,"[14] he could be paraphrasing Diodotus's as well. Just as Diodotus warns the Athenians that they will make enemies of those they need not make enemies (3.47.2–3), so too do the Melians warn the Athenians that if they destroy Melos they will make enemies of all neutrals, who will fear similar treatment from Athens (5.96–98).[15] Inasmuch as the word translated as "neutral" in Greek means literally to remain "at peace" (or "at rest"), the complaint of the Melians about the Athenians echoes that of the Corinthians in their earlier description of the Athenians, who are neither at peace nor allow others to remain so (1.70.9)

It is the very neutrality of Melos, however, that the Athenians find so problematic. If Athens allows an island such as Melos to remain independent, Athens will look weak and fearful (5.97). But this would be a false impression. Athens is not afraid. Although the subjection of Melos thus contributes to Athenian security, the Melians should know that Athenians "have not once ever yet withdrawn from a siege out of fear of others" (5.111.1). Athens's superiority to others trumps what it shares with them. This is why, they argue, Melos should capitulate.

When the Melians imagine that help might come to them from the Spartans, who are their kindred, they claim that the sea is "wide," and that it is possible to escape interception. But the Athenians reply that they are "commanders of the sea" (*naukratores*). The sea is no wider than their reach. They verge on asserting command of the unlimited or infinite (5.109–110, 5.97, 5.99).[16] So too when they warn the Melians not to follow the many, who place their hopes in the unseen, such as oracles or prophecy, they suggest that the gods no more than the Spartans limit their power.[17]

---

14. Connor, *Thucydides*, 153; see also Dobski, "Incomplete Whole," 26.

15. Liebeschuetz makes a good case that Diodotus's arguments in favor of the Mytileneans are even more supportive of the Melians—inasmuch as Mytilene is an ally who revolted and Melos an independent city. He therefore understands the Athenians at Melos to hold "a more extreme version of Cleon's position [concerning Mytilene]." "Structure and Function," 74. Orwin agrees with him that Diodotus's arguments with regard to Mytilene indicate that clemency is also appropriate to Melos, but in contrast to Liebeschuetz he finds that the arguments of the Athenians at Melos lead in this direction as well. He thus disassociates the Athenian envoys there from the harsh decision against the Melians, which was made by the assembly in Athens. *Humanity of Thucydides*, 112. Also Bruell, "Thucydides' View," 16–17; Pangle and Ahrensdorf, "Classical Realism," 18. I argue that the Athenians at Melos have more in common with Alcibiades than with Cleon (Liebeschuetz) or with Diodotus (Orwin and Bruell).

16. When Pericles makes a similar claim to the Athenians depressed from the plague, he tells them that their control of the sea in effect gives them control of the land (2.62.1–2). That is, they have no need for further conquests.

17. In his comedy *The Birds,* Aristophanes portrays an attempt by an Athenian Peisthetairos to control the intercourse between gods and human beings by founding a city in the skies. Controlling

The Melians admit that they place their hope in the gods as well as the Spartans, for they are pious men fighting against unjust ones (5.104). In response, the Athenians claim to do nothing more than the gods do among themselves, echoing the Unjust Speech in Aristophanes' *Clouds* in the play's *agon* (*Clouds* 1075, 1080–82). Indeed, neither divinity nor humanity can do otherwise, they insist, but all follow "a necessity of nature"—the strong rule. This is a "law" that they did not make, they say, nor were they the first to use it, and they will leave it behind "forever," knowing that Melos and others would follow it as well if they had "the same power" (5.105.1–2). That law has little in common with the law that Pericles thinks the Athenians heed out of a sense of shame except that it is unwritten (2.37.3). The Athenians at Melos attempt to imitate the gods, imposing their power on others without limitation, while hiding their hubris behind their appeal to a necessity that applies to god and human alike. They are like Phidippides, the young man corrupted by Socrates in Aristophanes' *Clouds*, who also appeals to the necessities of nature to justify his hubristic act of father-beating (*Clouds* 1075, 1427–28).[18] Like Phidippides', their frankness is deceptive.

The Melians' trust in the Spartans, the Athenians say, is also misplaced. The Spartans make use of virtue when it comes to the laws in their own country, but with regard to others they demonstrate that they consider the pleasant noble and the advantageous just (5.105.4). The Athenians' description of Sparta manifests their pride in Athens, which does not regard the pleasant as noble or the advantageous as just. Accordingly, they do not dismiss shame—and therewith the noble—rather they reinterpret it. "Shame that follows from folly," "willingly incurred," they say, "is more shameful" than disaster that comes from chance. Indeed, those who go straightest "do not yield to equals, bear themselves nobly to their superiors, and act with measure [*metrioi*] toward their inferiors." There is no shame in succumbing to "the greatest of cities" (5.111.3–4). The noblest course of action for the Melians

---

passage through the air—and therewith human access to the gods—underlies the Athenians' control of the sea. The play is performed in Athens in 414 BCE, soon after the expedition to Sicily sails.

18. Orwin offers a different reading of the Athenians' appeal to the necessities of nature. "If they reject the subjection of human beings to divine law," he writes, "it is not because they arrogantly impute to them a godlike freedom. Indeed they deprive them of such freedom as tradition had held them to possess, that of transgressing or not, of choosing 'blamelessness' over 'injustice.'" Orwin finds the Athenian subjection of the gods to nature "their most daring innovation in presenting the divine"—one that "foreshadow[s] Plato." *Humanity of Thucydides*, 106. See also C. W. Macleod, "Form and Meaning in the Melian Dialogue," *Historia* 23 (1974): 395.

is nothing other than to yield to Athens.[19] They may offer "moderate" terms to Melos, but they are the superiors to whom the Melians must succumb, and the Melians the inferiors who must find their nobility in doing so. It is difficult to know who from this perspective might be "equals" to the powerful. Equality would be demonstrated by resistance, and resistance will lead to one or the other succumbing. An equal is as problematic as a neutral (see 5.89).

The Athenians thus conclude that the Melians' trust in both the gods and the Spartans manifests an "irrational hope" of safety that will lead to their destruction (5.105.4, 5.111.2–3). Their reference to "irrational hope" recalls Diodotus's warning to the Athenians themselves about the irrational sway of hope and *erōs* that leads to destruction (3.45.5; see also 4.62.4). But when the Athenians at Melos claim that hope brings ruin through its false comfort, they gratuitously exempt those overly endowed (*perousia*). When such individuals hope, even if they suffer harm, they will not come to ruin (5.103.1). They themselves manifest hope that those endowed with the talents of an Alcibiades succeed.

After deliberating among themselves, the Melians refuse to capitulate, and the Athenians lay siege to the city. After holding out for several months, "some treachery" in the city leads the Melians to surrender to the Athenians. The Athenians proceed to kill all the adult males they capture, and sell the women and children into slavery (5.113–16). The case of Melos is a test for the Spartans, who do not come. It is also a test for the Athenians themselves. As Connor states, "Whatever our reactions to what happens to the Melians, it is hard to escape a feeling of horror at what is happening to the Athenians."[20] The Athenians' punishment of Melos is that which Cleon recommends for Mytilene but which Diodotus prevents from taking place. Diodotus's outlook is represented by the Melians on their own behalf with

---

19. Orwin also points out the Athenians' pride in Athens and their appeal to the noble, but argues that it indicates that "their understanding was itself somehow 'Melian,'" and that they "have failed to wash their own souls of the just and noble." *Humanity of Thucydides,* 111, 114. See also Ahrensdorf, "Thucydides' Realist Critique," 254–55; Pangle and Ahrensdorf, "Classical Realism," 25; Dobski, "Incomplete Whole," 26. I argue, in contrast, that the Athenians' pride in their city and refusal to follow other cities in assimilating nobility to pleasure, or justice to advantage, shows that they are still identifiably Athenian (see 2.40.3), or that they have succeeded in not washing their own souls of the just and the noble. How little Thucydides could approve of such an assimilation of the pleasant to the noble is clear from his description of this happening during the plague: "no one made efforts on behalf of what seemed noble, supposing it unclear whether he would perish before attaining it." It therefore "became settled that the pleasant and everything contributing to it were both noble and useful" (2.53.3).

20. Connor, *Thucydides,* 154.

no effect. That Thucydides reports some "treachery" in Melos suggests an opening for Diodotus's argument about sparing the people of captured cities, and the Melian officials' exclusion of the people from hearing the Athenian proposals would only strengthen it.[21] But Thucydides mentions no debate among the Athenians about how they should treat Melos once it is captured.

Plutarch reports that Alcibiades was "the principal cause of the slaughter of all the inhabitants of the isle of Melos who were of age to bear arms, having spoken in favour of that decree."[22] Forde argues, in contrast, that by mentioning just before his account of the Melian dialogue that Alcibiades is engaged elsewhere, Thucydides in effect "exempt[s] Alcibiades rather pointedly from any connection with the Melian episode itself."[23] It is possible, however, that Thucydides keeps Alcibiades' role in events out of plain sight, while suggesting his involvement. Thucydides has done this before—and will do it again.[24] He teaches us to look beyond the public face of events for explanations, especially in the case of Alcibiades, at the same time he leaves uncertain just what we should see when we look. In doing so, he helps us see the slippery, formless character of Alcibiades. If it is the spirit of Alcibiades that speaks for the Athenians at Melos, as I argue, it is Alcibiades who is the human face hidden behind the law of necessity to which they appeal.

The Melians, for their part, may not have acted as unreasonably as it might seem in deciding to resist the Athenians. Thucydides recounts an earlier Athenian expedition to Melos, led by the Athenian general Nicias, but when the Melians resist, the Athenian fleet leaves (3.91). The Melians may not

---

21. Liebeschuetz, "Structure and Function," 74n11.

22. Plutarch, *Lives*, 244. See Kagan, *Peace of Nicias*, 153; Malcolm F. Macgregor, "The Genius of Alcibiades," *Phoenix* 19, no. 1 (1965): 32.

23. Forde, *Ambition to Rule*, 196.

24. Whereas Alcibiades' role in effecting the Athenian alliance with Argos is unseen by the Athenians but revealed by Thucydides to the reader of his history, on other occasions, Thucydides keeps Alcibiades behind the scenes that he presents to the readers. While Alcibiades is a major character of book 6, in which the Sicilian expedition is launched, and book 8, after its defeat, he is barely mentioned in book 7. And yet he hovers over the Athenians' suffering there, just as much as he hovers over the Melian dialogue. Thucydides mentions Alcibiades' name only once in book 7, when he recounts that Alcibiades continues to advise the Spartans to follow up one of his recommendations against Athens (7.18.1). By doing so, Thucydides reminds us of his complicity with the Spartans and hence of the role he plays in the disaster we witness in Sicily. As we have seen, Thucydides' first detailed account of Alcibiades' role in Athenian politics shows him a master of operating behind the scenes.

realize that the Athenians with whom they are dealing differ from Nicias, who is sent on a different mission at the time of this second invasion of Melos (5.83.4). Nicias is no longer the moving spirit of Athenian policy, if he ever was.[25] He should not be taken by others as a representative Athenian any more than Brasidas should as a representative Spartan. It is appropriate that Thucydides mentions in passing not only the whereabouts of Alcibiades but those of Nicias just before turning to Melos. The misplaced reliance on the gods for safety that we see in the Melians will be reflected in Nicias's similar error in Sicily (7.77.3–4),[26] just as the Athenian insistence on their unlimited rule reflects Alcibiades' speeches and deeds.

Introducing Sicily

Thucydides structures his work so that he provides what appears to be a second beginning: his introduction of Athens's desire to conquer Sicily is the occasion of what has been called a "second archeology," a detailed account of the settlement of Sicily over time, of the migration and expulsions of its diverse peoples, and of the cities that now inhabit the island (6.1–5), which parallels Thucydides' similar account in book 1 of the settlement of Hellas (1.2–19).[27] This is not the first time Thucydides mentions Sicily in his work (see, e.g., 3.86.1–4, 3.88), or even the Athenian desire to subdue Sicily (4.65.3). And he has given us the speech of the Syracusan leader Hermocrates at a conference of Sicilian cities at Gela (4.59–64). By providing an archaeology of Sicily as his introduction to the Sicilian expedition, however, Thucydides gives the reader the sense that his work is starting anew. He is, in effect, introducing a new world, Sicily, with a different location, and a different past, an outlier of the Hellenic world he has been discussing, although its inhabitants include Hellenes as well as barbarians. And so his writing starts anew as well, as it focuses on Sicily, the alien or the faraway, as does Athens itself. The war continues, in spite of the "peace" of Nicias, but its new form makes it almost unidentifiable in terms of the past.

---

25. Perhaps this might have been true during the period when he helped negotiate the peace with Sparta, i.e., after Cleon, who had been opposed to peace, died at Amphipolis (5.16.1), and while Alcibiades was still young.

26. Many point out the resemblance, e.g., Connor, *Thucydides*, 155, 201–2; Orwin, *Humanity of Thucydides*, 123.

27. Hunter R. Rawlings, *The Structure of Thucydides' History* (Princeton: Princeton University Press, 1981), 65–67.

As at the beginning of his work, where Thucydides distinguishes the "truest cause" of the war between the Peloponnesians and the Athenians from its alleged causes, he now distinguishes the "truest cause" of the Athenians' expedition to Sicily—their "aiming to rule the whole [of it]," from what the Athenians claim—that they are going to help their kin and allies there (6.6.1). If Athens hopes to rule "the whole" of Sicily, this must include its kindred, such as the Leontines, and its allies, such as the Egestaeans, whom it claims it is going to help.

The Athenians lack experience of the island they desire to rule, Thucydides tells us, both its size and number of inhabitants (6.1.1).[28] For example, the voyage around Sicily on a merchant ship takes almost eight days.[29] And in spite of the size of the island, not much more than twenty stades of sea (about two miles) between Sicily and Italy prevent Sicily from being mainland (6.1.1–2). In other words, Sicily is much larger than Melos, and less isolated from help. As Lattimore observes, Thucydides' "display of knowledge accentuates Athenian ignorance."[30] Kagan argues that Thucydides' claim that the Athenians were ignorant of Sicily's geography and population is suspect, given the numbers of Athenians on the expedition to Sicily nine years previously and their length of time in Sicily.[31] Thucydides' emphasis on Athenian ignorance and inexperience of Sicily, however, highlights the undefined or unlimited character of the _erōs_ he attributes to Athens. As Kagan notes, although the expedition may have at first had more limited goals, by the time the expedition left Athens, the more limited venture became "a bold and unlimited commitment."[32]

Although Thucydides himself knows much more about Sicily than the Athenians do, his knowledge goes back only so far, for he "has nothing to say" about its first inhabitants, the Cyclopes and the Laestrygones, where they came from or where they went. For this we must rely on the poets, he says (6.2.1). In Homer, the Cyclopes and the Laestrygones are giants who threaten Odysseus and his men on their voyage home from Troy. The latter

---

28. Connor points out how often in his history Thucydides has used "experience" to characterize the Athenians. "A thematic reversal begins with book 6." _Thucydides_, 159n5.

29. According to Dover, Thucydides exaggerates the time it would take a ship to sail around Sicily. _HCT_, 4:197–98. See also Connor, _Thucydides_, 161n7. The longer the voyage around the island, the greater its size, and the more difficult to gain experience of it.

30. Lattimore, _Peloponnesian War_, 306, note on 6.2–5.

31. Kagan, _Peace of Nicias_, 165.

32. Ibid., 190–91.

destroy all of Odysseus's fleet and sailors except Odysseus's ship and its crew (*Odyssey* 10.80–132). Odysseus fares better against the one-eyed Cyclopes, contriving a crafty escape from Polyphemos's cave after blinding him with a burning poker (*Odyssey* 9.375–470). That Thucydides imagines that such monsters once inhabited Sicily makes it a more alien and foreboding place, and provides an ominous foreshadowing of what the Athenians will encounter there, especially since that Athenian master of craft Alcibiades will not be there to assist their escape. Thucydides earlier connected Sicily with Odysseus's troubled homecoming: the strait between Messana on the northeast coast of Sicily and Rhegium on the tip of the boot formed by Italy is where Odysseus "was said to have sailed by Charybdis" (4.24.5). But he sailed by Charybdis in Homer's account only by steering toward the opposite shore, where he did not sail so easily by Scylla (*Odyssey* 12.244–50). One of the first disappointments that the Athenians encounter when they arrive in Sicily is that neither Rhegium nor Messana receive them, as they expect (6.44.2–3, 6.66.2, 6.48.1, 6.50.1). Other disappointments—and eventually disasters—follow.

Whereas at the beginning of his work Thucydides warns against the poets' mythical adornments and exaggerations, including Homer's tales about Troy, now when he approaches his account of the Athenian expedition to Sicily, he recommends the poets' tales of terror-inspiring monsters, ugly in both their appearance and brutality (1.21.1, 6.1.3). Poetry, like Pericles' rhetoric itself, does not merely evoke confidence and daring by its appealing images of conquest and glory, as in stories of the heroes at Troy. Poetry also curbs undue enthusiasm by arousing fear (2.65.9, 2.64.5). In spite of Pericles' dismissal of the poets (2.41.4), they are his progenitors in arousing confidence and evoking fear. And in spite of Thucydides' dismissal of the poets, he appeals to them now to support his warning about human limits.

The Debate between Nicias and Alcibiades

When the Egestaeans come to Athens for help in their war against the Selinountines, allies of Syracuse, they make their proposal more appealing by offering "sufficient funding" for the war (6.6.2). Apparently, Athenians are suspicious, for after hearing this "many times" in the assembly, they send envoys to Egesta to see if such wealth is really available (6.6.3). The Egestaeans show the Athenians a great quantity of gold and silver both in the temples and in private homes, but their wealth is a ruse, for they "contrive" to borrow gold and silver from nearby cities to fool the Athenians. The report the Athenians bring back to their city is therefore "appealing but untrue"

(6.8.2, 6.46.3–5).[33] Whereas Nicias does not trust the Egestaeans' claims to wealth (6.22.1), Alcibiades says nothing about them in the assembly. Whether or not he is complicit in the Egestaeans' deception, however, the false report supports the involvement of his city in the Sicilian expedition that he advocates.[34]

Although the envoys do return with a favorable report, the issue seems lost in the debate about the expedition that Thucydides proceeds to report. After the Athenians vote to send an expedition to Sicily, Nicias attempts to revisit the issue to persuade them otherwise. It is not the first time Nicias's rhetoric misfires, nor the last (4.28, 7.16).

Nicias emphasizes how foreign and alien the island is, and how pressing are problems closer to home. He tells the Athenians that they have been persuaded by men "of another tribe" (*allophuloi*) (6.9.1), as he calls the Egestaeans. Although he later acknowledges that the Egestaeans are allies, he also refers to them as "barbarians" (6.10.5, 6.11.7). And he does not mention by name the Athenians' kin, the now-dispossessed Leontines, whom they claim they want to help against Syracuse, except to allude to them as liars (6.12.1). In other ways as well, he highlights how remote and distant is the enterprise under consideration. Even if we conquer the Sicilians, he warns, they could be ruled only with difficulty, inasmuch as there are so many of them and they are so faraway (6.11.1). Nicias admits that his speech would fail if he offered advice contrary to Athens's character (*tropoi*), specifically, if he "urges the city to preserve what it has and not to endanger what is at hand for what is unclear and in the future" (6.9.3). He says, in other words, that he cannot ask Athens to act like Sparta, as the Corinthians described that city—to care more for preserving what they have than for acquiring more,

---

33. The Egestaeans, Thucydides tells, are Trojans who escape the Achaeans after the fall of Troy and settle in Sicily (6.2.3). As the Achaeans trick their way into Troy, these Trojans trick the Athenians to come to Sicily.

34. When it is later confirmed that Egestaean wealth is a fabrication, this is nothing more than Nicias expects, Thucydides reports, but for the other two commanders, it is "incredible" or unspeakable (*alogōtera*) (6.46.2). Thucydides does not mention Alcibiades and the third commander, Lamachus, by name. Perhaps he refrains from mentioning the name of a man who has appeared himself as a master of deception—and whose deception by the Egestaeans might therefore seem incredible. According to Gottfried Mader, for the other two generals, especially for the cynical and manipulative Alcibiades, the Egestaean deception could not have been unexpected. Rather, he argues, Thucydides means that the *disclosure* of the deception was unexpected by Alcibiades, for it produces an unexpected hitch in planning their strategy with fellow commander Nicias. That is, their alliance with the Egestaeans seems less and less a reason for the Athenians to remain in Sicily. "Rogues' Comedy at Segesta (Thucydides 6.46): Alcibiades Exposed?" *Hermes* 121 (1993): 192–93. By "Alcibiades exposed," Mader refers to his imperial ambitions in Sicily, not to any complicity with the Egestaeans.

for staying home more than for being away (1.70.2). But this is exactly what he advises the Athenians to do. Haste now, he insists, is inopportune. The peace with Sparta is not secure, many points are contested, many of Sparta's allies have not accepted the treaty, and the Chalcidians in Thrace are not yet subdued (6.10). As we have seen, Thucydides makes many of the same points in arguing that Athens's "peace" treaty with Sparta does not secure the end of the war (5.25–26). They now come from Nicias himself, the Athenian most responsible for the treaty.[35] There is work, in other words, to be done at home, work that Nicias began—securing peace.

Nicias tries to occupy the middle ground that Pericles urges earlier—no new conquests while at war—but his rhetoric falters in the face of the very Athenian character that he says he cannot gainsay. He advises that because the farthest away is most terrible, Athenians will be most feared by the Sicilians if they remain faraway, that is, if they do not go to Sicily at all, or if they do go they will be most feared if they briefly display their power and leave (6.11.4).[36] It is the difficult and the faraway, however, that now attracts the Athenians, and Nicias's suggestion that they should bask in a reputation they do not test reeks of Sparta's earlier proposal for peace: quit now while you have luck on your side and chance has not deprived you of your reputation (4.18.3). Nicias would have done better to associate his advice with that of Pericles. Instead, he attacks his current opponent, a man with enough standing to be appointed as one of his fellow commanders of the expedition in spite of his youth.

Nicias claims that Alcibiades wants to be admired for his stable of horses, that he is too young to command, and that he endangers his city for the sake of his "private brilliance" (6.12.2). Nicias calls on the elders in the assembly to oppose Alcibiades and his followers and their "craving [duserōs] for the faraway" (6.13.1). As Nicias does of the Leontines, he alludes to Alcibiades without mentioning him by name. He seems to want to keep him, like the Leontines, faraway. He urges his addressees to leave the boundaries (horoi) between the Athenians and the Sicilians intact, boundaries against which they should not complain, the Ionian Sea and the Sicilian Sea. Athenians such as

---

35. Nicias uses a striking word to refer to Athens's current unsettled condition: Athens is still "at sea" (6.10.5). For Nicias, the city's being "at sea" is a dangerous condition, whereas for the Athenians at Melos (and Alcibiades) the Athenians are at home on the seas. See discussion by Taylor, *Thucydides, Pericles*, 140–45.

36. Nicias's formulation echoes the chorus in Sophocles' *Oedipus at Colonus*: "Not to be born surpasses speech," while the second best "once one appears lies in going back as swiftly as possible to whence one came" (1225–29).

those at Melos, however, would have complaints against these "boundaries" if, as they claim, they "command the sea" (5.109). The word for "craving" Nicias uses, *duserōs,* implies an *erōs* that is sick or diseased.[37] As Nicias presents it, a diseased *erōs* has no object other than the "faraway," literally "the absent" (*aponta*). Liberated from the restraint of particular purposes and objects that it seeks or loves, without destination or goal, its motion is infinite. Perhaps this is the meaning of Thucydides' statement at the beginning of his work, when he claims that with the Peloponnesian War came "the greatest motion" yet to take place (1.1.2).

Before Thucydides reports Alcibiades' response to Nicias, he confirms some of Nicias's claims about him. His extravagant tastes for horse breeding and other luxuries lead him to spend beyond his means. Like the Egestaeans, Alcibiades gives an inflated impression of his wealth. He now desires to command the expedition to Sicily in order to increase his private wealth and reputation. Alluding to his later removal from command in Sicily, Thucydides observes that the people suspected him of aiming at tyranny, and by turning to others to direct the war effort they contributed to the city's ruin (6.15.2–4). While revealing Alcibiades' desire to profit financially from the expedition and to enhance his reputation, Thucydides does not comment on the extent to which the people's suspicions about his inclinations to tyranny are correct. Even if Alcibiades intends to conquer Sicily and points beyond (see 6.15.2), he may serve Athenian interests. Exactly what he aims at—beyond wealth and reputation—is elusive. What does he want to do with his wealth? For what does he want to be remembered? Like Sicily, he remains distant, faraway.

Alcibiades begins his speech by proclaiming that it is more fitting for him to rule (*archein*) than for others, and that he thinks he is worthy of doing so (6.16.1). Whereas other Athenians have asserted that Athens is worthy of rule (*archē*) (e.g., 1.73.1, 5.89.1, 6.82.1), Alcibiades asserts this of himself. As Palmer observes, Alcibiades applies "the principles that Athens uses to justify her rule over fellow Greeks to justify his own rule over his fellow Athenians."[38] Is not the best way of life for cities also the best way of life for individuals (*Politics* 1323a14–1325b31)? By what logic could a tyrant city, as not only Athens's enemies but even Athenians themselves refer to Athens

---

37. The word stands out for its rarity. It is used nowhere else in Thucydides' text and appears very few times in classical Attic literature. In Euripides' *Hippolytus*, it is associated with disease (193).

38. Palmer, *Love of Glory*, 97. Also Forde, *Ambition to Rule*, 116; Rahe, "Thucydides' Critique of Realpolitik," 129, 131, 134.

(2.63.3, 3.37.2), refuse to be ruled by a tyrant? And yet if Alcibiades' understanding comes from "thinking the Periclean position through to its end,"[39] Alcibiades' path is not one that Pericles himself took. Periclean rhetoric, as we have seen, is based on fear as well as confidence, and Pericles speaks of the daimonic things such as the plague that are "beyond reason" (2.61.3, 64.2). And unlike Alcibiades, who concedes very little to Athens's authority over him, Pericles offers in effect a defense speech when, after the plague, the Athenians blame him as the cause of the war. He acknowledges that he can be held to account. When Alcibiades is summoned to face charges at Athens, he does not come.

By attacking him, Alcibiades says, Nicias "has compelled" him "to begin" by claiming he deserves to rule. In Greek, "to begin" (*archesthai*) is the verb "to rule" (*archein*) in the middle voice, in a reflexive sense. If one "rules oneself," one begins or causes what one does. To rule oneself is to be free. Alcibiades' coupling of "ruling" and "beginning" (or ruling oneself) undercuts his being "compelled" by Nicias to speak of himself. So does his playing with words when such serious matters are at stake. According to Diodotus, as we have seen, "rule" is one of the two greatest things. Freedom is the other, but Alcibiades' play on words covers that. In claiming that he is worthy of ruling, he is like the great-souled individual whom Aristotle later describes in the *Nicomachean Ethics*, who also claims that he is worthy of the greatest things (1123b2). Whereas Aristotle claims that the great-souled is indeed worthy of what he claims, Thucydides gives us only Alcibiades' claim about himself.[40]

The outcry against him, Alcibiades objects, involves matters that in fact bring repute to his ancestors and benefit his fatherland (6.16.1). While in his earlier introduction of Alcibiades, Thucydides says that he is honored in spite of his age because of his ancestors (5.43.2), Alcibiades reverses the relation: his ancestors are honored because of him. He thus goes a step further than Pericles: although Pericles praises the deeds of his contemporaries as greater than those of their ancestors (2.36.2), Alcibiades claims in effect that he shines glory on his ancestors. The effect gives luster to its cause. He does not deny the past; he re-creates it. If his reference to Athens as his "fatherland"

---

39. Palmer, *Love of Glory*, 97.

40. In the *Posterior Analytics*, Aristotle describes two types of greatness of soul, one characterized by an inability to endure insult, the other by an indifference to good and bad fortune. He includes Alcibiades among the former (*PA* 97b14–28). Alcibiades is only one example of one type, and not the most self-sufficient of the types.

suggests filial piety, he is a young man who does more for his father than his father does for him.[41]

Because of his own brilliance, he continues, the Hellenes, who thought Athens was brought down by the war, now think its power greater than it is (6.16.3). Pericles too, in his funeral oration, points to the discrepancy between reputation and truth, but that is because Athens proves superior to its reputation when tested (2.41.3). In claiming that his deeds give his city greater repute than it would otherwise have, Alcibiades, like Nicias, comes close to insulting his city for an undeserved reputation. But its reputation is not due to its being untested, as Nicias suggests, or to chance, as the Spartan envoys imply (4.18.5). It is due to Alcibiades. Athens deserves its reputation because of him. When Alcibiades urges the Athenians "to appear contemptuous" of the present peace with Sparta by sailing to Sicily (6.18.4), he is not suggesting that they appear to be what they are not. Rather, the greatest contempt lies in letting one's contempt be seen.

In his funeral oration, Pericles paints a beautiful city by describing Athens's form of government and way of life and asks his audience to become its lovers (2.36.4, 2.43.1). It is Athens who is "brilliant" (2.64.5). In contrast, Alcibiades presents his own brilliance (6.16.3). He is implicitly asking his audience to become his lovers. It is not surprising, then, that Alcibiades dismisses the envy that Athenians feel for him.[42] Even though those who have "grand thoughts" and do not deserve to be on an equal level with others may pain others in their own lifetimes, he observes, later generations will claim kinship with them even when it does not exist.[43] They will be thought of by posterity, not as having committed errors, but as having performed noble deeds, not as "alien" or other (*allotrioi*), but as their own (*spheteroi*). These are the things he "desires," he says (6.16.5–6). Alcibiades desires to belong to his

---

41. Orwin, *Humanity of Thucydides*, 123; Forde, *Ambition to Rule*, 79–80.

42. Macleod points out that Pericles made a similar point in his funeral oration about the envy (and hatred) that Athens incurs by ruling others, but that will be short-lived compared to the immortal reputation it will achieve (2.64.4–5). What Pericles says about empire, however, Alcibiades says of individuals like himself. The echo of Pericles "sets in relief Alcibiades' individualism." "Rhetoric and History," 75.

43. See Plato's *Lysis*, where a young boy, Lysis, shows an interest in ruling not only his own father but also the Athenians, and even the great king of Asia himself (209d). Socrates leads him to admit that all will become his friend—"and his kin" (*oikeioi*)—only if he is wise enough to be good and useful to them (210d). Socrates may detect in Lysis something we see in Alcibiades here—a desire for others to consider him their own, or a desire for home. Just before this exchange in the *Lysis*, Socrates has questioned whether Lysis's parents could love him as long as he is useless to them (207d–10c).

city, to be considered by future Athenians not as "alien" but as "their own." He desires a city in which he can be perfectly at home, even if this requires his alienation in his own lifetime, if this is a way for him to so distinguish himself that later generations will consider him their own.

What has Alcibiades achieved that makes him worthy of rule? He "makes himself splendid" (*lamprunomai*), he says, by the choruses he sponsors at the dramatic performances and by the chariots he enters in the Olympic games. He placed seven chariots in the races—a number greater than any private person had ever done, he boasts—and took first, second, and fourth places (6.16.2–3). Alcibiades' command is so great that the hole in his triumph is irrelevant to him.[44] Nor does he note that fewer than half of his entries were among the winners.

Alcibiades also takes credit for negotiating Athens's alliance with Argos and other cities on the Peloponnesus. Given the defeat of Athens and its allies at Mantinea, however, one might suppose that the less he says about that alliance the better. But Alcibiades seems able to convert even defeat into victory: "I brought together the strongest powers on the Peloponnesus without great danger or cost to you and made the Spartans contest everything in a single day at Mantinea." And "even though [the Spartans] prevailed in the battle, their confidence is still not restored to this very day" (6.16.6). Thucydides gave a different account: "by this single deed" the Spartans redeem the reputation for weakness they incurred after the disaster at Pylos, and show themselves to be the same men they had ever been (5.75.3). Alcibiades engages in a sort of revisionist history.[45] When referring to his success in securing the Argive alliance against Sparta, Alcibiades claims that his "youth and apparent unnatural folly" countered Peloponnesian power (*dunamis*) with fine-seeming speeches, and "by my ardor [*orgē*] gave them credibility [*pistis*]" (6.17.1). He converts youth and folly that his detractors attribute to him into a source of strength. Alcibiades even uses a word that ordinarily means "anger" (e.g., 3.36.2, 5.46.5) to mean "ardor," as several translators present it. His passion becomes a praiseworthy means of persuasion, even the basis for others' "trusting" his arguments (cf. Aristotle, *Rhetoric* 1356a1–5). As

---

44. There is an alternate tradition that Alcibiades' chariots won the first three places. Dover, *HCT,* 4:246–47; Isocrates 16.34. Perhaps Thucydides found the change to be required by the circumstances, that is, by what would most reveal Alcibiades.

45. According to Dover, during this period to which Alcibiades refers, Spartan prestige was enhanced, the Argive alliance broke apart, and an oligarchy was temporarily established in Argos. *HCT,* 4:248. Macleod uses Alcibiades' account of his activities in the Peloponnesus to illustrate how Alcibiades "deals above all in semblances." "Rhetoric and History," 73, 75.

Alcibiades recounts it, power seems to give way to speech, at least his own passion-inspired speech.

Alcibiades says much more about himself than about Sicily, about the individual who will lead the Athenians away than about their destination. Alcibiades admits that what he knows about Sicily, he "knows from hearsay" (6.17.6). He is one of the Athenians "without experience" of Sicily whom Thucydides mentions just before his archaeology of the island. Alcibiades informs the Athenian assembly that Sicily's cities are heavily populated with rabble and readily exchange and take in citizens. They lack the benefit of established customs, are given to faction, and are not furnished with arms. They have no sense of a fatherland. Nor do they have the number of hoplites they claim (6.17.2–5). The Sicilian cities from this account seem to have no forms of government or ways of life that give them an identity. Sicily is mere opportunity, a space for Alcibiades' activity. He has no need for experience of Sicily.

Even if many cities in Sicily hate Syracuse, Alcibiades knows that he must work to bring them into alliance with the Athenians once they arrive (6.17.6, 6.48). He must use the talents that brought the Peloponnesian cities to ally with Athens against Sparta, the most powerful force on the Peloponnesus, to bring together cities on the island of Sicily against Syracuse, the most powerful city there. Thus when the expedition arrives in Syracuse, he persuades his fellow commanders not to attack Syracuse until they win over the other cities in Sicily to their side (6.47–50). The world has yielded to his rhetoric and persuasion before, and he supposes it will do so again. He will conquer not by the sword, but by force of his words, and by force of the passion underlying them. If the world is essentially unformed, alliances made and broken in succession, Alcibiades already knows what he needs to know about Sicily, because he knows all that is to be known. He is not impressed by the fact that Athens and its allies whom he assembled lost the battle of Mantinea.

Athens would do well, Alcibiades continues, to allow him and Nicias to share command of the expedition to Sicily, since he is in his prime (*akmazein*) and Nicias appears fortunate (6.17.1). By claiming that he is in his prime, Alcibiades leaves no room for the middle-aged, for those who might be considered in the prime of life (also 6.18.6).[46] For Alcibiades, youth is the

---

46. In his *Rhetoric,* Aristotle distinguishes the different characters of the young, the elderly, and those in the prime of life, which combines the characters of the other two. Among the characteristics of the young is confidence, among those of the old is fearfulness. His descriptions of the young and the old have much in common with the characters of Alcibiades and Nicias, as Thucydides presents them. *Rhetoric* 1389a3–1390b12.

prime of life, and those who are not young are the old (see Xenophon, *Memorabilia* 1.2.40–46). Alcibiades' reference to Nicias's good fortune has been understood as a criticism of Nicias—"a veiled sneer which implies the lack of more substantial merit."[47] Alcibiades' appeal to the expedition's need for Nicias's good fortune, however, is ominous. So too is his appeal to his youth. As Macleod notes, Alcibiades "can appeal more urgently for the campaign by making its success depend on things which do not last, fortune and youth."[48] In doing so, Alcibiades implies that the campaign depends not only on things that change in time, but things that are beyond human control (see 7.77.2). Seizing the moment may seem to indicate decisive action, but that is only because the moment will not last.

The youthful Alcibiades nevertheless appeals to the old ways: "the safest course for human beings is to dwell within the character and laws that presently exist, even if they are inferior, and to conduct one's politics with the least variance from them." Since Athens's traditional way of life is an active one, Athens should not cease its activity but send an expedition to Sicily (6.18.7).[49] So speaks Alcibiades, who finds a way to present himself as the conservative follower of the ways of his fathers, recommending the "safest" course, adhering to one's character and laws, even if others are better.

After Alcibiades speaks, Nicias realizes that "the same arguments" that he made before will not work. The conservative Nicias therefore tries a new approach to alter the Athenians' resolve—describing the great size of the preparations they would need because of the difficulties they face in Sicily. Where Alcibiades sees disunity on the island as a result of large fluctuating populations without a sense of a fatherland, Nicias sees large cities that are independent and free, and hence likely to fight hard against subjection. Other than Naxos and Catana, who will likely join the Athenians because of their kinship with the Leontines, there are seven more cities on the island with military ways similar to those of the Athenians, especially Syracuse and Selinus, their primary foes. "Kinship," in other words, does not extend very far, and the "similarity" of the Sicilian cities in other ways with Athens intensifies its danger (6.20.2–3). Nicias's reference to "seven" cities on Sicily

---

47. Macleod, "Rhetoric and History," 77. Consider Pericles' claim that Athens's preeminence proceeds from "intelligence" (*gnōmē*) rather than fortune (*tuchē*) (1.144.3).

48. Macleod, "Rhetoric and History," 77.

49. Herodotus's Xerxes takes a similar approach in urging the Persians to send an expedition to conquer Athens: he proposes "not introducing a new law but accepting the one that is established," a law of conquering and adding to the empire (Herodotus 7.8a1).

that pose a threat to Athens echoes and renders comic the "seven" chariots that Alcibiades says he entered in the Olympic contests. Alcibiades has been paying more attention to his horses, Nicias implies, than to the opposition Athens faces in Sicily. While the Sicilians have hoplites, archers, dart throwers, ships, and money, Nicias points out, one of their chief advantages lies in their number of horses (6.20.4)—something the horse-racing Alcibiades seems to have neglected. The Athenians will have to rely on friendly cities there to furnish their cavalry, a rather risky dependence for something that makes a major difference in the fighting (6.21.1).

Moreover, they are not going to friendly territory, where additional provisions are easy to obtain, but are cutting themselves off in a completely alien land, where in winter a messenger might take even four months to get out (6.21.2). The alien, the distant, and hence foreboding character of Sicily that Nicias describes makes the preparations for the expedition huge. The requisite number of hoplites, archers, mercenary soldiers, and ships, and the quantity of food and other supplies and money seems astronomical. Indeed, "we must think that we are going to found a city among aliens and enemies," he says, in order to emphasize the enormity of the undertaking (6.23.2). Like a tragic protagonist, he says more than he intends, for a founding is closer to the Athenian purpose that Thucydides avers than is their helping kin and allies. Nicias's attempt to find a "new" approach rather than to give "the same arguments" may be fitting, but appealing to the "size" of the undertaking and using "founding" imagery do more to attract than to dissuade. As Thucydides says, the result of Nicias's speech is "the opposite" of what he intends (6.24.2). He attempts to point out dangers, and thereby to arouse fear. But he has in fact given the Athenians confidence, for the preparations that Nicias recommends seem to assure safety (6.24.1–2). It is only after Nicias's speech that "*erōs* for sailing away" falls upon everyone.[50] The Athenians' *erōs* is based on an illusion that Nicias inadvertently fosters, an illusion not about Sicily but about themselves. They can go forth in utmost security, and that security erodes caution and unleashes desire. The Athenian propensity to take risks, to which Alcibiades appeals, is based on their confidence in themselves.

---

50. Thucydides here echoes the words of Aeschylus's Clytemnestra. When hearing of the fall of Troy she wishes that "*erōs* not so fall upon the soldiers that they ravage what they should not" and prevent their "safe homecoming" (*Agamemnon* 341–44). Cornford, *Thucydides Mythistoricus*, 214. For the Athenians, *erōs* prompts not their excesses while on the expedition but the very expedition itself.

Nicias concludes by offering to give up his command to anyone who thinks the enterprise can be undertaken with fewer men and supplies (6.23.3). Earlier Nicias yielded his command at Pylos to Cleon, who insisted that he did not want it, and the more Cleon insisted, the more eager the Athenians became for him to lead the expedition (4.27–28). Nicias should have known from this experience that nay-saying can intensify the Athenians' desire. Nicias's nay-saying now has this effect, not only on the Athenians' desire for the expedition itself but also on their desire to include Nicias among its leaders. Just as the Athenians believe that the larger force provides safety, they suppose that Nicias's caution makes safe Alcibiades' daring. It is no less a stable combination than is Alcibiades' youth and Nicias's good fortune. Kagan speculates that the Athenians "saw the impossibility of naming to one command two generals who were political and personal enemies and who disagreed on all aspects of the projected campaign." They therefore appointed a third general, Lamachus, to share in the command, who presumably favors the expedition but who respects Nicias.[51] As events unfold, Alcibiades is removed from command, and Lamachus dies in battle. Nicias's caution, which comes to characterize his command in Sicily, leads to disaster.

When Nicias speaks of the difficulties that the Athenians face in Sicily, he uses the same words as Alcibiades did: both recount what they "know from hearsay" (6.20.2, 6.17.2). Alcibiades does not require experience of Sicily, if all alike yield to him, whereas no experience of Sicily could persuade Nicias that a land that faraway could come under his sway. Thucydides gives us a kind of experience of Sicily from his account of an earlier expedition Athens took there. There is, for example, an assembly of the leading cities on the island at which the Syracusan leader Hermocrates appeals for unity against the threat from Athens. He succeeds in forestalling Athens's ambitions there (4.58). Although differences among the cities exist, there is also a potential for leadership and cooperation. Thucydides concludes his account of this earlier foray to Sicily with Athens's reaction to its fleet's returning home—banishing two of the generals, and fining a third, in the belief that they brought the fleet home as a result of bribes when they might have subdued Sicily. Thucydides comments then that Athens's good fortune leads it to think that it could "accomplish the possible and the impenetrable alike" (*aporōtera*) (4.65.3–4). The Greek word for impenetrable means, literally, "without passage." The Athenians will eventually face a situation in Sicily in which they have no way or passage home. At the end of his account of the earlier expedition,

---

51. Kagan, *Peace of Nicias*, 171.

Thucydides ominously comments that the Athenians confuse their strength with their hopes (4.65.4), reminding us of Diodotus's warning about *erōs* and hope, and reminding us as well of Alcibiades, who describes only those things about Sicily that are "favorable" to Athenian success, literally, those things that make for a good passage (*eupora*) (6.17.4–6).

Hermocrates warns the Sicilian cities that the Athenians want the goods the Sicilians possess (4.61.3). Alcibiades expresses his aims in more abstract terms. Echoing the Athenians at Melos, he claims that Athens must undertake the expedition to Sicily because unless it rules others it is in danger of being ruled by them (6.18.3). There are only those who rule and those who are ruled, just as the Athenians at Melos deny that there can be neutrals. Alcibiades observes that there is "no reckoning for how far we wish to rule" (6.18.3). Alcibiades rejects all "measure," or what Thucydides praised in Pericles' politics (2.65.5). The Athenians at Melos also imply that there can be no limits to Athens's rule, but they were speaking to the Melians. They were trying to arouse fear. Alcibiades now presents an image of endless or infinite increase to Athens itself. He provides no image of a beautiful Sicily that Athenians might love, and thereby want to make their own, as Pericles does of a beautiful Athens. What attracts them about Sicily is not what they might find there, but what they might found there, as even Nicias suggests when he describes the supplies the Athenians need in Sicily as those required to found a city. If the world is unformed, one becomes the object of one's own desire, displayed visibly for viewing, by oneself. Not its goal, but the expedition itself, as the fleet leaves the Piraeus, becomes the beautiful object of longing.

The debate between Nicias and Alcibiades that Thucydides records revisits a decision that has already been made. This is true in the case of Mytilene as well. With respect to Mytilene, the Athenians come to a different decision, whereas in the case of Sicily Athens's reopening of the debate results in sending a much greater force to Sicily.[52] Unlike the Athenians of that earlier period, these refuse to reverse themselves. Later, when they hear from Nicias about the troubles of their expedition in Sicily, and that they should either withdraw or send a force equal in size to the first, they send a second expedition (7.11–16). No ship carries a command to the forces in Sicily to reverse the previous decision; there is only a fleet that reproduces it. The Athenians have become like Pericles urges them to be—always remaining

---

52. Connor, *Thucydides*, 162n11.

the same (2.61.2)—in a situation that blatantly contradicts his war policy by attempting new conquests while still at war (1.144.1), or at least while the city at home is, as Nicias says, still "at sea."

Sailing Away

Although "an *erōs* for sailing away fell upon all alike," different groups in Athens have different purposes for signing on to the expedition: "the older men go to conquer the places they are sailing against, believing in any case that they will be safe; those in their prime long for sight [*opsis*] and contemplation [*theoria*] of the faraway [*apousa*, literally, 'the absent']; and the masses in the army seek wealth in the present and pay forever." As Alcibiades suggests, there are in Athens only the elderly and those in the prime of life, that is, no one to moderate or combine the propensities of the old and the young. We should not expect Lamachus to have an influential role in Sicily as a fellow commander with Nicias and Alcibiades. Moreover, "all" are overcome by *erōs* only because some fear to appear ill-intentioned toward the city by holding up their hands in opposition (6.24.2–4). That is, they are overcome by the *erōs* of others, and their own fear. The "everlasting" glory that Pericles promised to those who sacrifice themselves for their city (2.43.2) was eclipsed earlier by a desire to be safe forever from invasion by enemies, which motivates the Athenians at the battle of Mantinea (5.69.1). And now Athenian soldiers are looking for "everlasting" pay. The "philosophizing without softness" for which Pericles praises Athens (2.40.1) has degenerated into a longing for sight and contemplation "of what is absent." If *erōs* has no object but the "absent," it can never be satisfied, just as the Corinthians' description of Athenians as ever "away from home" (*apodēmētai*) (1.70.4) places them nowhere in particular. Hermocrates' supposition that the Athenians want "the goods" that the Sicilians possess (4.61.3) is superficial. The "faraway" or "absent" and "safety" have this in common—both (like wealth itself) are infinite.

The expedition sails from Athens, Thucydides reports, in the middle of the summer (6.30.1), reminding us of Nicias's reference to the difficult winters in Sicily. The atmosphere at the Piraeus, however, is more of celebration, although there are lamentations mixed with hope from those escorting the sailors to their ships (6.30.2). "The whole city, so to speak," Thucydides says, accompanies the sailors to their ships, as if the whole city is drawn into the expedition itself. He also mentions that the onlookers include both Athenians and foreigners, giving us a sense that the expedition itself has become a spectacle (6.30.2; see also 2.36.4). Indeed, Thucydides uses several different words for looking or seeing as the crowd sees the expedition off, including *opsis* and *thea* (6.30.2–31.1), reminding us of the faraway sights and spectacles Athenians seek from the voyage. Athens has become the very thing that it is seeking, seen rather than seeing. That this characterized Cleon before the defeat of his troops and his own death at Amphipolis (5.6–8) does not bode well for the expedition.

The expedition, Thucydides observes, is "the most extravagant [*poluteles-tatē*] and lavish preparation" that had ever sailed out from a single city (6.31.1). The "love of beauty without extravagance" (*met' euteleias*) that Pericles attributes to Athens (2.40.1) gives way to excess. The expedition's extravagance, Paul A. Rahe observes, attained "a scale more reminiscent of the barbarians than of the Greeks," marked by "a splendor" and "unrestrained daring" for which Alcibiades was notorious.[53] The expedition is outfitted not only by the city but by the commanders of the triremes themselves, who compete with one another for their ships "to excel in good looks" (6.31.3). The effect of the whole is more "like a display" (*epideixis*) of power and capacity than a preparation against an enemy, and celebrated no less for the wonder of its boldness and the brilliance of its sight than for any superiority to its foe (6.31.4–6). Athens's expedition seems to exist for its own sake rather than for any purpose outside itself.

To be sure, the Athenians took their city to sea before—in the defining moment when they deserted their city to the invading Persians, in order to save themselves from subjection and take their chances in a naval battle.[54] But then they abandoned their city for the sake of preserving their freedom, in response to an enemy closing in on them and therefore near at hand (see 1.73.4). As soon as the Persians left, the Athenians, as Thucydides recounts, "immediately" brought back their women, children, and property and started to rebuild their city and walls (1.89.3). Now the Athenians are displaying their daring and luster, and their goal is simply "sailing away." The past is prologue, and the future irrelevant. The present, initially so paltry compared to the absent, has come to hold within itself the fullness of time. The expedition might as well stay home. And surely anyone who reads Thucydides' moving description of its almost complete destruction in Sicily will believe that it should have stayed home. Alcibiades' politics could avoid tragedy only if politics, while moving, could stay in place. This is the very goal—and

---

53. Rahe, "Thucydides' Critique of Realpolitik," 133.
54. J. Peter Euben, "The Battle of Salamis and the Origin of Political Theory," *Political Theory* 14, no. 3 (1986): 359–90.

accomplishment—of Pericles' politics that Thucydides presents and that his successors were not able to achieve.[55]

When describing the size of the expedition, Thucydides observes that in number of ships and hoplites, the force that Pericles took earlier in the war to the coast of Peloponnesus was not inferior, although that expedition went on "a short voyage with scanty equipment" (6.31.2–3). That expedition had the numbers without the liberated *erōs* that now impels Athens to Sicily. This is the only time that Pericles' name appears in Thucydides' history after Thucydides announces his death. Unlike the Athenians at the time of the expedition to Sicily, Thucydides remembers Pericles, and the shorter, less brilliant expedition that was his last in Thucydides' history.[56]

Just before heading to sea, the Athenian fleet offers customary prayers and pours libations in gold and silver cups (6.32.1). Thucydides' reference to the Athenians' gold and silver cups reminds us of those in which the Athenians are served at Egesta, when they go to find out whether the Egestaeans have the wealth to furnish the expedition. The lavish but deceptive display in Sicily forms the background of the even more lavish one in the Piraeus.

In the next chapter, I trace the aftermath of the Sicilian expedition, with its liberation of *erōs*. First, Alcibiades is recalled home to stand trial for charges of impiety, and escapes to Sparta and conspires with the enemy so that, he claims, he might repossess his city. Even then his goal is going home, as it is for Nicias with the expedition in Sicily. Alcibiades comes closer than Nicias to returning home by moving, it seems, even further away—to intrigues with the Persian satrap Tissaphernes: specifically, he hopes to show the Athenians that he is useful to them if he can bring them an alliance with Tissaphernes and Persia. To negotiate with Tissaphernes is to negotiate his return to Athens (8.47.1). By making homecoming a theme, Thucydides indicates that

---

55. Others see a direct line between Pericles' appeal to the citizens to become lovers of Athens and the *erōs* for sailing that takes the Athenians to Sicily. E.g., Strauss, *City and Man*, 226; Palmer, *Love of Glory*, 105; Taylor, *Thucydides, Pericles*, 149–50.

56. Taylor argues that Thucydides' reference to Pericles' earlier expedition in commenting on the size of the fleet sailing for Sicily has the effect of presenting the latter expedition as Periclean. *Thucydides, Pericles,* 155–57. Pericles' expedition, however, remained closer to home, whereas the other goes far away. One effect of this difference is that Pericles' expedition was able to take three hundred horses for the Athenian cavalry (6.32), whereas the Sicilian expedition took only one horse transport carrying thirty horses (6.43.1). Hans–Peter Stahl, "Speeches and Course of Events in Books 6 and 7 of Thucydides," in *The Speeches in Thucydides*, ed. Philip A. Stadter (Chapel Hill: University of North Carolina Press, 1973), 66–69. Given Nicias's claim that one of the chief advantages the cities on Sicily will have over the Athenians lies in their cavalry, whereas the Athenians will have to rely on allied cities to furnish horses (6.20.4), the contrast Thucydides makes is telling.

human action (and therefore the freedom it manifests) is possible only in response to time and place. Its objects are those that are here and now, or can become so, rather than the merely absent. That is why homecoming, which of course presupposes a voyage, can appear as the consummate human activity, metaphorically speaking, for it combines a freedom from home that is manifest in traveling away, with a recognition that actions are one's own only because they involve the particularities of time and place.

CHAPTER 5

Homecoming and Freedom

The issue of homecoming arises in the last books of Thucydides' history as a consequence of the Sicilian expedition. Will those who go so far away be able to return home? Homecoming and its problems have emerged previously. As we have seen, the Spartans on Sphacteria become alienated from their city not merely by surrendering to the Athenians, but also by questioning what they should do, for Spartan laws and customs hold surrendering to be shameful. As a result, they lose the trust of their city, and cannot resume their place in the regime once they return home. The Spartans have even greater reason to distrust Brasidas than they do their soldiers who surrendered on Sphacteria, for Brasidas acts even more independently of his city than those soldiers (see also 5.63). Brasidas does not even ask Sparta what to do when he is in the field, he simply decides himself. He finally resists Sparta's directives (4.122).

Whereas Brasidas's freedom strikes at the heart of Spartan identity, Nicias's compliance with necessity strikes at the heart of Athenian freedom. Consequently, neither has a home in his city. Pericles boasts that the virtue of Athenians comes from within themselves rather than from the harsh discipline of the law. Only if the actions of the Athenians are theirs, rather than compelled by necessity, do they merit eternal fame. Achievement that is deserved and recognized serves as a tribute to and hence a confirmation of freedom. By the same token, failure in Sicily, indeed any failure of such magnitude, not only means the loss of lives and resources, but strikes at Athens's self-understanding by demonstrating the limits of its freedom to act. Nicias knows that if he orders retreat in Sicily, the Athenians will blame him rather than acknowledge such limits, just as they held their generals responsible for not conquering Sicily on an earlier venture (4.65.3). They would hold him responsible for the very failure he foresaw and warned them against. Failure would be Nicias's undoing, although or precisely because it would prove him correct—Athens should have stayed closer to home. Athens should have acted more like Sparta, because it is more like Sparta than it admits. Nicias cannot return home without grand achievement, and grand achievement is impossible for him in Sicily. To make the decision to retreat, and thereby to bring himself and his troops home in safety, would require an independence or freedom from his city. It would require the very freedom in which Athens takes pride, but which Nicias does not achieve. Nicias is more like a Spartan than his undying loyalty to Athens acknowledges.

Alcibiades is a more complicated case. He seems to embody Athenian freedom, in that he proclaims the active character of the city and manifests that character in his own life. But if the virtue of Athenians comes from within themselves, those who exercise the freedom in which Athens takes pride are those who owe least to the regime and most to their own efforts. The people are correct not to trust Alcibiades. Just as he believes that he can bestow glory on his ancestors, he thinks that he can repossess his city. His homecoming would be an even greater problem than Nicias's. Repossessing one's city—and thereby making it one's own—is the ultimate demonstration or proof of one's freedom. If Alcibiades could succeed in coming home, he would be an Athenian by virtue of his own act. His homecoming would mean not that he belonged to Athens, but that Athens belonged to him. If Athens could become the home of a man who acts as freely as Alcibiades—and who therefore must repossess his city himself—it would no longer be a free city.

When Alcibiades and Nicias leave together in command of the Sicilian expedition, the people who celebrate onshore expect a successful homecoming. But that requires the cooperation of these two commanders, and one has his eyes on points even beyond Sicily, the other on problems nearer home. It is appropriate that Thucydides himself remembers a previous expedition led by Pericles when the fleet departs, one equal in size but with a destination closer to home (6.31.2). Pericles is a general who led many an expedition, but he always came home. Homecoming for him, unlike for Nicias and Alcibiades (and also for Brasidas), never appeared as a problem. It is Thucydides' Pericles who holds together respect for Athens's regime, laws, and way of life with the freedom for human action that the regime made possible and that made it worthy of respect.

In this chapter, I discuss Thucydides' account of the efforts of both Alcibiades and Nicias to return home once they leave Athens on the Sicilian expedition, and the problems that their homecomings present for human freedom. Alcibiades' exceptional abilities make it difficult for him to play only a part in whatever he undertakes, and he cannot easily find a place even in a regime such as Athens. His independent action obscures the extent to which he owes his freedom to the Athenian regime. Nicias, in contrast, does not achieve the independence necessary to lead, and therefore cannot lead his troops home. He does not grasp the freedom that is Athens's characteristic excellence. In this chapter, I discuss Alcibiades' speech at Sparta, then Nicias's command and defeat in Sicily, and finally the intrigues of Alcibiades throughout the Hellenic world that Thucydides recounts in book 8. Thucydides concludes his work with the need to recall liberated *erōs* home, inasmuch as virtue must both come from oneself and find expression in a political community if it is to be simply good. Thucydides' portrayal of Alcibiades and Nicias in his last books prepares us to reflect on the ways in which Thucydides himself is an Athenian, as I do in my concluding chapter. His writing of a history of the war, I argue, not only manifests his freedom but also serves as a homecoming, and therefore allows Thucydides to claim his identity as an Athenian.

Alcibiades in Sparta

Shortly before the expedition departs for Sicily, herms are mutilated throughout the city, Thucydides says, and the event is thought to be an ill omen for the voyage. Those resenting Alcibiades for standing in the way of their own influence over the people implicate him in this act as well as in mockeries of the sacred mysteries. Moreover, many become convinced that these acts of impiety are part of an oligarchic or tyrannical conspiracy. Although Alcibiades would like to face a trial head-on before he leads the expedition to Sicily, his accusers fear his support from the army and the people, and hope to make a stronger case against him "in his absence" (*apōn*) (6.27–29, 6.53, 6.60.1). The man who leads the Athenians in the pursuit of the faraway must obviously go far away himself in doing so. And he is more vulnerable to his enemies at home when he is away. Shortly after the expedition arrives in Sicily, a ship comes from Athens to fetch Alcibiades and others who have been accused so that they might stand trial for charges of impiety. Opposition has mounted in his absence (6.53).

Before leaving Sicily, Alcibiades informs Messana of a plot within the city to bring Messana over to the Athenians. He betrays the very men with whom he was conspiring on behalf of Athens (6.48, 6.50). The conspirators are put to death (6.74.1). We see how quickly Alcibiades can switch sides. The death of the Athenian supporters in Messana in which Alcibiades is instrumental foreshadows what happens on a larger scale to the Athenians in Sicily.

En route to Athens, Alcibiades and the others accused with him escape, doubting their chance of a fair trial there. Later the exiles cross in a boat from Thurii on the coast of Italy to the Peloponnesus, and then to Sparta (6.61.6–7). At Melos the Athenians boasted that because no one was likely to escape them at sea the Melians should not count on aid arriving from Sparta. The Athenians are masters of the sea (*naukratores*) (5.109). But Alcibiades escapes them. It is he who masters the sea. Before the outbreak of the war, the Spartans received an oracle from the god at Delphi that told them that the god would come to their aid, "whether summoned or not," as long as they prosecute the war "with all their strength" (1.118.3). Alcibiades comes without being summoned to offer help, and he comes to encourage them to throw all their strength into the war.

When Alcibiades and his fellow exiles arrive in Sparta, they find Syracusan envoys and their Corinthian supporters there as well, in the process of requesting that the Spartans send aid to Sicily against Athens. As at the beginning of Thucydides' account of the war, Corinth comes to Sparta to advocate war against Athens. The representatives of the only city in Thucydides' work who have given speeches at both Athens and Sparta are now aided by the only man who does this. Whereas the Corinthians appear Spartan when they speak at Athens, and Athenian when they speak at Sparta—to speak in terms of the Corinthians' distinction between the traditional Sparta and innovative Athens—Alcibiades appears Athenian at Athens and Spartan at Sparta. It is he who has a flexibility that Pericles associates with Athens (2.41.1), and his speeches are more persuasive than those of the Corinthians. At Athens, the Corinthians cannot prevent the Athenian alliance with Corcyra, whereas Alcibiades arouses his city's enthusiasm for the Sicilian expedition. When Alcibiades comes forward to speak at Sparta, the Corinthians have acquired Spartan support for Syracuse, but Sparta plans merely to send envoys to encourage Syracuse to hold out against Athens, with no assistance beyond that (6.89.10). The Spartans offer words rather than deeds. Once more, the Corinthians find it difficult to move the Spartans to actions. As Corinth reproached them earlier, they are inclined to stay at home rather than to come to the aid of their allies. Thucydides shows us, although he does not say it explicitly, that the Spartans are "the same men that they ever were" (see 5.75.3). As Thucydides presents the sequence of events, Alcibiades makes the difference.[1] This time the Athenians in Sparta—Alcibiades and his fellow exiles—support the Corinthians' request.

Had Alcibiades returned to Athens he would have stood trial for impiety, and for his disloyalty to the Athenian regime. He would have had, we assume, an opportunity to deliver a speech in his defense. About fifteen years later, Socrates was also accused of impiety and disloyalty to his city, even of corrupting the young, such as Alcibiades himself (Xenophon, *Memorabilia* 1.2.12). While Socrates does not flee prosecution, and even refuses an opportunity to escape from prison once he is condemned to death (Plato, *Crito* 50b–c), Alcibiades flees prosecution, suspecting the outcome as surely as Socrates does (Plato, *Apology* 36a). Whether or not Thucydides had Socrates in mind, his account of Alcibiades in similar circumstances offers us a dramatic contrast between the world-traveling Athenian traitor and the Athenian philosopher, who never left home except to serve in his city's army (Plato, *Crito* 52b). In Thucydides' account of the war, Alcibiades appears more often away from home than in Athens. And while he delivers no defense speech in an Athenian court, he delivers one in effect in Sparta, for he must defend himself to the Spartans before they will listen to the advice he comes to offer them.

There are at least three reasons why Sparta might not trust him, and Alcibiades addresses each in turn. Alcibiades has been no friend to Sparta at Athens, but the contrary, even bringing together the Argive alliance against the Spartans. In the second place, he supported democracy, a form of government to which the Spartans are adverse. Most important of all, a traitor to one's own city might be thought a potential traitor to whatever city accepts his aid. "It is necessary," he begins his speech at Sparta, "for me to speak first about the prejudice that has arisen against me, so that you will hear me on public matters without suspicion" (6.89.1). Like Socrates, who also addresses the "prejudices" that have arisen against him when he defends himself against charges of impiety and disloyalty to his city (e.g., *Apology* 19b, 23a), Alcibiades does so, but in the city that he now tries to make his own.

---

1. Brunt finds it incredible that Alcibiades was so much more persuasive than ambassadors from Syracuse and Corinth, and suggests that Thucydides exaggerates Alcibiades' importance. "Thucydides and Alcibiades," 70–72. See also Kagan, *Peace of Nicias*, 257. Thucydides' "exaggeration" of Alcibiades' role, however, if that is what it is, is not necessarily favorable to Alcibiades, inasmuch as the greater his role in Spartan decisions, the greater his harm to Athens. If Thucydides does exaggerate, he allows us to see more clearly the danger Alcibiades holds for his city. See Gribble, *Alcibiades and Athens*, 24, 176–77, 191–92, 204.

Alcibiades claims that Sparta itself is to blame for his past opposition to it. When Alcibiades tried to renew his family's role as *proxenus* to Sparta and to serve it in Athens after the Pylos disaster, Sparta rejected his efforts when it negotiated the peace with his "enemies" in the city, giving them power, and dishonoring him. Alcibiades' enemies are therefore not Spartans, but those Athenians who oppose him, especially Nicias, who supported the peace that Sparta desired and whom Alcibiades does well not to mention now by name. Nicias has been a friend to Sparta. Alcibiades' harming Sparta by turning to Mantinea and Argos, he asserts, was therefore just (6.89.1–2). He is nevertheless approaching Sparta again, in effect giving the city a second chance. When Plataea asked Spartans for help against the Thebans, they reply that they live too far away, and that Plataea should seek help instead from Athens, their "near neighbor" (3.55.1). Alcibiades now asks the Spartans to go even farther away, to Sicily, to help the Syracusans against Athens. He expects success where others have failed, even with Sparta.

As to Alcibiades' support of democracy, he explains, anyone who hates him for inclining to the people is wrong to do so. We were ever the opponent of tyranny, he assures the Spartans—perhaps referring to his family, or his class, or his political associates—and all resistance to tyranny is called popular. Moreover, since Athens had a democratic government, "it was necessary to conform to existing circumstances," while "tempting to be more moderate in political matters than the prevailing license." As to democracy, men of judgment know it for what it is, and he more than anyone has cause to complain (6.89.3–6). Socrates too had cause to complain against democracy, which tried and found him guilty of corrupting the young. But if he voices his concerns about the authority of the people in his interrogation of Meletus at his trial, he leaves his complaint against the regime itself implicit (*Apology* 24d–25b; see also *Crito* 44d). Alcibiades refrains from criticism in his own way as well, for "nothing new [*kainon*] can be said about such acknowledged folly" as democracy. He does not introduce the new, the novel (see *Apology* 24c and 26b), just as he did not when he lived under the Athenian democracy. His side supported the democracy, but they were simply preserving the received government. Moreover, they could hardly think of overthrowing the democracy, he claims to the Spartans, "with you entrenched as enemies" (6.89.3–6). Once more Sparta is to blame—for preventing the very revolution in government that would have established a regime more friendly to Sparta.

Alcibiades uses the first person plural four times in rapid succession within a few lines of Thucydides' text (6.89.4–6). The individualism that appeared in his speech at Athens can hardly serve him here, at least not at the outset.

Presenting himself as a loyal citizen of Athens, Sparta's traditional enemy, would not necessarily create more sympathy, however, not to mention its lack of credibility under the circumstances. By identifying himself with his family or class, Alcibiades becomes someone with whom Spartans can sympathize, a man who follows in the ways of his ancestors, even trying to revive his family's connection with Sparta, and conforming to the received ways. Once again, he presents himself as a family man, although not the sort he claims to be in Athens, one whose ancestors shine in his reflected glory (6.16.1).

After excusing his opposition to Sparta and his support of democracy, Alcibiades goes on to reveal the purpose of the Athenian expedition, something about which he claims to know more than anyone: "we sailed to subdue Sicily, if possible," he says, and then Italy, and then the Carthaginians and their empire. With all the resources from these conquests, including men from those territories, ships built from timber in Italy, and barbarians such as the warlike Iberians in Athenian pay, "we hoped to subdue the Peloponnesus, and then to rule all Hellas" (6.90.2–3). It is not clear whether Alcibiades' suggestion that Athens must conquer the known world before conquering Sparta compliments the strength of his addressees, or indicates contempt—the conquest of Sparta is an afterthought, for subduing what is closer to home will occur only after more glorious achievements. That Athens is planning such a conquest of the world is of course more than Alcibiades mentioned in his speech at Athens, but who could speak for the intention of the Sicilian expedition better than Alcibiades himself? Alcibiades informs them further that Athens remains committed to these goals, for "the remaining generals if they are able will do these things" (6.91.1). Once again, he finds it convenient not to mention the name of Nicias, this time because it might well belie his statement. Even Hermocrates knew from the outset that Nicias was not eager to lead the Athenians on this expedition (6.34.6). If the Syracusan envoys at Sparta know this as well, this is not the time or place for them to mention it. As Alcibiades describes it, no threat to Hellas could be greater than the one Athens currently presents, and nothing less than a full and immediate effort from the Spartans can meet it. Without substantial reinforcement, Syracuse is in danger of falling.

Alcibiades' advice is specific. Spartans must send troops as well as a Spartan commander to inspire confidence and bring those cities who are still neutral over to the Syracusan side. So too they should carry on the war against Athens in Attica, making it difficult for the Athenians to send reinforcements to Sicily. In particular, they must fortify Decelea in Attica. While Spartan forces invaded Attica many times during the first years of the war, they always came home for the winter. Alcibiades' advice requires them to remain in Attica, just as the Athenians fortified Pylos in Spartan territory. They must come to imitate Athens in order to succeed against it. Such a fortification in Attica, as Alcibiades well knows, would cause major problems for the Athenians, cutting Athens's supply route over land from Euboea (7.28.1). This is the very thing the Athenians most fear, Alcibiades says, "and the surest way of harming an enemy is to discover what he most fears" (6.91).

Can any man who so clearly betrays his city be trusted? Alcibiades concludes his speech by addressing this issue explicitly. He does not expect, he says, the Spartans to think less of him as a lover of his city although he now joins its worst enemies in attacking it. The greater enemies, in fact, are not those (like the Spartans) who harm their enemies, but those (like the Athenians) who compel their friends (such as himself) to become enemies (6.92.2–3). Just as Sparta is to blame for Alcibiades' earlier opposition to Sparta, so Athens is now to blame for his helping Sparta. Alcibiades is consistent, for he is always reacting against being wronged, although he turns one way and then another. Acting unjustly to Alcibiades, Athens has made itself his enemy, Alcibiades asserts. Alcibiades' argument implies that one's city owes one justice, and when the city does not render it, one is permitted, even required by justice itself, to punish it. It is an argument that Socrates rejects when he refuses to escape from prison because the city has wronged him (*Crito* 50b–c). Alcibiades, in contrast, claims that he is not attacking a fatherland that still exists but rather trying to repossess one that does not. The lover of his city (*philopolis*) is not one who loses it to injustice without fighting but one who tries to recover it by any means whatsoever (6.92.4).[2] Although he asserts that there are no limits to what he would do to recover Athens, he implies that the Spartans should think him worthy and use him with no fear of danger.

Alcibiades concludes his speech by offering the Spartans the prospect of "destroying both the present and future power of Athens, and achieving the supremacy of all Hellas not by force but voluntarily and with goodwill" (6.92.5; cf. 4.20.4). Of course, "all Hellas" includes Athens, the city that Alcibiades loves and wants to repossess. And it presumably will have to be taken by force (see Isocrates, 5.58). Moreover, can Alcibiades repossess his

---

2. Nathan Marsh Pusey argues that Alcibiades' attitude toward his city here is not treasonous, but was common to the Greeks, inasmuch as the city was only one association among many to whom Greeks owed allegiance, such as families, tribes, religious groups, or political clubs. "Alcibiades and *to philopoli*," *Harvard Studies in Classical Philology* 51 (1940): 215–18. It is nevertheless his city that Alcibiades claims to love and to want to repossess—not any of these other associations. See also Forde, *Ambition to Rule*, 107n27.

city if it is subject to Spartan hegemony? Once again, we cannot know what Alcibiades is up to.[3]

Although the Spartans have good reason to be wary, they are persuaded by Alcibiades, believing that they have heard from the one who knows matters most clearly (6.92.1, 6.93.1). They do not yet know how elusive Alcibiades is. They send a Spartan, Gylippus, to command the united forces against Athens in Sicily, as Alcibiades advises, but they do not send the troops Alcibiades recommends.[4] They agree to the fortification of Decelea, but seem to proceed with their customary slowness. Alcibiades does not join this new expedition to Sicily, whether by his own choice or that of Sparta and its allies. The possibility of his accompanying the forces against Athens does not arise in Thucydides' text. Indeed, Thucydides barely mentions Alcibiades again during his account of the next two years of the war and during his dramatic and moving narrative of the devastation of the Athenian forces in Sicily.

Alcibiades is not the sole cause of Athens's defeat in Sicily, however. Nicias, the Athenian commander in Sicily who never wanted to leave home in the first place, and who wanted to return as soon as possible (6.11.4, 6.47), makes decisions that lead to the deaths of most of those who go on the expedition, including his own and that of Demosthenes, who joins him with reinforcements from Athens. We now turn to Nicias and the fate of the Athenians in Sicily. After all, in recommending the two of them as joint leaders of the expedition, Alcibiades suggests that both are necessary for its success (6.17.1). It turns out that both contribute to its defeat.

Nicias in Sicily

Although Nicias leads the Athenians to several military successes in Sicily, the tide turns toward Syracuse when Gylippus and the Peloponnesian reinforcements arrive (6.88.5, 6.93.4–103, 7.2.1, 7.6–8). By the following winter, the Athenians are in desperate straits, and Nicias sees no prospect of survival unless they quickly return home or substantial help comes from Athens (7.8.1). Although the commanders were given full authority on the expedition (*autokratores*) (6.26.1),[5] and Nicias has inherited sole command

---

3. Palmer, *Love of Glory*, 101. Also Forde, *Ambition to Rule*, 114–15.

4. Kagan points out that the force that Sparta sent was "pitifully small," and that the men were Helots or former Helots. "No Spartiate soldiers went to Sicily." Gylippus, whom they sent in charge, moreover, was the son of a Spartiate and a Helot mother, and was also burdened by accusations against his father. *Peace of Nicias*, 257–58.

5. See ibid., 277. Consider also the implications of their discussion at 6.47–50.

with the removal of Alcibiades and the death of Lamachus, he proceeds to ask the Athenians what he should do. He sends them a letter rather than trusting a messenger to convey the complexities of the situation (7.8.2–3). Swift action in Sicily is imperative, and of course Athens is some distance away, but Nicias cannot bring himself to act without the backing of the city. He worries about the reaction of the Athenians. This is not the first time that we are told that Nicias "fears returning" to Athens with his mission unaccomplished (5.46.4–5). Nicias's letter reveals his fear of Athens, as he glosses over the expedition's failure by referring to Athens's successes in Sicily in the same breath as he describes their desperate situation (7.11–15).[6] Successes do not indicate desperation. Nicias told his troops that they must suppose the necessity they face in Sicily is more fearful than the enemy himself (6.68.4), and now he himself seems to fear the faraway Athens more than the enemy in front of him.

After listing their initial successes, Nicias describes the worsening conditions: the growing number of enemy troops arriving, the cities of Sicily joining Syracuse, and the deteriorating Athenian navy, for they have not been able to beach their ships to dry them out. Members of their crews were killed by Syracusan cavalry when gathering supplies on land, and their mercenaries are leaving or even increasing enemy ranks. A crew's "prime" (akmē) is brief, Nicias says, implying that it is past (7.11.1–14.1; see also 1.1.1). Nicias nevertheless holds back from telling the Athenians that their cause is lost and that they have no choice but to summon the expedition home. Instead he flatters them into supposing that they are free to deliberate and therefore to choose (7.11.1, 7.14.4). He presents two options. They must either recall the expedition or send out another just as large, as well as a large sum of money (7.15.2). He has tried a similar tactic before, when he tried unsuccessfully to dissuade the Athenians from the expedition because of the size and expense required. He implies that it is still possible to conquer Sicily, with additional force, and passage home will be possible later as it is now. Thucydides earlier praises Pericles for instilling fear when the people are overconfident and fostering confidence when they are despondent (2.65.9). Nicias, in contrast, tries to do the former and accomplishes the latter, because he himself is moved more by fear of his addressees than by confidence in himself. Thucydides lets us see

---

6. According to Lattimore, Nicias "seldom mentions a difficulty (actual or exaggerated) [in his despatch] without attaching some form of self-justification." *Peloponnesian War*, note on 364n7.8–15. Also Westlake, *Individuals in Thucydides*, 194.

that when he earlier criticized Pericles' successors for flattering the people (2.65.10), his criticism applies to Nicias.[7]

The Athenians repeat their earlier decision to go against Sicily, and send another expedition there, just as Nicias repeats his failure to persuade the Athenians to stay at home. It is almost as if Alcibiades were still in Athens, influencing its decisions, and Nicias were the one in exile. Nor do the Athenians concede to Nicias's request that he must be removed from command because of his illness. Although Nicias tells them that he is "unable to remain" because of his kidney disease (7.15.1), the Athenians decide that Nicias must continue in command. They do not allow him to come home even to die. Like the Spartans on Sphacteria, Nicias sends to Athens to ask what to do when he faces insurmountable odds. For them to ask Sparta means that they have already asked themselves. When Nicias asks Athens, in contrast, he refuses to ask himself. Both the Spartan soldiers and Nicias get what they merit, when the Spartans leave it up to their soldiers, and the Athenians tell their general what to do.

When Demosthenes arrives with reinforcements, he recommends they assault Syracuse at once, in order to end the war in the shortest time possible, and if they fail to take Syracuse, he advises they return to Athens and not wear out the expedition and indeed the whole city (7.42.4–5). When that attack proves disastrous for the Athenians, Demosthenes is ready to depart while it is still possible to sail away. Nicias refuses. In the first place, he claims to have information from sources in Syracuse that the situation in that city is also deteriorating and that there are some who want to surrender. Moreover, Nicias "knows well" that it would be unacceptable to the Athenians if the expedition left Sicily without voting on the matter themselves. If those in Sicily return to Athens without being recalled, they will be judged by men who will not be able to see their situation in Sicily as clearly as they themselves can, he says, and who will listen to the criticisms of others (7.7.43–44, 7.47.3, 7.48.2–3). Nicias does not consider the possibility that he himself— or Demosthenes—might succeed, once they return, in defending their decision to withdraw. Moreover, if the Athenians cannot see clearly enough to judge correctly the decision to withdraw should the generals make it, how can they see clearly enough to make the decision instead of the generals themselves?

---

7. Yunis's analysis of the exchanges in the Athenian assembly over Pylos gives further evidence of Thucydides' reservations about Nicias. *Taming Democracy*, 103.

Nicias nevertheless refuses to return on his own initiative to Athens, even if it costs him his life. If die he must, he would prefer to run the risk as an individual (literally, "in private") at the hands of the enemy than to perish unjustly at the hands of the Athenians because of a shameful charge against him (7.48.4). But Nicias's preference for what he thinks is the more honorable death neglects the extent to which he is not a private man, but a general, who has the lives of his soldiers in his care. Once again, he takes the safer course in his dealings with the Athenians—for himself—but he does so under the cover of making the more honorable choice.[8] When Thucydides describes the predominance of private concerns in Athenian politics among Pericles' successors (2.65.7), his observation applies to Nicias as well as to Alcibiades.[9] Nicias, once again, acts out of fear of the Athenians to the detriment of the expedition. Whereas the Athenians at Melos cover their rule of the weak with an appeal to necessity, Nicias refuses to rule, while covering what he supposes is necessary with an appeal to honor. The man who wants to stay at home now does not want to go home. He must act independently of his city in order to serve it. Nicias is too dependent on his city to go home.

When Gylippus recruits further reinforcements, and the Athenian situation worsens, even Nicias agrees to sail home. As they prepare to depart, however, there is an eclipse of the moon, which the seers interpret to mean they must not sail for "thrice nine days." The majority of the Athenians want to obey the seers, as does Nicias, who, Thucydides says, is "overly attached to divination and such things" (7.50.4).[10] Thucydides does not report his asking Demosthenes' opinion, nor does he tell us what it is. The expedition remains. The Syracusans, for their part, seem to take no notice of the eclipse and prepare another attack. Nicias has delayed retreat for so long that he has no choice but to engage his troops in yet another battle. Athens's foes, Thucydides tells us, no longer aim at merely driving the Athenians away, but at attaining the glory that would come with capturing the whole Athenian force, with the result that "the rest of Hellas would be either liberated immediately or released from fear [of Athens]" (7.56.2, 7.59.2). Thucydides thus reminds us of Brasidas's promise on behalf of the Spartans, but how does Thucydides know the intentions of Athens's foes now? Nicias's "inside

8. Westlake, *Individuals in Thucydides*, 198.

9. Gribble, *Alcibiades and Athens*, 211–12, 185. Cf. Nicias's statement at 6.9.2, with Pericles' at 2.60.2.

10. The "thrice nine" days of the seers' advice echoes the prophecy that Thucydides tells us about earlier—that the war will last for "thrice nine" years (5.26.4). That prophecy did not prevent Nicias from pushing for the peace with Sparta in 421 BCE.

information" from Syracuse, which to be sure does not always prove as accurate as he supposes, favors complicity with Athens, not liberation of all Hellas from its rule. As both sides gear up for one last battle, "the Syracusan generals and Gylippus" (7.65.3, 7.69.1) give an encouraging speech to their troops that says nothing of the goal of liberating Hellas but emphasizes the sweetness of revenge (7.68.1).

On the Athenian side, Nicias addresses the troops, telling them that their struggle is for the sake of "security and fatherland" as much as this is so for the enemy. Victory will allow them "to see their own cities again," whereas if they suffer defeat the enemy will immediately sail against their own land (7.61.1, 7.64.1). He speaks to the hoplites about the need to man the ships and to wage land battle from their decks, for the Syracusan ships will try to block their passage to the open sea. He speaks to the sailors who are admired throughout Hellas, for their participation in the Athenian way of life (7.62–7.63.4). Finally, just before the ships sail, Nicias goes to each of the men commanding a trireme, "addressing him by his father's name, by his own name, and by his tribe, and whenever someone had some luster [*lamprotēs*] he urges him not to betray it or the virtues of the fatherland with which their ancestors shone." He reminds them that their fatherland boasts the greatest freedom and provides for "an unfettered daily life," and uses traditional words (*archaiologein*) about their wives and children and the ancestral gods (7.69.2; see 2.39.1). If there are traces of Sparta in Nicias's appeal to the ancestral, there are also traces in his speech of Pericles' appeal to freedom. Pericles' image of Athens remains at work, even if it cannot muster the enthusiasm of Gylippus's appeal to revenge and anger. The Athenian who is most like Sparta is superior to the Spartan who will soon defeat him. Nicias's exhortation may be his finest moment in Thucydides' work, even if it is too late to earn him passage home.

Thucydides reports the shock of the Athenian defeat, as their ships are either disabled or driven back to shore. Indeed, they are so overwhelmed by the immensity of their loss that they do not even think of asking their enemies to allow them to take up their dead (7.72.1). Thucydides is reminded of Pylos, for what the Athenians now suffer resembles what they inflicted there (7.71.7, 4.36.3). They are in fact trapped on an island like the Spartans were on Sphacteria, with no way to escape by sea. They must retreat by land, in the hope of finding refuge somewhere. As for the Spartans on Sphacteria, the island provides no refuge.

When the Athenians begin their retreat, they hear the lamentation (*olophurmos*) of the sick and the wounded whom they must leave behind, and see the corpses that they have been unable to bury (7.75.2–4). Nicias's supposedly comforting words to his troops that they will be able to constitute a city wherever they establish themselves (7.77.4) indicate that he does not expect them to return home. They echo his words before departing that the expedition must take so many people and supplies that they would be enough to found a city in a foreign land (6.22–23.2). The retreating army, however, goes without sufficient supplies, especially food and water, again resembling the Spartans on Sphacteria, who suffer from want of provisions (7.76.6; see 4.15.2, 4.36.3, and 4.39.2). The lamentations of the sick and wounded as they are left behind by those departing sound like lamentations for the dead (cf. 2.34.4; 2.46.2). The Athenians are mourning themselves. The speech Nicias delivers to his men as they begin their retreat has the flavor of a funeral oration: they have suffered so greatly that the gods must now feel more pity for them than envy, he tells them. They can therefore hope that the gods will be "kinder" to them now (7.77.4).

Nicias has been wrong before, but he is never more wrong than he is now. As Kagan observes, the retreat is "like a terrible nightmare from which there is no waking."[11] Demosthenes and his troops, who retreat in the rear, are surrounded first, and surrender on the condition that no one be killed, either from violence or prison or lack of the necessities of life (7.82.2). Demosthenes knows enough about his enemies to insist on these humane conditions, but if they would act inhumanely without the agreement, will they honor the agreement? They do not, and Thucydides does not mention the conditions again. After Demosthenes and his men surrender, the Syracusans soon overtake Nicias's contingent. Like departed souls in myth, the Athenian troops led by Nicias make their way to a river, which they seek to traverse to safety. But they trample one another as they try to cross, find the enemy on the opposite bank as well as behind them, and are slaughtered as they seek to quench their thirst in the river. Very soon they are drinking water filled with their own blood (7.84.3). Athens is consuming itself.

At last making a decision without considering what Athens might expect of him, Nicias surrenders to the Spartans, telling them to do whatever they like with him if only they stop slaughtering his soldiers (7.85.1). Nicias does not ask his men to uphold their honor by dying fighting; he is trying to prevent their dying slaughtered. His surrender to the enemy entails surrendering what he claims to value most—his good name (see 5.16.1). It is also an act of kindness toward his men, who he believes have suffered enough. The "kindness" he expects the gods to show his long-suffering army (7.77.4) he must render himself.

---

11. Kagan, *Peace of Nicias*, 337.

Like the Plataeans, who insist on surrendering to the Spartans rather than to the Thebans in hope of fair treatment, Nicias surrenders to the Spartan commander rather than to the Syracusan forces as a whole. But like the Plataeans, his expectations are disappointed. Just as the Spartans yield to their allies in executing the Plataeans, the Spartan Gylippus now follows the bidding of Sparta's allies in executing Nicias: the Corinthians fear that the wealthy Nicias will bribe his way to freedom and cause them more damage, and those Syracusans who had sent information to Nicias now fear that he will reveal their complicity with the Athenians (7.86.4). As in trusting informants from Syracuse (7.73.3), Nicias's trust is again misplaced, and Sparta shows itself "the same city that it ever was" (see 5.75.3). Nicias receives more kindness from the Athenian Thucydides than the Spartans he had favored, when Thucydides announces that of all the Hellenes of his time, Nicias was least worthy of the misfortune to which he came, inasmuch as the law-bred (*nenomismenē*) practices of his life were directed to every virtue (7.86.5).

The virtue that Athens represents for Pericles is not simply law-bred, for it comes "from within" (2.39.1). Law-bred virtue asks too much of human beings when it leaves no room for choice, and too little when it does not require choice. When Nicias finally makes a decision in Sicily and acts, his action is one of surrender rather than homecoming. His independent act is only in yielding to the enemy's superior force rather than fighting to the death. After that he no longer has a say in what happens to him or his men. Brasidas, the Spartan most like Athens, saves almost all of his soldiers at Amphipolis because of his stratagem (5.8.2–3, 5.11.2), although he himself dies fighting. When Thucydides praises his virtue, he says nothing about it being law-bred (4.81.2–3). Like Nicias, Brasidas is an outlier from his city. Thucydides accepts Pericles' standard in this regard: the superior city is the one that not merely allows, but requires freedom. If Nicias's decision to surrender shows that he has learned this, it takes him a long time to learn what Pericles knows. When Thucydides suggests that Nicias's life was informed by law and thus directed to virtue, his praise may also entail some blame.

Gylippus yields to his allies' wish to kill Nicias, although unwillingly, Thucydides tells us, for he thought that bringing Nicias and Demosthenes alive to Sparta would be "a noble prize" (*kalon agōnisma*) for himself (7.86.2).[12] Gylippus's "noble prize" is all that is left of the "noble prize"

---

12. In charge of the fighting at Sphacteria, Demosthenes stopped the slaughter in order to bring the prisoners back alive to Athens (4.37.1). Thucydides does not tell us there whether Demosthenes is like Gylippus looking for glory, or whether he just wants to stop the slaughter of men who are

(*kalon agōnisma*) Thucydides claims that the Syracusan side sought in capturing the whole Athenian force, noble insofar as it would either liberate the
Hellenes or release them from their fear of Athens (7.65.2). As for Demosthenes, in spite of the conditions under which he surrenders, he is executed
along with Nicias. Neither is asked whether he did anything to benefit
the Peloponnesians during the present war, as were the Plataeans. Although
Demosthenes is hated by the Peloponnesians because of his command at
Pylos, Nicias might have mentioned his attempt to procure the release of
the Spartan prisoners from Sphacteria (7.86.3). Demosthenes is almost pre-
scient in his insistence as a condition of his surrender that no one be killed
by violence, prison, and lack of life's necessities. After he and Nicias are
executed, the captured Athenians and their allies, "not fewer than seven
thousand," are imprisoned in quarries where miserable conditions, including
the lack of life's necessities, result in a great number of deaths. The corpses
that now pile up unattended in the quarries remind us of Athens during the
plague (7.87.1–4), but here we have human not daimonic forces at work (see
2.64.2). We hear of no Spartan—or Syracusan—who attempts to procure
their release, as Nicias did in Athens for the Spartans captured on Spachteria.
Whereas the Spartan prisoners taken to Athens from Sphacteria return to
Sparta after the "Peace of Nicias" is signed (5.24.2), and Thucydides mentions no outrages committed against them, of the Athenian prisoners taken
in Sicily "few out of many return home" (7.87.5).

Thucydides concludes his account of the "greatest deed of the war,"
hence the greatest deed of the greatest war, "the most splendid for those
conquering, and most unfortunate for those ruined" (7.87.5). But while the
suffering is clear, the splendor that was once Athens's, and that Thucydides
now attributes to the victors, is not so apparent. As Thucydides has warned
us, under the pressure of events words change their meanings (3.82.4). Or,
rather, Thucydides is like the Athenians who refrain from questioning the
honor of the Spartan prisoner: Thucydides never explicitly questions that of
Syracuse and its Peloponnesian allies (4.40.1).[13] He does assert, however, that

---

defenseless. Perhaps it is his perception of the latter possibility that moves Strauss to comment without explanation that Demosthenes is "the most lovable of Thucydides' characters." *City and Man*,
197. And perhaps he is moved as well by Thucydides' praise of Nicias's virtue in contrast to his silence
about that of Demosthenes, Nicias's fellow commander, who, if he had sole authority, would have
brought the expedition home when homecoming was still possible.

13. When the Spartan prisoners arrive in Athens and all are surprised that Spartans would surrender, one of the Athenian allies taunts one of the prisoners, asking whether those who died were
noble men. Strauss finds it gratifying to see that this "mean question" about Spartan honor is not
raised by an Athenian. *City and Man*, 218.

the "greatest deed" of this war, or of any war, is one of the greatest suffering, for the carnage in Sicily was exceeded by none in the war (7.85.4). The Sicilian expedition, "the fleet, the army, all perished," even if a few Athenians, such as those sold as slaves who then escape (7.87.5, 7.85.4), make it home.

Alcibiades in the East

Alcibiades escapes destruction in Sicily, just as he escapes trial and execution in Athens. His very homelessness seems to save him. He can go to Sparta, and serve his city's enemy. Book 8 opens with Alcibiades in Sparta, supporting envoys from Chios and Erethrae who want Spartan help when revolting from Athens.[14] Sparta agrees to send aid, but its fleet encounters a few mishaps on the way to Ionia. When Sparta plans to recall its forces, Alcibiades intervenes. If he goes quickly to Chios, he explains, before news of the Spartan failures arrives, he will persuade Chios and other cities to revolt, when he informs them of "Athenian weakness" after its disaster in Sicily and "Spartan eagerness" (8.12.1). Thucydides has just shown how little eagerness Spartans have for the expedition, inasmuch as they are about to call it home. As to Athenian "weakness," it is not as great as many claim (8.2.2, 8.24.5). In fact, Athens shows more "eagerness" to send reinforcements against the revolting cities than Sparta does to send them support (8.15.2; see also 8.22.1).

Once again, Alcibiades is trading on his own words and ardor (see 6.17.1), including the impression he creates of himself, especially of one who can provide inside information. When he tells Spartans of Athens's intentions in Sicily, as we have seen, they suppose they are listening to the man who knows more clearly than anyone (6.93.1). Now Alcibiades claims that when he arrives in Ionia he will be considered "more trustworthy" than anyone (8.12.1). The

---

14. There has been much discussion of the unfinished character of book 8—as well as the unfinished character of Thucydides' history as a whole, which breaks off in 411 BCE, whereas Thucydides tells us that the war lasted "thrice nine years," that is, until 404 (5.26.1). While scholars have traditionally viewed book 8 as a draft in need of revision, more recent scholarship argues that the changes in Thucydides' literary technique in book 8 reflect the new character of the war after the Sicilian disaster. Connor, in particular, presents a strong case that the movement of book 8, in which "individuals appear with momentary prominence and then swiftly disappear in disfavor, obscurity, or death," reflects "the tendency toward civic disintegration or moral atomism" belonging to the last decade of the war. *Thucydides*, 215. Also Marc Cogan, *The Human Thing: The Speeches and Principles of Thucydides' History* (Chicago: University of Chicago Press, 1981), 165; Rood, *Thucydides' Narrative and Explanation*, 253; Andrewes, *HCT*, 5:369–755; John A. Wettergreen, "On the End of Thucydides' Narrative," *Interpretation* 9 (1979): 93–110; Munn, *School of History*, 325–26; Pouncey, *Necessities of War*, 142–43; Johnson, *Thucydides, Hobbes*, 216–17; Mara, "Thucydides and Political Thought," 121–22.

Spartans decide to send him to instigate revolt, with five ships and the Spartan commander Chalcideus. When they arrive, "they" inform the Chians that more ships are on the way. They do not mention, Thucydides tells us, that Athenian ships are preventing Spartan ships from leaving the Peloponnesus (8.14.2). Chios revolts, and other cities follow suit (8.14.2–3, 8.17.2).

Having once led the Athenian expedition west to Sicily, Alcibiades now takes Peloponnesian forces east to instigate the revolt of cities there from Athenian rule. In this he is like Brasidas, although Alcibiades goes by sea. Alcibiades seems to open up possibilities rather than foreclose them, whereas Brasidas's deception of the Thessalians restricts Spartan passage through their territory. Soon after Alcibiades and Chalcideus arrive, Chalcideus and the Persian satrap Tissaphernes conclude an alliance between the Persian king and the Spartans (8.17–18). We can assume Alcibiades is present, perhaps responsible (see 8.17.2).[15] But Thucydides does not mention him by name. Alcibiades is only a private man. He cannot form alliances, he has no resources with which to bargain. He cannot commit Sparta to the terms of the alliance as can Chalcideus, such as waging war against Athens "in common" with the Persian king (8.18.2). Unlike Brasidas, he has no army to lead, even if Sparta considers the army it gives Brasidas negligible.

Alcibiades is eventually suspected by the Spartans, who send a message to the Spartans in the field ordering them to execute him. Thucydides does not go into the details except to say that he was the enemy of the king Agis and in other things appeared untrustworthy (8.45.1).[16] Once again, Alcibiades eludes his enemies, this time taking refuge with the Persian satrap Tissaphernes, and becoming his adviser. Alcibiades is a protean figure, as he appears on one side, then another.[17] As Tissaphernes' adviser "in everything," he now

---

15. Forde observes that "Alcibiades is singlehandedly responsible for the prosperous beginning of the Peloponnesian and Spartan campaign in the East during this phase of the war." *Ambition to Rule*, 124. See also Westlake, *Individuals in Thucydides*, 235–36.

16. Plutarch tells us one reason why Agis may have felt hostility toward Alcibiades: while King Agis is abroad with the army, Alcibiades corrupts his wife, and she has a child by him. Alcibiades acted not out of passion, but that his race might one day be kings over the Spartans. *Lives*, 249. At Athens he proclaimed that later generations of Athenians will claim "kinship" with him because of his service, even though no kinship exists (6.16.5). In Plutarch's story, Alcibiades' desire for kinship takes a more concrete form.

17. Plutarch even more explicitly presents Alcibiades as a protean figure. He describes Alcibiades' "conformity to Spartan habits" during the time he was there, such as "eating a coarse meal, and dining on black broth." He had a talent, Plutarch observes, for embracing the habits and ways of life of others, and "chang[ing] faster than the chameleon." *Lives,* 249. Compare 8.50.3 with Homer, *Odyssey* 4.454–56. Forde argues that Athenians distrust Alcibiades as "an unknown quantity," and experience "sheer uncertainty of who he is." *Ambition to Rule*, 169. Also Gribble, *Alcibiades and Athens*, 26–27.

does as much as possible to harm Peloponnesian affairs, such as advising Tissaphernes to cut the pay of the Peloponnesian navy to keep the sailors from luxury, to bribe the Peloponnesian commanders to agree to this policy,[18] and to delay in putting the Phoenician fleet he is equipping into the hands of the Peloponnesians (8.45.1–3). In each case, Alcibiades' advice serves the larger plan he proposes to Tissaphernes—that of serving Persia's (and Tissaphernes') interests by wearing out both sides in the conflict. Besides, it is better for Tissaphernes to incline more to Athens than to Sparta: if the Peloponnesians liberate Hellenes from Athenian rule, Alcibiades tells him, they would want to liberate them from Persian rule as well (8.46.2–3). Although in his initial appeal to the Spartans Alcibiades asked them to imagine defeating the Athenians and gaining hegemony over all Hellas (6.92.5), he now appeals to the image of Spartans as liberators to make them suspect to Tissaphernes. He puts the noble image of Sparta's purpose to work against the city.[19]

Although Alcibiades seems to betray all of Hellas to Persia by advising Tissaphernes, Thucydides tells us that Alcibiades aims at facilitating his recall to Athens: his Persian "connection" will be useful to Athens in its war with Sparta. Alcibiades is using Tissaphernes as a way back to Athens, as he previously was using the Spartans to aid his repossession of his city. He therefore sends a message to Athenian military leaders in Samos that he wishes to return and can make Tissaphernes their friend if they replace the democracy that threw him out with an oligarchy. Only then, with a more trustworthy form of government, he tells them, could the Persian king trust the Athenians (8.47–48.1).

The Athenian general Phrynichus opposes Alcibiades' proposal, objecting that Alcibiades cares no more for oligarchy than for democracy, but seeks "an overturn of the order of the city" only that he might be recalled. Alcibiades is indifferent to regimes and to Athens's regime in particular. He wants simply to go home, and acts to bring about whichever regime he believes would be most favorable at the time to his return (8.48.2–5). Disregarding Phrynichus, the oligarchic faction in Athens uses Alcibiades' promise of Persian aid in order to appeal to the Athenians for a change in regime. One

---

18. Thucydides tells us that Alcibiades' bribery plan works with all the commanders on the Peloponnesian side except the Syracusan Hermocrates (8.45.3). Spartans, away from home, remain corruptible (see 1.95.7).

19. The only Spartan voice in Thucydides' text that objects to Persian rule of the cities "liberated" from Athens in the East is that of the negotiator Lichas. His brief echo of Brasidas hardly confirms Alcibiades' warning to Tissaphernes about the Spartans, since he seems to have no other effect (8.43.3–4, 8.52.1, 8.84.4–5).

of their leaders, Pisander, tells them of Alcibiades' offer to help with Tissaphernes, including their need to change to a more moderate government, with the offices in fewer hands, in order to gain the Persian king's trust. In the present circumstances, Pisander claims, they must deliberate about "the safety" of Athens more than about "the regime," for "it is possible for us to change [the regime] later if something does not please us" (8.53.3). Regimes themselves are ever changing, and no decision need be final, just as no alliance or law precludes change if a better one is discovered, and if not a better one, perhaps merely one that better pleases. It is appropriate that Pisander makes an argument that carries the Athenian propensity "to innovate" to the very regime itself (see Aristophanes, *Ecclesiazusae* 455–57; see also 1.70.2, 1.71.3) in the context of arguing that the city that once banished Alcibiades should now turn to him for help. If Athens becomes as protean as Alcibiades himself, Alcibiades can save his city.

This brief statement by Pisander is the only speech in direct discourse in book 8 of Thucydides' work. It is a speech that Pisander makes not to a public assembly, but by "taking each of his opponents aside" (*paragōn*), Thucydides says, using a verb that can also be translated as "leading astray, or misleading" (8.53.2). Pisander's speech occurs in the midst of much "controversy" (*antilogia*) (8.53.2), a word that ordinarily refers to opposing speeches (e.g., 1.31.4), but which looks like "anti-speech"—that is, "opposed to speech." These observations confirm Forde's speculation about the almost complete absence of speeches in direct discourse in book 8: speech no longer animates the political life of cities during this period, which "have been reduced to the most minimal concerns of the public good."[20] Pisander's brief speech is hardly an exception: it is spoken not to an assembly, but "to each" of his opponents; and it argues against considering the question of regime (as opposed to that of safety).

When the oligarchic forces gain ascendancy in the city, they send Pisander and others to Tissaphernes with the expectation that Alcibiades will help them obtain Persia's aid against the Peloponnesians. As Thucydides says with some understatement, Alcibiades is not "altogether certain" of Tissaphernes, who wants to wear out both sides of the conflict, the very thing Alcibiades advised him to do. Alcibiades tries to conceal his inability to control Tissaphernes by making the negotiations between the Athenians and Tissaphernes miscarry. He presents such excessive demands on behalf of Tissaphernes that the Athenians must finally refuse and break off the negotiations. Alcibiades'

---

20. Forde, *Ambition to Rule*, 120–21.

plan itself nevertheless miscarries, for the Athenians conclude that they have been deceived by Alcibiades and leave in anger (8.56). In his brief narration of this event, Thucydides twice describes Alcibiades as "unable" (*adunatos*) to bring about what he had promised.

The oligarchs in Athens do not recall Alcibiades, as he hoped. They decide, Thucydides reports, that Alcibiades is "unsuitable for joining an oligarchy," or, as Crawley translates it, that "he is not the man for an oligarchy" (8.63.4). Phrynichus, it turns out, is suitable, and he joins the oligarchic forces, now that they are opposed to Alcibiades' recall (8.68.3). Phrynichus is open to any regime that is opposed to Alcibiades' return, just as Alcibiades favors whatever regime is open to his return from exile. It is Phrynichus, after all, to whom Thucydides credits this understanding of Alcibiades. The concept of "regime" that for Pericles gives a city its way of life and distinguishes one city from another appears to be fading into insignificance.

In place of the democracy, the oligarchs proclaim a government by the Five Thousand, who are qualified to rule by virtue of their persons or wealth. The "Five Thousand," according to Thucydides, is only a specious gesture toward the multitude, for the few who accomplish the change remain in control. The oligarchs maintain the charade of a larger governing class than exists by convening the democratic assembly and council, but reviewing the speakers and their speeches in advance (8.65.3–66.2). The oligarchs do not include Alcibiades, but they imitate his politics, as when he teaches the Spartans what to say in the Athenian assembly in order to achieve his own purposes (5.45.3). The Five Thousand exist only "in name," whereas in fact a few oligarchs rule. Although Thucydides refers to Athens in Pericles' time as a democracy only in name (2.65.9), the Athenian assembly does exist in his time as an independent force. At one point, Pericles does not convene it when he knows there will be opposition to his policy (2.22.1), but Thucydides does not suggest that he ever programs who speaks in the assembly or what they say. If he did, he would not have to avoid convening it.

The name of the Five Thousand leads the people to suspect one another, uncertain whether their neighbors are members of the Five Thousand. Each is restrained from acting by what he wrongly imagines of his neighbor (8.66.3–5). The Five Thousand do not exist. The Athenians have countless misleading images of one another. The general distrust that prevails makes it easier for the oligarchs to act with impunity. Some opponents are killed in secret, while others are imprisoned or banished (8.65.5, 8.70.2). The regime change to oligarchy produces not a more trustworthy regime—the reason Alcibiades gave for the change from democracy (8.48.1)—but one that keeps subjects powerless by fomenting distrust among them. This is the very thing for which tyrants were known in the ancient world (see, e.g., Plato *Symposium* 182b–c and Aristotle, *Politics* 1313a41–b6). Eventually, only Four Hundred are allowed to participate in governing, but even this group stems from five oligarchs, who together choose a hundred men, who each in turn choose three more. Each of the Four Hundred, Thucydides reports, carries a concealed dagger, and the group employs one hundred and twenty youths for violence when it is needed. Little remains of the free regime with liberal tolerance and lack of suspicion of fellow citizens that Pericles describes (2.37.2). And little remains of Athens's active citizen who participates in public life (2.42.2). Those ruling can convene the Five Thousand whenever they please, but find no occasion to do so (8.67, 8.69.4, 8.72.1).

When the oligarchy tries to negotiate peace with the Spartans, claiming to the oligarchic Spartans that they are more trustworthy than the former democracy, even the Spartans do not trust them (8.70.2–71.1). Commenting on the oligarchic revolution at Athens, Thucydides observes that, almost a hundred years after the removal of the tyrants, it is no light matter to deprive the Athenian people of their freedom (8.68.4). The pathos that Thucydides expresses is not diminished by the irony that it was Sparta itself, Thucydides told us earlier (1.18.1), that drove the tyrants from Athens. An "oligarchic and tyrannical conspiracy," which the Athenians fear when they recall Alcibiades from Sicily to stand trial (6.60.2), has now been realized at Alcibiades' instigation, even if he is now excluded from it by the Athenians in power. No one can be at home in Athens now, neither the oligarchs, who are suspicious of one another (8.89.3), nor even Alcibiades himself.

Alcibiades at Samos

Rumors of outrages perpetrated by the oligarchy at Athens reach the Athenian army at Samos. When exaggerations circulate—that the wives and children of the soldiers are being abused and that the relatives of any of the soldiers who oppose the oligarchy will be imprisoned—the army considers attacking the city itself. An army trying to force a democracy on Athens struggles against a city trying to force oligarchy on the army (8.74.3–75.1). Indeed, it is not clear from Thucydides' description of the situation whether the city of Athens exists to a greater extent in the now oligarchic city located in Attica or in the democratically inclined army at Samos. The soldiers hold an assembly (*ekklesia*) that chooses new generals and captains sympathetic to democracy (8.76.2; also at 8.81.1–2). So too do they encourage one another, claiming that "the city revolted from them." They point out that they represent the greater number of Athenians than the oligarchs and have greater resources, even the fleet itself that could collect the tribute from the allies just as it has in the past. The army both controls the material resources and preserves the regime, "the ancestral laws" (*hoi patrioi nomoi*), that the oligarchs abolished. And if all else fails, they say, there are places to which they could withdraw and find land (8.76.2–7). Indeed, they sound like Nicias with his retreating army in Sicily, with little hope of returning to Athens, who encourages his men that the city will exist wherever they settle (7.77.4).

The "democratic" army at Samos, rather than the oligarchs in the city, finally recall Alcibiades, hoping to procure his help in obtaining aid from Persia. The democratic soldiers have not discovered, as the oligarchs did, Alcibiades' bluff; nor do they suppose, as had the city that tried to bring him home to stand trial (6.60.1), that Alcibiades is not the man for a democracy. With his recall by the army, Alcibiades nevertheless seems to be on his way home. When he arrives at Samos, Alcibiades speaks to the "assembly" of soldiers. His speech, which Thucydides recounts in the indirect discourse characteristic of book 8, does not bode well for Athens's future. Scholars describe his speech as "little more than a harangue," and find it disappointing as a speech of public deliberation.[21] Not only does Thucydides credit Alcibiades with magnifying his influence over Tissaphernes to increase his standing and to arouse fear. He also presents him as "wailing loudly" (*anolophuresthai*) about "the personal [*idia*] misfortune" his exile brought to him (8.81.2). That is, even though Alcibiades has been condemned to death by both Athens and Sparta, even though he is by no means "sure" of Tissaphernes, and even though he has not yet been able to return to Athens itself, Alcibiades remains unchastened.

Alcibiades' bold exaggerations of the help he can secure from Tissaphernes succeed with the soldiers, who are so elated that they elect him general, and are ready to sail to the Piraeus if Alcibiades will lead them (8.82.1). But Alcibiades is more interested in promoting the image of his influence and power than engaging in a military operation—a pattern we have seen when the Athenian expedition arrived in Sicily. He leaves immediately to visit Tissaphernes, purportedly to coordinate matters with him, Thucydides recounts, but actually to try to frighten Tissaphernes with his influence over the Athenians and Athenians with his influence over Tissaphernes (8.82.3). When Alcibiades sets sail to join Tissaphernes, he promises the army either to bring the Persian fleet back for the Athenians or at least to prevent it from going

---

21. Ibid., 163–64; Westlake, *Individuals in Thucydides*, 250.

to the side of the Peloponnesians. He "likely knows Tissaphernes does not intend to bring the fleet" to either side, Thucydides observes, for Tissaphernes would not want to upset the balance of power between the Athenians and the Peloponnesians (8.88.1). In other words, Alcibiades will take credit for effecting what he thinks is going to happen anyway.

Throughout his narrative about Alcibiades, Thucydides has been presenting and correcting the images that Alcibiades has constructed of himself, as someone who can deliver Tissaphernes' aid, for example. In other words, Alcibiades acts as if his words can take the place of facts or deeds. Thucydides' repeated presentations of his failures indicate the limits of his power. Like Thucydides, Alcibiades constructs speeches in accordance with his purposes, without Thucydides' recognition that his speeches must come as close as possible to what was in fact said, and to the world his speeches reflect (1.22.1). Alcibiades' speeches do not reflect a world, they create a world. Thucydides contrasts himself with Alcibiades by his deeds. As we have seen, Thucydides points out that he records both speeches and deeds in his history and suggests that the deeds should serve as a test of speeches (1.21.2). He also presents only deeds when Alcibiades becomes the focus of his history in book 8. He leaves even the lengthy speeches of Alcibiades in indirect discourse.

There is one time, however, when Thucydides vouches for a good deed Alcibiades renders to Athens. When the army at Samos remains eager to sail to the Piraeus—and presumably overthrow the oligarchy and restore the democracy—Alcibiades prevents it. If the army had attacked Athens, Thucydides points out, Ionia and the Hellespont would have "most certainly" gone to the enemy. Athens would have left itself vulnerable, and the fall of Athens might have followed the fall of its empire in the East. No one else except Alcibiades, according to Thucydides, would have been able to hold back the army, to reproach the soldiers for their anger, and to stop the expedition against the city. This was the first time, Thucydides reports, that Alcibiades benefited his city (8.86.4–6).[22] For the moment, Alcibiades saves his city.

Alcibiades also sends a message to those in charge in Athens. In the first place, he does not simply oppose the oligarchy, at least not the Five Thousand, which we know exists only in name, but only the Four Hundred. In effect, he asks them to live up to their word. The name is not sufficient but

---

22. That this was "the first time" (*proton*) that Alcibiades benefited his city appears to many as a harsh judgment on Thucydides' part, and various explanations and emendations have been suggested. For discussion, see Westlake, *Individuals in Thucydides*, 253n1; Lattimore, *Peloponnesian War*, 454, note on 8.86; Forde, *Ambition to Rule*, 165n47; Gribble, *Alcibiades and Athens*, 186–87, 203.

must reflect the facts. Alcibiades uncharacteristically insists on the facts. In the second place, he urges the city to hold out against the Peloponnesians, contrary to the oligarchs in the city who have been trying to capitulate. If the city were preserved, as Thucydides paraphrases his message, there would be hope for reconciliation between those in the city and those in the army (8.86.7). As Forde points out, Alcibiades' advice "is both moderate and conciliatory and is scrupulously attentive to the interests of the city as a whole." It is also "a brilliant piece of strategy" to undermine the more extreme of the oligarchs by driving a wedge between them and the moderate elements among them.[23]

It is perplexing how such moderate advice could come from Alcibiades, especially since even his recent harangue to the soldiers at Samos was anything but moderate.[24] Thucydides offers no speculation concerning why the man who was ever attentive to his personal or private interests now acts in the interests of the city as a whole, or why the man who up to now showed so little restraint now performs this act of moderation. What—or who—could have restrained him? Thucydides claims that Alcibiades "taught" Tissaphernes about playing both sides off the other, while he pursues his own interest in returning to Athens, but who teaches Alcibiades to try to moderate both Athenian factions in the interests of the city and to refrain from returning when he has the opportunity to do so? In the Platonic dialogues, we see that Socrates attempts to teach Alcibiades a kind of restraint that comes from examining his own life, but that Alcibiades flees Socrates' speeches as if they were Siren songs that would prevent him from engaging in political affairs (*Symposium* 216a). What accounts for Alcibiades' exercise of Socratic "moderation" now to restrain himself and the army from going home?

Alcibiades of course might have supposed that the army's withdrawal from its strategic station at Samos would leave Athens's possessions in Ionia vulnerable to the enemy, and eventually expose Athens itself. Pouncey speculates that Alcibiades simply "wants there to be something left when he reaches

---

23. Forde, *Ambition to Rule*, 165–66; Westlake, *Individuals in Thucydides*, 253–54.

24. Westlake also notices the contrasting portrait Thucydides gives of Alcibiades when he first speaks at Samos after his recall, and this account that shows "another side of [Alcibiades]," and presents "a totally different [assessment]." Given how pronounced Thucydides makes these different visions of Alcibiades, Westlake thinks that "the contrast in tone . . . is surely intentional." Thucydides shows us, Westlake concludes, that in spite of his selfishness and passion for double-dealing, Alcibiades could perform services in the public interest beyond any of his contemporaries. *Individuals in Thucydides*, 253–54. Westlake does not speculate about what moved Alcibiades to do so, that is, why one "side" of Alcibiades would control rather than another.

Athens."[25] But Thucydides doesn't say that Alcibiades is concerned with this. It is Thucydides who points out the possible domino effect of the army's attack on Athens, and who therefore understands why Alcibiades' action benefits his city. Considering the details that Thucydides knows of Alcibiades' intrigues, scholars speculate that Alcibiades was one of Thucydides' informants about events of the war. This seems even more likely insofar as Thucydides tells us of his efforts to obtain the truth, and that he was present with both sides during his exile—which we assume cannot mean at Athens (5.26.5).[26] If Thucydides were present with the Athenians on Samos, might he have shown Alcibiades a benefit of moderation that Socrates could not provide? Even if he were present with Alcibiades at any point during his exile, Alcibiades would have known about Thucydides' work. Regardless of whether or when Alcibiades and Thucydides meet, however, by writing about the war Thucydides offers Alcibiades the prospect of being remembered—in this case, for serving and even saving his city. After all, in his first speech in Thucydides' work before the Athenian assembly Alcibiades claims to desire that later generations claim kinship with him by thinking that he has performed noble deeds (6.16.5).

If Alcibiades is moved to restraint in some way because of Thucydides, if only out of concern with what Thucydides will remember of him in his account of the war, the man who once failed to bring the Athenian fleet to Amphipolis would now contribute to preventing another Athenian fleet from arriving at the Piraeus. Just as that failure earns him his exile, such a public-spirited accomplishment, we might speculate, could earn him his homecoming. Thucydides' reticence about himself would be nothing new. Nor would his generosity or liberality toward many of his fellow Athenians be anything new, when he now praises Alcibiades for benefiting Athens.

Alcibiades' message to the oligarchs in Athens finds at least many of them already discontent and looking for a safe way out of their difficulties. Reconciliation with the Athenian army at Samos offers them, at least some of them, more security than would surrender to Sparta. They therefore urge that the Five Thousand participate "not in name but in fact, and a more equal regime be established." To be sure, their appeal to a more equal regime,

---

25. Pouncey, *Necessities of War*, 110.

26. P. A. Brunt presents substantial evidence that Alcibiades himself was an informant of Thucydides, on the basis of information that Thucydides includes in his history that only Alcibiades or a close confidant could have known. "Thucydides and Alcibiades," *Revue des Études Grecques* 65 (1952): 59–81. Also Edouard Delebecque, *Thucydide et Alcibiade* (Aix-en-Provence: Centre d'Études et Reserches Helleniques, 1965), 233; Westlake, *Individuals in Thucydides*, 24–26, 240–41, 244–45.

Thucydides informs us, was "a political guise" that served their private ambitions, which were not satisfied by their places in the oligarchy (8.89.1–3). In any case, with the help of Phrynichus's assassination, and the desertion of some of the oligarchs to the Spartans who hold Deceleia, another revolution takes place in Athens, in fact if not in name, from the oligarchy to the Five Thousand, to the very regime that the oligarchy claimed existed. The Four Hundred are deposed, Thucydides says, and matters turned over to the Five Thousand—to all who can afford a suit of hoplite armor. This balanced (or measured, *metria*) mixing of the few and the many, Thucydides claims, at least in its first phase, seems the first time the Athenians govern themselves well in his lifetime (8.97.2).

By reference to its "first phase," Thucydides implies that the regime of the Five Thousand, at least in its moderate character, is short-lived. Because Thucydides' history breaks off shortly after this regime is established at Athens, he does not tell us what its "other phases" might have been, or even how long the regime lasts. Monoson and Loriaux refer to Thucydides' statement that the Five Thousand was Athens's best regime in his lifetime to support their argument about Thucydides' criticisms of the regime under Pericles.[27] Thucydides' praise of only "its first phase," however, and his reference to the private ambition of those who support establishing this more moderate regime, warn us to be wary of its stability. According to Forde, we do not know "what to make of Thucydides' praise of the Five Thousand," because the short life of its historical existence made it "so shadowy."[28] His praise of this regime serves less as an implicit criticism of Periclean Athens than a reminder of the balance that he attributes to Pericles, and of the statesmanship of which his successors fall short.[29] Thucydides praises the blending of the few and the many in the regime of the Five Thousand as "measured," the very word that he uses to characterize Pericles' rule, when he associates his rule with Athens's attainment of its height of greatness (2.65.5).

Thucydides tells us of only one action taken by the regime of the Five Thousand—a vote to recall Alcibiades from exile (8.97.3). We do not learn

---

27. Monoson and Loriaux, "Illusion of Power," 292. Also Hornblower, *Thucydides*, 160; Palmer, *Love of Glory*, 113. Connor suggests that Thucydides' praise of Periclean government and his subsequent praise of the Five Thousand show a major development in Thucydides' attitude in his work. *Thucydides*, 228n34. Also Mara, *Civic Conversations*, 116.

28. Forde, *Ambition to Rule*, 159n42. See also Mara, "Thucydides and Political Thought," 122.

29. Finley, *Thucydides*, 248; Dobski, "Incomplete Whole," 26; Cynthia Farrar, *The Origins of Democratic Thinking: The Invention of Politics in Classical Athens* (Cambridge: Cambridge University Press, 1988), 186–87.

of Alcibiades' reaction to his long-awaited recall, for he is with Tissaphernes, making it appear that he is preventing the satrap from bringing his fleet to the aid of the Peloponnesians. His return to Samos with the message that he has succeeded in persuading Tissaphernes is the last word that Thucydides gives us of Alcibiades in his history (8.108.1), which soon ends abruptly. Although Alcibiades eventually returns to Athens, a few years later, only to be exiled once again, and eventually assassinated,[30] Thucydides' history breaks off before these events. Thucydides leaves Alcibiades busy engaging in his politics of appearances. Alcibiades' base of operations remains at Samos, with an army that is only trying to be a city, for it no longer has a home.

Alcibiades' Long Road Home

When Thucydides refers to Alcibiades' desire to be recalled from exile, the word he uses for returning is, literally, "a road or way back" (*kathodos*) (8.47.1, 8.49.1, 8.50.1, 8.76.7, 8.81.1, 8.83.1). Whereas Alcibiades comes unsummoned to the Spartans, he cannot return to Athens unless the Athenians summon him, and there remains resistance in the city to his recall. His homecoming cannot be merely of his own making, however much he tries to make it so, but depends on Athens itself. He attempts to create images of himself as shortcuts home, especially the image of the help he can bring from Tissaphernes. But to the extent that they are only images, as we have seen of his supposed influence over Tissaphernes, he cannot sustain them.

Thucydides captures the problem Alcibiades represents when he explains that Alcibiades "knows that if he does not destroy [his fatherland] he might persuade his way back" (8.47.1). Could Athens trust a man, however, who might destroy it? Odysseus finds it necessary to destroy the leading men of Ithaca on his return home (Homer, *Odyssey* 22). So too Alcibiades' recall occurs only after many of the leading men at the time, the more extreme oligarchs, take refuge with the Spartans, and Phrynichus, the Athenian most opposed to Alcibiades' homecoming, is assassinated.[31] Thucydides thus raises

---

30. On Alcibiades' assassination, see Munn, *School of History*, 234, 415n36.

31. Thucydides tells us that Phrynichus's assassin escaped. His accomplice, an Argive, Thucydides reports, was captured and tortured by the Four Hundred, but did not reveal anything further about the matter (8.92.2). Neither does Thucydides. Earlier in book 8, when Phrynichus is still at Samos opposing Alcibiades' overtures to return, Thucydides recounts intrigues between him and the Spartan commander Astyochus, who betrays Phrynichus's communications to Alcibiades. Phrynichus then sends Astyochus false information, counting on his revealing it again to Alcibiades, in order to trap him. This time Phrynichus takes advantage of the outcome (8.50–51). Forde observes that Phrynichus is "the only person in the History to outsmart Alcibiades." *Ambition to Rule*, 138n24.

the question of the effect of Alcibiades' homecoming: Would Alcibiades' return in some way destroy his fatherland?

When Phrynichus asserts that Alcibiades is indifferent to regimes, Thucydides finds it important enough to interrupt his account of the events in order to confirm the truth of his claim: "this very thing was the case," he says (8.48.4). Thucydides has already provided some evidence—when Alcibiades fudges the very issue of his past support of democracy in Athens in his speech to an oligarchic Sparta. Alcibiades supported the established democracy, he says, because the hostility of Sparta meant it was not a good time to undertake its overthrow (6.89.6). It is therefore apart from any regime that Alcibiades "loves his city" (*philopolis*) (6.92.2). It seems that for him there is something more fundamental to Athens than the regime and way of life that Pericles praises in his funeral oration and by which he identifies Athens. But if a city can be identified only by its regime and way of life, is there anything that persists when a regime changes, as Athens does several times in Thucydides' lifetime? Is there something that limits or conditions change? Thucydides presents this question through his portrayal of Athens without answering it (as does Aristotle, *Politics* 1274b33–76b15).

When Pericles speaks of the power or potential of Athens, that potential is specific to Athens. In loving his city, Alcibiades in contrast seems to befriend pure possibility, just as he shares the Athenians' *erōs* for "sailing away." It is therefore not merely that Alcibiades is indifferent to regimes; rather, he is hostile to all regimes. Regimes establish institutions and determine who is to rule, and those rulers do not merely rule, they are dependent on the regimes for their rule. Regimes stand between the individual and his city, structuring their relationship and interaction. In this light, we can understand Forde's observation that "in [Alcibiades'] hands, the city becomes an almost non-political association," and why Forde is reminded of Aristotle's description of a kingship that is so total that it turns the city into a household (*Politics* 1285b29–34).[32] Thucydides indicates such an effect of Alcibiades' rule when Alcibiades acknowledges his desire to be regarded by succeeding generations as "kin," as "their own" (6.16.5). But a household does not come into its own until it has become part of a regime. It loses its autonomy, at least according to Aristotle, in order to fulfill its potential (see Aristotle, *Politics* 1252b22–24). Alcibiades refuses to do the former, and consequently never does the latter, unless at the moment he acts for the first time to benefit his city.

---

32. Ibid., 166.

It is fitting that Alcibiades thinks of repossessing his fatherland rather than of merely possessing it. In Greek, the verb "to possess" is the perfect form of "to acquire." One possesses what one has acquired. As the perfect form of the verb, however, "to possess" also refers merely to the present: to possess is a perfect state, free of the moment of acquisition. Alcibiades never lets the perfect rest, just as he proclaims that there is no end to the activity of an active city such as Athens (6.18.7). Consequently, he never takes the received for granted. He thinks of himself as granting more than he receives, as when he imagines shining his light on his ancestors and his city (6.16.1). The Corinthians' exaggeration about the Athenians—that they do not enjoy what they possess because they are ever acquiring (1.20.8)—applies especially to Alcibiades. For Alcibiades, possession is always repossession. He may seem like the Athenian playboy—with his horses and chariot races—but he never relaxes from his labors. He ill fits the way of life for which Pericles praises Athens (2.38.1).

Nor is Nicias a good fit. Although he prefers rest to motion, peace to war, Thucydides tells us of no activities that occupy his leisure, as he tells us of Alcibiades' horseracing and sponsoring choruses in dramatic productions. Nicias leads the army to their deaths in Sicily, cutting off their homecoming, just as he does his own. For Nicias, there is no road home, long or otherwise, because he never breaks free from his city. Nicias cannot repossess his city, because he never possesses it. To possess, one must have acquired, or make one's possession one's own. Whereas, metaphorically speaking, Alcibiades does not act as if he knows that "to possess" is a perfect verb, Nicias does not know that the perfect comes from the present form of the verb for acquiring. He does not understand the active sense or the origin of possession. The virtue of Athens is that it cannot be taken for granted, in the way Nicias takes it for granted. He is in name a commander in Sicily, but he is in fact ruled by the people in Athens, by the Athenian forces in Sicily (7.14.2), and finally by the seers.

Thucydides finds a failure of political realism in Athens's disaster in Sicily, but the failure lies not in Athens's loss of nerve out of fear of the gods and recall of Alcibiades from command, but in Athens's following Alcibiades' advice to go to Sicily, and especially in deciding to send a second expedition to help the first.[33] Thucydides presents Alcibiades not as the great leader

---

33. When Thucydides refers to the bad decisions the Athenians made concerning their army in Sicily (2.65.11), he is usually thought to refer to removing Alcibiades from command. His presentation of Nicias's failure to withdraw in time suggests that he refers as well to the Athenians' decision to send reinforcements rather than to bring the army home when they have the opportunity to do so. Connor, *Thucydides*, 189n9.

who would have accomplished the conquest of Sicily and indeed the greater part of the Hellenic world had he not been removed from his command, but as a man who overreaches by creating expectations that he cannot sustain. Against Alcibiades, and an Athens under his sway, Thucydides defends a political realism. It is a realism to which freedom is essential. His portrayal of Nicias makes this clear. Nicias fails to secure the survival of the Athenian army—and ultimately of Athens itself—due to his inability to achieve the freedom required for ruling. Nicias's subservience to the seers is as central to his character as his subservience to the Athenian demos. Out of fear for his life, he risks his life by refusing to return to Athens. Out of fear for his reputation, he risks the lives of the men under his command and his reputation can only suffer from the result. His politics of caution or self-preservation is as self-destructive as Alcibiades' politics of innovation and aggrandizement.

Thucydides' Pericles is the better political realist. Like Nicias, he warns against grandiose political adventures of conquest. But whereas Nicias's caution, fear, and sense of limits make it difficult for him to act, Pericles praises the choice of the noble over the pleasant, the just over the advantageous, and the public good over private interest. Indeed, the choice of the former in each case constitutes noble deeds, and manifests freedom. Such choices may serve the pursuit of power, but they also moderate it because they give it a purpose. Purpose both restrains freedom and calls for its exercise. None of these difficult conflicts ever appear to give Alcibiades pause, any more than they move Nicias to act. Alcibiades' image of Athens as unlimited motion is a reflection of himself (6.18.2–3, 6.18.6–7), whereas Nicias tries to maintain Athens at rest, at least he tries to do what is necessary to achieve the very state of peace he negotiated for it with Sparta and that is still not secure (6.10). Thucydides' reflections on their shortcomings indicate his preference for Pericles, or at least for the potential he represents. In my last chapter, I examine two digressions that Thucydides makes concerning Athens's past, and how they shed light on his own freedom, on what he as a historian owes to this city.

Conclusion

Thucydides, an Athenian

          Why Thucydides calls himself an Athenian at the outset of his history is as perplexing as his view of his role as a historian. We have seen arguments that Thucydides writes as a realist, a scientist, a postmodern, a constructivist, or a philosophic historian. The question of his approach to history is related to that of his identity as an Athenian. A constructivist, for example, might recognize that he, along with the actors in his history, is formed by the institutions and conventions of his world, and identify himself with his city at the beginning of his work. From this perspective, historians might help their readers understand their past, their accomplishments, their failures, and more generally the traditions that nurture their present and future. Such a historian would himself contribute to the identity of his city by writing its history, making his city his own, by repossessing it, as Alcibiades says he wants to do.

    Thucydides also claims to be a historian committed first and foremost to a "search for the truth," one that corrects the easygoing propensity of others to accept whatever comes readily to hand. Here Thucydides seeks a more impartial view than that of any city or its citizens, whether he is best understood as a scientific historian who investigates cause and effect, or a philosophic historian who seeks universal truths in particular events. After introducing himself as an Athenian at the outset, he finds no other occasion in his work to call himself an Athenian. He later mentions his twenty-year exile from Athens after his command at Amphipolis. His exile separated him from his city. By identifying himself as an Athenian only at the beginning of his work perhaps he indicates a perspective he was able to transcend.

Athens, however, as Thucydides presents it to us, differs from other cities, and that difference may make it easier for a historian committed to the truth to call himself an Athenian. There are more speeches by Athenians in Thucydides' work, for example, than by members of any other city. And there are more speeches in Athens than in any other city, whether delivered by Athenians or others (Corcyrians, Corinthians, and Spartans). Athens is a city that likes to listen to speeches, as the violent Cleon claims by way of reproach (3.40.2–3). The word "philosophy" or its derivatives appear only once in Thucydides' history, used by an Athenian, Pericles, to describe Athenians. Pericles claims that in Athens neighbors do not become angry with one another for doing what they please in their private lives; nor does the city close itself off to foreigners (2.37.2, 2.39.1). Athens is a city in which one can inquire about the events of the war, as did Thucydides. It is Athens that has the custom or law of funeral orations, which naturally lead the speaker to reflect about why its soldiers give their lives for their city. Athenians stand out in Thucydides' work for their self-reflection. Thucydides' two most obvious digressions, moreover, concern Athenians and their past. Thucydides too engages in the self-reflection that characterizes the Athenians he describes. As digressions from the war he recounts, they serve, as it were, as speeches of Thucydides himself.

Of course all the speeches in his work are Thucydides' speeches, inasmuch as he chose to include them and wrote them up as parts of his history. But these two digressions cannot be explained as the speeches of his history might—as speeches that were delivered in the course of the war he is narrating. The digressions tell stories about another, earlier time. We can ask their relevance to the present Thucydides is recounting, just as we might ask about the relevance of the Peloponnesian War to the future. In the digressions, we can see Thucydides reflecting on his own work, on what we might learn from the past, and why we should remember it. At the same time, by means of his digressions Thucydides enacts his freedom as a historian, as he steps back from the course of events he is narrating and thus from the necessary progression of time in order to reflect on the past and its relation to the present. Because both digressions involve Athens's past, they shed light on the character of Athens. Thucydides' self-reflection in the digressions therefore touches not only on his identity as a historian but on his identity as an Athenian. I will conclude by discussing the two digressions in turn, first, the place of the supposed Athenian tyrant slayers in Thucydides' work, and second, his digression on the Athenian statesman Themistocles.

Aristogeiton and Harmodius

In illustrating early in book 1 that human beings accept what they hear without testing it, Thucydides mentions the mistaken beliefs of the Athenians about an event in their past over eighty years before the outset of the war, concerning Aristogeiton and Harmodius and their plot against Athens's tyrant (1.20.1–3). Thucydides returns to Athens's misunderstanding of this incident in a digression from his account of Athens's recall of Alcibiades to stand trial for impiety (6.54–61). The digression strikes one commentator as "one of the most unusual passages in the entire work."[1]

The Athenians make a number of mistakes about this event. In the first place, they celebrate Harmodius and Aristogeiton as slayers of tyrants. Their plot, however, failed to kill the tyrant Hippias, and hence to drive tyranny from Athens. The man they did kill, Hipparchus, was not the tyrant, as Athenians think, but his younger brother. Moreover, Hippias and his father before him were virtuous and intelligent, and their rule was not harsh. It was only after the botched attempt on Hippias's life that his rule became oppressive. Third, the conspirators' action against tyranny not only failed; it was counterproductive. The would-be assassins were moved not simply or even primarily by a love of freedom, as Athenians think, but by Aristogeiton's love for Harmodius, and his anger when the tyrant's brother Hipparchus tried to seduce his beloved (6.54–59).[2] The lovers are not the models for fighters against tyranny that popular opinion made them. To make matters worse for Athens, it was the Spartans, not the Athenians themselves, who four years after the murder of Hipparchus freed Athens from its tyranny by driving

---

1. Elizabeth A. Meyer, "Thucydides on Harmodius and Aristogeiton, Tyranny, and History," *Classical Quarterly* 58, no. 1 (2008): 13. For an account of diverse scholarly opinion about Thucydides' digression on the Athenian tyrants, see ibid., 13–15. Michael W. Taylor refers to "the Tyrannicide excursus" in Thucydides as "a jarring detour." *The Tyrant Slayers: The Heroic Image in Fifth Century B.C. Art and Politics* (New York: Arno Press, 1981), 162. While some scholars consequently suppose that Thucydides simply could not resist a historian's temptation to clear up confusion about the past regardless of its relevance, others find deliberate parallels between Athens's situation at the time of the attempted assassination and its situation at the time of the recall of Alcibiades, which is the occasion for his digression.

2. Thucydides reports that Harmodius and Aristogeiton did not involve many in the conspiracy for the sake of security, but that they hoped that once they attacked the tyrant, others would join them to fight for their liberty. It is not clear from his account that anyone joins them for this purpose (6.56.3–57.4).

Hippias out. The Athenians are not responsible for their own freedom from tyranny, but owe it to Sparta. The truth, in this case, explodes their pride in themselves and their past.[3]

In the legend of the "tyrant slayers" Athenians "embellish" the facts, like the poets Thucydides criticizes at the outset (1.21). The truth damages not merely the verses of the poets (2.41.4), but Athens's understanding of its past. Indeed, Athenians themselves hid the truth about the tyrants, when they erased an inscription to the tyrants from an altar in the marketplace (6.54.6–7). The Athenians literally rewrite, or at least erase, the past in a deliberate act of forgetting.

The Athenians' discovery of the truth about this incident, made soon after the Sicilian expedition sails, fuels their frenzy over the mutilation of the herms and their suspicion that Alcibiades is plotting tyranny (6.53 and 60).[4] Although the "hearsay" about the tyrants that Thucydides earlier calls "untested" is now corrected, learning the truth only leads the Athenians to become more fearful of tyranny, savage toward those they suspect of plotting against the government, and ready to act on "untested hearsay" in the present (6.60.2–3). Having cleared up mistaken conceptions of the past, they act on mistaken conceptions of the present, as they execute citizens on the basis of untested allegations about the mutilation of the herms (6.60.4). Athens has become almost unrecognizable as the tolerant people whom Pericles describes (2.37.2). Connor sees a resemblance between the Athenians during this period and the tyrants themselves, at least "in their last stages, when fear and suspicion lead [the tyrants] to repression."[5] Athens becomes "a tyrant city" not merely toward the cities it subjugates (see 1.122.3, 1.124.3, 6.85.1) but also toward its own citizens. Meyer points out that whereas the Athenians know "nothing precise" (6.54.1) about what happens in 415 in the matter of the herms, Thucydides describes his effort to gain as much "precision" as possible about the events of the war (1.22.2). She concludes, "Thucydides is different, and better [than the Athenians in 415], because of his methods."[6]

---

3. Shanske, *Thucydides and the Philosophic Origins*, 75.

4. Munn speculates that Alcibiades' enemies appealed to Herodotus's account of Athenian tyrants to increase fear of Alcibiades. *School of History*, 114–18.

5. Connor, *Thucydides*, 179–80; also Meyer, "Thucydides on Harmodius and Aristogeiton," 21, 24.

6. Meyer, "Thucydides on Harmodius and Aristogeiton," 27. Also Scanlon, "Thucydides and Tyranny," 291; Hans-Peter Stahl, *Thucydides: Man's Place in History* (Swansea: Classical Press of Wales, 2003 (an expansion of the edition in German published in 1966), 1–11; Shanske, *Thucydides and the Philosophic Origins*, 75.

Thucydides' methods enable him to learn the truth in writing his history, whereas the Athenians remain ignorant of what is happening, even in the present.

Thucydides is "better" than the Athenians of that time also because in the matter of the herms, he admits that it remains "unclear whether those who were punished were justly punished or not" (6.60.5). "Conjectures can be made on both sides [of this question], and no one either then or later was able to say clearly who did the deed" (6.60.2). It is a case in which inquiry does not yield the truth. The Athenians think they know but do not, and act swiftly and harshly against those they accuse of the crime. Had the Athenians shared Thucydides' awareness of ignorance, they might not have committed what he presents as terrible injustices. In an apparently irrelevant anecdote about the Athenian tyrant Hippias, Thucydides quotes an inscription on the tomb of his daughter Archedice, which praises her moderation (her mind was without reckless presumption), although she was the daughter, sister, and wife of tyrants (6.59.3). She is one of the few women whom Thucydides mentions by name in his history (see also 4.133.1–3). Her name in Greek sounds like "just rule." By implication, she possessed a moderation that the Athenians of 415 would have done well to emulate.

Thucydides' claim of uncertainty about these events in Athens leaves open the question of whether Alcibiades is guilty of mutilating the herms, which he is rumored to have done. If Alcibiades was one of Thucydides' informants about various events of the war in which he participated, either Alcibiades did not tell Thucydides whether he was guilty of the impiety of which he was accused, or Thucydides does not trust what he says enough to report it to his readers. Unlike the Athenians in the case of the revelations about the herms, Thucydides does not simply trust his informers. Athens at any rate supposes that Alcibiades is clearly guilty of impious deeds—for the city condemns him to death when he does not appear in court to face the charges against him—whereas Thucydides claims not to know who is responsible. He professes not to know what the Athenians think they know. Whether or not he trusts Alcibiades, he does not trust the Athenians on this issue. Thucydides leaves the cause of the crime obscure.

What is "manifestly clear" (*periphanēs*), however, is that regardless of whether the accused suffer unjustly in the matter of the herms, the rest of the city benefits once the executions take place. Confidence appears to be restored when the Athenians believe they know what they do not, and hence think that they have found relief from their uncertainty (6.60.5). In his funeral oration, Pericles characterized the Athenians as philosophizing without softness (2.40.1). If that involves knowing what one does not know, however, Pericles was wrong to attribute it to the Athenians. At least this description does not apply to them in 415. It is Thucydides, in his claim of ignorance, who preserves the spirit of Athens that Pericles describes. He is more like Socrates than like those who brought him to trial and executed him. Socrates of course, not only his executioners, is an Athenian.

Thucydides' digression is first and foremost a criticism of Athens—for its simplistic understanding of its past that exalts the city as a home for freedom. Athenians were not the freedom fighters that they boast themselves to be, they owe more to Sparta than they acknowledge, and even the "tyrants' rule" was not simply tyrannical until the "tyrant slayers" caused it to become so. Thucydides, in contrast to the Athenians who believe the legend, shows his freedom of thought, for love of his own does not hinder his pursuit of the truth. The legend of the tyrant slayers, however, not only demonstrates the Athenians' misplaced pride. It also shows their aspiration to freedom in what they like to think about themselves. That aspiration to freedom is found even in Aristogeiton, who defends his beloved from the overtures of the tyrant's brother. Love of one's own can lead to acts in defense of freedom, even if the plot of the lovers in this case was a debacle. The Athenians are a people who are open to Pericles' funeral oration, which describes Athens as the home of freedom, and with the guidance of a statesman they can at times live up to this characterization.

In the second place, and consistent with this observation, learning the truth about one's past does not by itself make one free. The truth intensifies the Athenians' suspicions of one another and their fear of tyranny. There is no one to act the part of Pericles—who restored their confidence in themselves when they lost it, and who was able to contradict them in their anger because of his "worth and judgment" (2.65.8–10). Thucydides mentions no one in the city at the time of the mutilation of the herms who moves others to restraint, or even who shows restraint. He mentions no leader by name. Alcibiades, to be sure, leads, at least some in the city, but he is en route to Sicily, and the city's fears are directed against Alcibiades himself. Athens has become leaderless, faceless. The people come to act like tyrants themselves, in prosecuting citizens in the matters of the herms without evidence. There is no one like Archedice in the city to act as a model. Calm is restored only by widespread executions. In more ways than one, Thucydides' devotion to the truth distinguishes him from his countrymen, for he knows that the identity of the perpetrators remains uncertain. This truth, his knowledge of his ignorance, frees him from the frenzy that captures the Athenians. His freedom does not merely demonstrate his distance from the blinding passions that consume others or his resignation at the injustices of political life, but is a model of political restraint that Athens lacked at the time.

Themistocles

The other digression that most obviously interrupts Thucydides' narrative involves another Athenian from the past, Themistocles. As one of Athens's outstanding statesmen and generals, Themistocles has already played a part in Thucydides' account of the fifty-year period prior to the Peloponnesian War (1.89–117). Themistocles guided Athens at the time of the Persian War, including the Hellenic naval victory against the invading Persians at Salamis (1.74.1, 1.91.5). After the Persian War, he was instrumental in Athenians' refortification of their city, as Thucydides describes it, advocating the completion of the "long walls" to the Piraeus, and deceiving Sparta about the progress of their construction (1.90–93). Thucydides completes his story of Themistocles later in book 1 in a digression that involves his exile in Persia (1.135.2–138).

Thucydides' occasion for the digression is his discussion of the charges and countercharges between the Athenians and the Spartans just before the outbreak of the war. After the Spartans ask the Athenians to drive out the descendants of those who incurred a curse for violating the rights of suppliants, who included Pericles, the Athenians ask the Spartans to do the same regarding a curse they claim the Spartans incurred in the past for a similar offense, which involved their treatment of Pausanias. When accused of treason, Pausanias takes refuge in a temple, Thucydides recounts, where the Spartans barricade him in. He ends up dying of starvation (1.126–135.1). Collecting evidence against Pausanias, the Spartans find evidence against Themistocles as well, and send it to the Athenians (1.135.2). Thucydides uses this observation as the occasion for his digression about the charges against Themistocles and his escape to Persia. Unlike the story about Pausanias, there is no obvious connection between that of Themistocles and the negotiations between the Spartans and the Athenians that precede the war. Thucydides' story of Themistocles' exile stands out as a digression from his account of the events leading up to the war.

Once Themistocles discovers the charges brewing against him in Athens, he proceeds to Persia. His route requires him to traverse Molossia, where he requests aid from its king, Admetus. The king's wife "instructs" (*didaskein*) Themistocles how to supplicate her husband—by sitting on their hearth (*hestia*) while holding their child. By following her advice, he succeeds in obtaining Admetus's help in his journey, even though Themistocles had not been friendly toward him when he had a say in Athenian affairs (1.136.2–137.1). Just as Thucydides' reference to Archedice is unnecessary to his account of the Athenian tyrants, his anecdote about Admetus's wife is not necessary to his tracing of Themistocles' passage to Persia. We meet her too in connection to her family, her husband and her child. (Thucydides does not even give her proper name, referring to her only as Admetus's wife.) But she takes the side of and instructs a foreigner, a fugitive from his own city, in how to succeed in obtaining her husband's help. Like Archedice, who maintains her virtue in spite of her family of tyrants, hers is no passive role within the family; rather, she is able to instruct her husband about how he should act toward Themistocles by advising Themistocles how he should proceed to ask for help. Both women, in effect, keep to their places within their families while transcending them.

At the end of his funeral oration, as we have seen, Pericles recommends silence about women as best, regardless of praise or blame (2.45.2). He follows his own advice, for he says little more about women in his speech than that. It has been observed that in writing his history, Thucydides himself follows Pericles' advice.[7] But not only does Thucydides speak about Archedice and Admetus's wife, he also tells us that it is the place of the women at the public funeral to lament the dead (2.34.4). He himself is not silent about the women; nor are they silent. Their cries of sorrow affirm the goodness of life that war and its emphasis on winning glory may obscure. Admetus's wife gains her husband's help for Themistocles by reminding him of their child, and therewith of his connection to generation, something more immediate and fundamental than the unwritten memory or fame Pericles promises those Athenians who give their lives for their city. She teaches Admetus to risk his own—Corcyra had already sent Themistocles away out of fear of both Athenian and Spartan reprisal (1.136.1)—to save another from persecution from his own. She is therefore able to serve as a model for what Thucydides' understands as human freedom: by virtue of her place within the family, she can support acts of freedom, Themistocles' escape and Admetus's facilitation of his escape. Pericles presents Athenian freedom as a model for Hellas, and therefore for Thucydides, but Thucydides finds in women a model as well. Like Themistocles, he is able to learn from women.

In the course of his digression, Thucydides refers to Themistocles' "native intelligence" (*oikeia sunesis*), unformed or undeveloped by education (1.138.3). Indeed, Thucydides' words foreshadow Pericles' contrast between the Athenians' courage and that of the Spartans—it comes from within rather than from the harsh discipline of the laws (2.39.1, 2.39.3). Themistocles' intelligence is his own, rather than law-bred like Nicias's

---

7. Shanske, *Thucydides and the Philosophic Origins*, 61.

virtue or Spartan courage. Themistocles illustrates the versatility whereby an Athenian is prepared for anything, for which Pericles praises the Athenians (2.41.1). When Themistocles arrives in Persia, as Thucydides recounts, he asks to delay his appearance in court for a year, during which time he studies the Persians' language and practices. Themistocles' intelligence is not owing to his education, but he knows that he must become educated, especially about those with whom he must deal. In this regard Thucydides implicitly contrasts Themistocles with Pausanias, who quickly dons Persian garb and follows Persian custom. Pausanias's knowledge of the Persians is superficial, and his imitation of them foolish. Whereas Pausanias requires the ongoing discipline of Sparta to maintain his Spartan identity, Themistocles continues to demonstrate the character for which Thucydides praises him, even when in Persia. As Forde observes, Thucydides' "parallel portraits of Pausanias and Themistocles demonstrate that Athenian genius, grounded in nature or natural talent, does not lose its force when operating apart from the city, whereas Spartan virtue, grounded in its conventional discipline, does."[8]

Although Themistocles' genius belongs to him, and goes with him wherever he goes, Thucydides carefully preserves an ambiguity in his presentation of Themistocles' deeds in relation to Athens. For example, when Themistocles arrives in Persia, he addresses the issue of his past enmity toward the Persians, as Alcibiades does in Sparta. Although Themistocles orchestrated the Persians' defeat by Athens at Salamis, as he acknowledges to them, he soon thereafter rendered them a service—warning them to retreat and preserving the bridges they needed for crossing home. Thucydides interrupts the message to tell us that Themistocles is lying (1.137.4): he is only pretending to have betrayed his city. But this is the evidence he offers that it is for his friendship to the Persians that he is now being persecuted by Athens, and thus why he has now come to render the Persians another great service. Themistocles holds out the hope of their subjugation of Hellas, Thucydides tells us, but he does not comment on Themistocles' intention (1.138.2). As Richard H. Cox asks, "Does Themistocles truly intend to help the king [of Persia]? Or is that what the king too credulously infers?"[9]

Although the Persian king gives him the rule over several of his territories (1.138.5), there are no further expeditions against the Hellenes while

---

8. Forde, *Ambition to Rule*, 69.

9. Richard H. Cox, "Thucydides on Themistocles," *Politikos II: Educating the Ambitious; Leadership and Political Rule in Greek Political Thought*, ed. Leslie G. Rubin (Pittsburgh: Dusquesne University Press, 1992), 104.

Themistocles is in Persia. Themistocles makes no effort to regain his city, even at the price of remaining in exile, whereas Alcibiades seeks to recover Athens regardless of any dangers to his city. So too the Athenian tyrant Hippias, once expelled from Athens, joins the Persians and accompanies them to Marathon on an expedition to enslave Athens (6.59.4). As is clear from Themistocles' famous advice to go to sea that saves Athens from the Persians (1.74), he is a man who knows that there are times when one must abandon one's city in order to save it.[10] He may be the greater patriot than Alcibiades, precisely because he makes no effort to go home within his lifetime, even when it means he must die in a foreign land.

Although "they say that Themistocles killed himself by poison, thinking that he was unable to accomplish what he promised the king," Thucydides reports that he dies from disease (1.138.4). Thucydides reports hearsay about the manner and cause of Themistocles' death in order to correct it. It is also said, Thucydides continues, that Themistocles "ordered his relatives to bring his bones home [*oikade*] and bury them in secret in Attica, because it is not permitted that one exiled for treason be buried [there]" (1.138.1–6). Whereas Thucydides denies the first report about Themistocles' death—that it was self-inflicted because of unfulfilled obligations to the Persian king—he does not deny the rumor about his burial. If true, Themistocles is unlike Brasidas—he wants to be buried at home. He does not want "the whole earth" as his tomb, the prospect that Pericles held out to those who sacrifice themselves for their city (2.43.2–3). He wants to be buried in Attica. He relies on relatives to make this possible. Although Athens rejects him, he does not reject Athens. His homecoming, if what is said is true, is one of the first mentioned in Thucydides' history.

Only of Themistocles does Thucydides use the expression that Pericles uses of Athens itself—"worthy of wonder" (1.38.3, 2.39.4). Thucydides thereby implies that the expression belongs less to Pericles' Athens than to an Athenian leader of the past. He reserves this praise not for Nicias, and not even for Pericles, but for Themistocles, a man whose relationship to his city is more ambiguous than that of either Nicias or Pericles, neither of whom is ever exiled from Athens. Not only Nicias, but Pericles himself is more dependent on his city than Themistocles is. According to Shanske, Themistocles' remarkable "native quickness *is* Athenian" (emphasis Shanske's), and it is because of this that he "loses his home." The case of Themistocles

---

10. Ibid., 105.

therefore raises the question, in Shanske's words, "whether it is also Athenian to end up alienated from yourself."[11] Themistocles' relationship to Athens is nevertheless more complex than that of other traitors whom Thucydides mentions, such as Hippias or Alcibiades. Either of these traitors is a better candidate for alienation from Athens than Themistocles. Shanske notes only the tragedy in that "the savior of Athens and Greece" must be buried at home "in secret."[12] But this savior of Athens and Greece wants to be buried at home, not in Persia, and his contrivance to do so "in secret" acknowledges the law of his land, to which he defers in part by keeping his violation secret. Thucydides' praise of Themistocles as worthy of wonder suggests that Themistocles is the Athenian most worthy of note in his work, although he did not live to see the war most worthy of note, as Thucydides did. What is most worthy of note does not depend on the war, whether its magnitude lies in its achievements or in its sufferings (1.23). What is most worthy of note lies in what Thucydides' reflections about the war enable him to see, such as the way in which Themistocles, like Thucydides himself, might, in spite of his exile from home, be called an Athenian.

Thucydides

Thucydides is not a philosophic historian if by that is meant one who reveals only what is universally true of all cities and all human beings. Athenian democracy rewards excellence, at least according to Pericles, and in doing so distinguishes itself from other cities. Thucydides is as concerned with the distinctive as the universal, and perhaps even more with the former. The universal, insofar as it is true only for the most part, acts as a foil for distinction. Fear and interest may move human beings, as many in Thucydides' history claim (e.g., 6.85.3), and the strong may everywhere rule the weak, which the Athenians at Melos say is a law of nature that applies even to the gods (5.105.2). But others appeal to honor as well as to interest and fear, and also refer to justice (e.g., 1.76.2–3). Thucydides states that "in peace and prosperity cities have better intentions [*gnōmai*] through not falling in with unwilling necessities" (3.82.2). Even during the plague, when the Athenians yielded to "lawless excess" (2.53.1), those with aspirations to virtue "did not spare themselves in going to their [sick] friends" at great risk to their own

---

11. Shanske, *Thucydides and the Philosophic Origins,* 62–63.
12. Ibid., 62–63.

lives (2.51.2).[13] Some conditions bring out the best in human beings, others the worst, and some human beings manifest the best even in the worst conditions. It is the rule that makes the exception worthy of wonder. And some exceptions are worthy of horror. When Thracian mercenaries, "the bloodiest of the barbarians," massacre the population of Mycalessus, even the school children, Thucydides says that "the disaster" was as unexpected and as terrible (*deinos*) as any during the war (7.29.5). Thucydides gives us no reason to think that others would not be as shocked as he. War may be "a harsh teacher," as Thucydides says (3.82.2), but that does not mean that the effect of its teaching is merely to harden.

Thucydides' inclusion of the two digressions I have discussed in this chapter confirms that he is no mere recorder of the events of the war and sheds light on his concerns as a historian. Just as his digressions stand out from the sequence of events, they refer to individuals who do so as well. In his digression about tyrant slayers, Thucydides distinguishes himself from the Athenians, for he knows what they do not about their past, and he knows that he does not know who desecrated the herms, when they think that they do. Thucydides' acceptance of his own ignorance serves as their foil and correction. It is not universally true that human beings act in ignorance, thinking that they know when they do not. In his digression about Themistocles, we see a human being distinguished by his intelligence, but also by his awareness that he does not know what he needs to know and by his willingness to learn, even from a woman, as he does from Admetus's wife. It is not universally true that men refuse to heed the advice of a woman (see Aristotle, *Politics* 1260a29–30). Themistocles is taught by a woman. Themistocles is even willing to learn about what might seem utterly foreign, as he does concerning Persian customs and language "as much as he is able" (1.138.1). The Athenian Themistocles serves as a model for Thucydides himself, who inquires about the events of the war, even from foreign sources. Like Themistocles, Thucydides knows what he does not know and also what he needs to know. And he makes the effort to do so, to the extent that he is able. And this requires that he travel to both sides during the war.

When Thucydides tells us that he was exiled from Athens for twenty years, he does not tell us for a fact that he went home when he was allowed to do so. Finley argues that Thucydides' giving us the exact length of his exile "suggests that he returned to Athens at its expiration." "Why otherwise,"

---

13. Johnson, *Thucydides, Hobbes*, 36–37.

Finley asks, "would he have recorded the exact length of his exile?"[14] There is nothing improbable about his return home after his exile, moreover, as there would be in Brasidas's going home from Thrace. Pouncey thinks that Thucydides felt an exile's eagerness to return home inasmuch as he mentions "apparently out of the blue" that the Athenian oligarchs did not recall the exiles because of Alcibiades (8.70.1). This small parenthesis to his account "seems quite irrelevant," according to Pouncey, "until we realize that for Thucydides this meant that his banishment had another seven years to run."[15]

Perhaps Thucydides leaves open the question of whether he returns to Athens not because of his famous reticence about himself, which he nevertheless violates from time to time, but because it is unclear whether Athens still exists. Athens surely undergoes many changes during the time Thucydides recounts—from Periclean democracy to the democracy of his successors, from a democratic regime to the government of the oligarchic and tyrannical Four Hundred, and then from that oligarchy to the government of the Five Thousand. Thucydides' dark description of his city in frenzy over the mutilated herms in 415—as well as the Athenians' widespread suspicion of one another under the Four Hundred in 411—illustrate signs of decline, a decline Thucydides leads us to expect in his contrast between Pericles and his successors. Like Pericles, who praises Athens's "regime and way of life," Thucydides is not indifferent to regimes. He offers a judgment about which is the best regime that Athens has in his lifetime (8.97.2). If there is an escape from tragedy for Thucydides, it lies not in an escape from political life, but in finding a balance resembling that which Thucydides attributes to Pericles' politics (2.65.7). Homecoming cannot be good if one's home is not. To be concerned about whether one's home is good requires considering one's city's regime. It is for this reason that even Themistocles is an insufficient model for Thucydides. For the latter, having his bones laid in Attica, or even going home to die, could not alone be the homecoming he desires, inasmuch as he understands Athens not merely as the land on which the city is located but, more important, as the regime that makes Athens a city in which freedom of thought and action can be found.

In judging Athens by its regime, Thucydides implicitly distinguishes himself as well from Alcibiades, who is indifferent to regimes (8.48.4). For Alcibiades, freedom lies in sailing away, rather than in a way of life that a regime

---

14. Finley, *Thucydides*, 11.

15. Pouncey, *Necessities of War*, 6. Crawley also points out that these exiles who were not recalled at this point include Thucydides. *Landmark Thucydides*, 521, note on 8.70.

makes possible, and homecoming is a return to whatever regime welcomes him back to the city. From him, Thucydides learns the futility of an idealism that severs the good from any particular good, with its limits of time and place, and of a realism that seeks power without measure or end. Through his presentation of Alcibiades' career, Thucydides thus teaches idealists Nicias's lesson that boundaries are necessary (6.13.1), even though he is more willing than Nicias to test them, and even to modify them. At the same time, he cautions those inclined to the outlook of one or another of these Athenian commanders that a politics that ignores the good in pursuit of security or power gives up too easily on human potential.

Athens can be Thucydides' home only insofar as its regime is good. He therefore appreciates Athenian democracy to the extent that it is a home for freedom, manifesting as Pericles claims opportunities for citizens to participate in ruling, toleration for individuals in their private lives, and liberality in foreign relations. To do so obviously requires leaders with the ability to balance liberality with the necessities of rule as new problems and challenges arise in time. This may be "a democracy in name" as existed during Pericles' time, or it may be a regime that mixes the few and the many as Thucydides says of the regime of the Five Thousand. The Syracusan leader Athenagoras defends democracy itself in just such terms, when he asserts, "the people [*demos*] means everyone, while oligarchy means [only] a part; the rich are the best guardians of wealth, the intelligent give the best advice, and the many are best at listening and judging; and in democracy these, individually and collectively, have a fair share" (6.39.1). Thucydides renders doubtful that Athenagoras is describing his own regime when "one of the generals" comes forward, and prevents anyone else from speaking on the matter before the assembly, and when his command replaces a vote (6.41). Although he is from Syracuse, Athenagoras's name sounds as if it means "an Athenian speaker," or perhaps "a speaker for Athens."[16] Thucydides apparently found that his own city of Athens came closer at times to the judicious balancing or mixing that renders democracy defensible than any other city that appears in his work.

---

16. Athenagoras is one of three figures in Thucydides' work who delivers a speech in direct discourse but who plays no other role, and who is unknown except for his appearance in Thucydides. The first is Diodotus, whom I have discussed in chapter 2. The other is the Athenian Euphemus, who attempts to assuage fear of Athenian imperialism in Sicily by claiming it grew out of necessity— rather than out of any ambition to rule that would move the Athenians to subdue Sicily (6.81–87). In each case the names of these otherwise unknown figures seem significant. Not surprisingly there has been speculation that Thucydides may have invented one or two or all three of these characters. See Palmer, *Love of Glory*, 125n22; Forde, *Ambition to Rule*, 40; Mara, *Civic Conversations*, 123; Bruell, "Thucydides' View," 16–17. For discussion of Athenagoras, see Connor, *Thucydides*, 171; Orwin, *Humanity of Thucydides*, 185–86; Pouncey, *Necessities of War*, 14.

Thucydides' evaluation of imperialism is as complex as his evaluation of democracy. Athenian virtues, intelligence and daring, led to the city's imperialism, and imperialism in turn encouraged the exercise of those virtues by providing opportunities for ruling others, for deliberation and planning, and for actions undertaken freely rather than out of necessity. Thucydides nevertheless shows that Athens frequently failed to exercise these virtues, as in its granting of power to Cleon, and in its action against Melos. His reservations against Athenian imperialism appear in his portrayal of such failures, as well as in his considerable sympathy for the Spartan Brasidas, especially in Brasidas's drive to liberate subject cities from Athens and his promise to them of autonomy. Most important, Thucydides' description of the Sicilian expedition leads us to question the extent to which a moderate or balanced foreign policy such as he attributes to Pericles can be maintained over time. The excesses of Athens during the time of Alcibiades, and the excesses of Alcibiades himself, suggest that even a city as resourceful as Athens could not maintain the freedom and restraint necessary to sustain its way of life for long.

Words can lose their meanings, as happens during the plague and civil war in Corcyra (2.53.3, 3.82.4). But the good and the bad do not change, even if our view of them changes under the pressure of events. Pericles, who claims that he "is the same and does not alter" (2.61.2), knows that Athens leaves behind everlasting memorials (*mnēmeia*) of both good and bad (2.41.4). Not only the good endures. In this, Pericles speaks for Thucydides, although Thucydides expresses greater sadness than Pericles that so many of the memories of the war are of the bad rather than the good. Thucydides' description of acts committed during the plague in Athens and during the civil war in Corcyra, the slaughter at Mycalessus, the destruction of Plataea, and the sufferings of the Sicilian expedition serve as a few illustrations among many. So too we can judge acts as good. The Athenians' reversal of their decision on Mytilene is an outstanding example. That Thucydides judges and enables us to judge what he remembers of the war in his history as good and bad does not mean he is not a philosophic historian, at least in a Socratic sense of philosophy. The philosopher loves the good, but he also desires the good to be his own (*Republic* 505d–e; *Symposium* 204e–205a).

Thucydides achieves his homecoming by his act of writing his history of the war as "a possession for all time," for he thereby repossesses his city through the active acquisition that Alcibiades craves for all his possessions, while attaining the perfect sense of possession that Nicias never risks enough to achieve. Moreover, whether or not Thucydides can find a home in Athens after his exile, he finds a homecoming time and again in the future, wherever his written memory of Athens survives, generates wonder, and can be brought to bear on human and political life. For there one would find, as Thucydides did for a time in Athens, freedom for thought and action. With the exception of Pisander's brief speech in favor of oligarchy in Athens, Thucydides records no speeches in direct discourse in Athens after those of Nicias and Alcibiades concerning the Sicilian expedition. He does quote Nicias's letter to the Athenian assembly about the army's situation in Sicily. Nicias puts his message in writing because he does not trust a messenger to describe the situation accurately, or sympathetically (7.8.2). This is the longest writing quoted directly in Thucydides' work, other than the many treaties and alliances that boast their longevity with as much certainty as Nicias announces his death in the letter he writes. Within the confines of Thucydides' history, the Athenian people do not hear another funeral oration after Pericles delivers his. When Nicias tries to tell them that he is dying, they insist that he remain in command in Sicily. They concede nothing to death. Nicias's letter that announces his approaching death from illness is a poor reflection of Thucydides' writing, which announces its own—not its author's—immortality, at least in principle. "A possession for all time" does not inevitably last forever, but it is worthy of doing so. Thucydides concedes to the destructive power of time only in part, and not with respect to his judgment of what is worthy of enduring.

❦ Bibliography

Adcock, F. E. *Thucydides and His History.* Cambridge: Cambridge University Press, 1963.

Ahrensdorf, Peter J. "Thucydides' **Realist** Critique of Realism." *Polity* 30, no. 2 (1997): 231–65.

Allison, June W. "Homeric Allusions at the Close of Thucydides' Sicilian Narrative." *American Journal of Philology* 118, no. 4 (1997): 499–516.

———. "Pericles' Policy and the Plague." *Historia* (1st qtr., 1983): 14–23.

Bedford, David, and Thom Workman. "The Tragic Reading of the Thucydidean Tragedy." *Review of International Studies* 27 (2001): 51–67.

Bluhm, William T. "Causal Theory in Thucydides' Peloponnesian War." *Political Studies* 10 (1962): 15–35.

Bolotin, David. "Thucydides." In *The History of Political Philosophy*, edited by Leo Strauss and Joseph Cropsey, 7–32. 3rd ed. Chicago: University of Chicago Press, 1987.

Bruell, Christopher. "Thucydides' View of Athenian Imperialism." *American Political Science Review* 68 (1974): 11–17.

Brunt, P. A. "Spartan Policy and Strategy in the Archidamian War." *Phoenix* 19, no. 4 (1965): 255–80.

———. "Thucydides and Alcibiades." *Revue des Études Grecques* 65 (1952): 65–81.

Burns, Timothy. "The Virtue of Thucydides' Brasidas." *Journal of Politics* 73, no. 2 (2011): 508–23.

Clinton, W. David. "Conclusion: The Relevance of Realism in the Post-Cold War World." In *The Realist Tradition and Contemporary International Relations*, edited by W. David Clinton, 234–56. Baton Rouge: Louisiana State University Press, 2007.

Cochrane, Charles. *Thucydides and the Science of History.* Oxford: Oxford University Press, 1929.

Cogan, Marc. *The Human Thing: The Speeches and Principles of Thucydides' History.* Chicago: University of Chicago Press, 1981.

Connor, W. Robert. "A Post Modernist Thucydides?" *Classical Journal* 72, no. 4 (1977): 289–98.

———. *Thucydides.* Princeton: Princeton University Press, 1984.

Cornford, Francis M. *Thucydides Mythistoricus.* Philadelphia: University of Pennsylvania Press, 1971. First published 1907 by Edward Arnold.

Cox, Richard H. "Thucydides on Themistocles." *Politikos II: Educating the Ambitious: Leadership and Political Rule in Greek Political Thought.* Edited by Leslie G. Rubin. Pittsburgh: Dusquesne University Press, 1992.

Crawley, Richard. *The Landmark Thucydides*. Translated and revised by Robert B. Strassler, with an introduction by Victor Davis Hanson. New York: Simon & Schuster, 1996.

Delebecque, Edouard. *Thucydide et Alcibiade*. Aix-en-Provence: Centre d'Études et Reserches Helleniques, 1965.

Dobski, Bernard J. "The Incomplete Whole: The Structural Integrity of Thucydides' History." In *Socrates and Dionysus: Philosophy and Art in Dialogue*, edited by Ann Ward, 14–32. Newcastle: Cambridge Scholars, 2013.

Ducrey, P. *Le traitement des prisonniers de guerre*. Paris, 1968.

Edmunds, Lowell. *Chance and Intelligence in Thucydides*. Cambridge, MA: Harvard University Press, 1975.

Euben, J. Peter. "The Battle of Salamis and the Origin of Political Theory." *Political Theory* 14, no. 3 (1986): 359–90.

———. *The Tragedy of Political Theory: The Road Not Taken*. Princeton: Princeton University Press, 1990.

Farrar, Cynthia. *The Origins of Democratic Thinking: The Invention of Politics in Classical Athens*. Cambridge: Cambridge University Press, 1988.

Finley, John H., Jr. *Thucydides*. Cambridge, MA: Harvard University Press, 1942.

Forde, Steven. *The Ambition to Rule: Alcibiades and the Politics of Athenian Imperialism in Thucydides*. Ithaca, NY: Cornell University Press, 1974.

———. "International Realism and the Science of Politics: Thucydides, Machiavelli, and Neorealism." *International Studies Quarterly* 39, no. 2 (1995): 141–60.

Garst, Daniel. "Thucydides and Neorealism." *International Studies Quarterly* 33, no. 1 (1989): 3–27.

Gillis, Daniel. "The Revolt at Mytilene." *American Journal of Philology* 92, no. 1 (1971): 38–47.

Gilpin, Robert. "The Theory of Hegemonic War." *Journal of Interdisciplinary History* 18, no. 4 (1988): 591–613.

Gomme, A. W. *Historical Commentary on Thucydides (HCT)*. 5 vols. With A. Andrewes and K. J. Dover. Oxford: Clarendon Press, 1945–1981.

Grant, John R. "Toward Knowing Thucydides." *Phoenix* 28, no. 1 (1974): 81–94.

Gribble, David. *Alcibiades and Athens*. Oxford: Oxford University Press, 1999.

Hanson, Victor Davis. Introduction to *The Landmark Thucydides*, translated by Richard Crawley, revised by Robert B. Strassler. With an introduction by Victor Davis Hanson. New York: Simon & Schuster, 1996.

Hegel, Georg Wilhelm Friedrich. *Lectures on the Philosophy of History: Introduction*. Translated by H. B. Nisbet, with an introduction by Duncan Forbes. Cambridge: Cambridge University Press, 1975.

Heilke, Thomas. "Realism, Narrative, and Happenstance: Thucydides' Tale of Brasidas." *American Political Science Review* 98, no. 1 (2004): 121–38.

Hornblower, Simon. *A Commentary on Thucydides*. 3 vols. Oxford: Clarendon Press, 1991–2008.

———. *Thucydides*. Baltimore: Johns Hopkins University Press, 1987.

Hunter, Virginia. *Thucydides the Artful Reporter*. Toronto: Hakkert, 1973.

Johnson, Laurie M. *Thucydides, Hobbes, and the Interpretation of Realism*. DeKalb: Northern Illinois University Press, 1991.

Kagan, Donald. *The Archidamian War.* Ithaca, NY: Cornell University Press, 1974.

———. *The Peace of Nicias and the Sicilian Expedition.* Ithaca, NY: Cornell University Press, 1981.

———. "The Speeches in Thucydides and the Mytilene Debate." *Yale Classical Studies* 24 (1975): 71–94.

Lattimore, Steven. *The Peloponnesian War.* Translated, with an introduction, notes, and glossary. Indianapolis: Hackett, 1998.

Lauriello, Christopher Lewis. "Diodotus and Thucydides." *Interpretation* (2009): 237–58.

Lebow, Richard Ned. "Play It Again Pericles: Agents, Structures and the Peloponnesian War." *European Journal of International Relations* 2, no. 2 (1996): 231–58.

———. "Thucydides the Constructivist." *American Political Science Review* 95, no. 3 (2001): 547–60.

Liebeschuetz, W. "The Structure and Function of the Melian Dialogue." *Journal of Hellenic Studies* 88 (1968): 73–77.

Ludwig, Paul. *Eros and Polis.* Cambridge: Cambridge University Press, 2002.

Macgregor, Malcolm F. "The Genius of Alcibiades." *Phoenix* 19, no. 1 (1965): 27–50.

Macleod, C. W. "Form and Meaning in the Melian Dialogue." *Historia* 23 (1974): 385–400.

———. "Reason and Necessity." *Journal of Hellenic Studies* 96 (1978): 64–78.

———. "Rhetoric and History." In *Collected Essays*, 68–87. Oxford: Clarendon Press, 1983.

———. "Thucydides and Tragedy." In *Collected Essays*, 140–58. Oxford: Clarendon Press, 1983.

———. "Thucydides' Plataean Debate." *Greek, Roman, and Byzantine Studies* 18, no. 3 (1977): 227–46.

Mader, Gottfried. "Rogues' Comedy at Segesta (Thucydides 6.46): Alcibiades Exposed?" *Hermes* 121 (1993): 181–95.

Mara, Gerald M. *The Civic Conversations of Thucydides and Plato.* Albany: State University of New York Press, 2008.

———. "Thucydides and Political Thought." In *The Cambridge Companion to Ancient Greek Thought*, edited by Stephen Salkever, 96–125. Cambridge: Cambridge University Press, 2009.

Meyer, Elizabeth A. "Thucydides on Harmodius and Aristogeiton, Tyranny, and History." *Classical Quarterly* 58, no. 1 (2008): 13–34.

Monoson, S. Sara, and Michael Loriaux. "The Illusion of Power and the Disruption of Moral Norms: Thucydides' Critique of Periclean Policy." *American Political Science Review* 92, no. 2 (1998): 285–97.

Munn, Mark. *The School of History: Athens in the Age of Socrates.* Berkeley: University of California Press, 2000.

Orwin, Clifford. *The Humanity of Thucydides.* Princeton: Princeton University Press, 1994.

———. "The Just and Advantageous in Thucydides: The Case of the Mytilenaian Debate." *American Political Science Review* 78 (1984): 485–94.

Ostwald, Martin, "Diodotus, Son of Eucrates." *Greek, Roman, and Byzantine Studies* 20 (1979): 5–13.

Palmer, Michael. *Love of Glory and the Common Good*. Lanham, MD: Rowman and Littlefield, 1992.

Pangle, Thomas L., and Peter J. Ahrensdorf. "Classical Realism." In *Justice Among Nations: On the Moral Basis of Peace and Power*, 13–32. Lawrence: University of Kansas Press, 2002.

Parry, Adam. "Thucydides' Historical Perspective." *Yale Classical Studies* (1972): 47–61.

Plutarch. *The Lives of the Noble Grecians and Romans*. Translated by John Dryden. 1683. Reprint, New York: Modern Library, 1932.

Pouncey, Peter R. *The Necessities of War: A Study of Thucydides' Pessimism*. New York: Columbia University Press, 1980.

Pusey, Nathan Marsh. "Alcibiades and *to philopoli*." *Harvard Studies in Classical Philology* 51 (1940): 215–31.

Rahe, Paul A. "Thucydides' Critique of Realpolitik." In *Roots of Realism: Philosophical and Historical Dimensions*, edited by Benjamin Frankel, 105–41. London: Frank Cass, 1996.

Rawlings, Hunter R. *The Structure of Thucydides' History*. Princeton: Princeton University Press, 1981.

Romilly, Jacqueline de. "Fairness and Kindness in Thucydides." *Phoenix* 28 (1974): 95–100.

———. *Histoire et raison chez Thucydides*. Paris: Les Belles Lettres, 1967.

———. *Thucydides and Athenian Imperialism*. Translated by Philip Thody. Oxford: Basil Blackwell, 1963.

Rood, Tim. *Thucydides: Narrative and Explanation*. Oxford: Clarendon Press, 1998.

Saxonhouse, Arlene W. *Athenian Democracy: Modern Mythmakers and Ancient Theorists*. Notre Dame: Notre Dame University Press, 1996.

Scanlon, Thomas F. "Thucydides and Tyranny." *Classical Antiquity* (October 1987): 286–301.

Shanske, Darien. *Thucydides and the Philosophic Origins of History*. Cambridge: Cambridge University Press, 2007.

Stahl, Hans-Peter. "Speeches and Course of Events in Books 6 and 7 of Thucydides." In *The Speeches in Thucydides*, edited by Philip A. Stadter, 60–77. Chapel Hill: University of North Carolina Press, 1973.

———. *Thucydides: Man's Place in History*. Swansea: Classical Press of Wales, 2003. An expansion of the 1966 German edition.

Strauss, Leo. *City and Man*. Chicago: Rand McNally, 1964.

———. "Preliminary Observations on the Gods in Thucydides' Work." *Interpretation* 4, no. 1 (1974): 1–16.

———. "Thucydides: The Meaning of Political History." In *The Rebirth of Classical Political Rationalism*, edited by Thomas L. Pangle, 72–102. Chicago: University of Chicago Press, 1989.

Stroud, Ronald S. "Thucydides and Corinth." *Chiron* 24 (1994): 267–304.

Taylor, Martha C. *Thucydides, Pericles, and the Idea of Athens in the Peloponnesian War*. Cambridge: Cambridge University Press, 2010.

Taylor, Michael. *The Tyrant Slayers: The Heroic Image in Fifth Century B.C. Art and Politics*. New York: Arno Press, 1981.

Thucydides. *Historiae*. Edited by Henricus Stuart Jones. Oxford: Oxford University Press, 1966.

Wassermann, F. M. "Post-Periclean Democracy in Action: The Mytilenean Debate (Thuc. III 37–48)." *Transactions of the American Philological Association* 87 (1956): 27–41.

Westlake, H. D. "The Commons at Mytilene." *Historia* 25, no. 4 (1976): 429–40.

———. *Individuals in Thucydides*. Cambridge: Cambridge University Press, 1968.

Wettergreen, John A. "On the End of Thucydides' Narrative." *Interpretation* 9 (1979): 93–110.

White, James Boyd. *When Words Lose Their Meaning: Constitutions and Reconstitutions of Language, Character, and Community*. Chicago: University of Chicago Press, 1984.

Wylie, Graham. "Brasidas: Great Commander or Whiz Kid?" *Quaderni Urbinati di Cultura Classica*. n.s. 41, no. 2 (1992): 75–95.

Yunis, Harvey. *Taming Democracy: Models of Political Rhetoric in Classical Athens*. Ithaca, NY: Cornell University Press, 1996.

Zuckert, Catherine H. "The Socratic Turn." *History of Political Thought* 25, no. 2 (2004): 189–219.

Zumbrunnen, John G. *Silence and Democracy: Athenian Politics in Thucydides' "History."* University Park: Pennsylvania State University Press, 2008.

🐚 INDEX

Acanthus, 93–94, 103

action: choices limited by, 16; freedom and, 6, 26, 84; necessity and, 5; speech and, 4, 52, 53, 59; voluntary vs. involuntary, 61

Admetus (Molossian king), wife of, 175–76, 180

advantage: and Athenian empire, motivation for, 5, 30; vs. freedom, in Pericles' image of Athens, 35; and Pericles' politics, 29

advantage vs. justice: in Melian case, 115–16; in Mytilenean case, 52, 61–62, 65, 66, 67–68, 115; in Plataean case, 53, 69n32, 70

Aeschylus, 73, 131n50

Agis (Spartan king), 100, 104, 155, 155n16

Ahrensdorf, Peter J., 108, 109

Alcibiades (Athenian leader), 106, 111–14, 126; and Athens, 108, 109, 111, 127–28, 145, 157, 161–62, 165–66, 168, 179; Brasidas compared to, 20, 155; on democracy, 143, 166; Egestaean deception and, 123n34; and freedom, 6, 19, 106, 139, 181; godlike hubris of, 21, 109; homecoming for, 20, 139, 140, 156, 165–66, 182; and Melian episode, 114, 119, 120, 133; mutilation of herms and, 108, 140, 172–73; peace negotiations and, 112; Pericles compared to, 20, 106, 110, 126, 127, 127n42, 133; in Persia, 155–59; Plutarch on, 119, 155n17; politics of, 11, 112–14, 119n24; protean nature of, 145, 146, 155–56, 155n17, 162n24; recall from exile, 164; recall from Sicily, 108, 140; and regime change in Athens, 156–57, 159; at Samos, 160–65; and Sicilian expedition, 19, 24, 110, 111, 113, 125–30, 135, 144; Socrates compared to, 142, 143, 145, 162; and Sparta, 19, 112, 113, 141–46, 154–55, 166; speeches of, 19–20, 141–45, 160, 161; Themistocles compared to, 178; Thucydides compared to, 22, 161, 181–82; as Thucydides' informant, 163, 173

Alcidas (Spartan general), 74, 75, 95

Amphipolis: battle at, 100–102, 152; Brasidas at, 18–19, 22, 95, 100–102, 105; Cleon at, 100, 101, 102, 105; Peace of Nicias and, 103; Spartan ruler of, 100, 101; Thucydides at, 22, 105

Archedice (daughter of Hippias), 173, 175, 176

Archidamus (Spartan king), 3, 28n10, 31, 78–79, 84–85, 91, 104

Argos, 83n8, 100n30, 111, 112, 113, 143

Aristogeiton (reputed slayer of tyrants), 21, 171, 174

Aristophanes: *The Birds,* 117n17; *Clouds,* 83, 113, 117; *Ecclesiazusae,* 157; *Knights,* 55n4

Aristotle: on city as household, 166; on good deeds, 70; on great-souled individual, 126; on history and historians, 1, 2n1; on poet vs. historian, 12–13; on work of men vs. women, 82; on young and old, 129n46

Athenagoras (Syracusan leader), 44n40, 182, 182n16

Athens: Alcibiades and, 108, 109, 111, 127–28, 145, 157, 161–62, 165–66, 168, 179; Athenian envoys at Sparta on, 35, 62, 64; Brasidas and, 102; and Corcyra, 28–29, 45; Corinthians on, 17, 38, 79, 110, 116, 167; decision to enter Peloponnesian War, 30–31; degeneration of, 102, 134, 135, 157, 174; digressions involving past of, 21, 170, 180; and *erōs* for faraway, 19, 136, 136n55, 166; and foreigners, openness to, 4, 34, 170; freedom of, 2–3, 5, 16, 19, 21, 25–26, 27, 34, 63, 139, 140, 174; hubris of, 107, 116; imperialism of, 2, 5, 25–26, 63, 183; legend of tyrant slayers in, 171–73, 174; and Melos, invasion of, 107, 109–10, 114–20, 133, 141, 149; mutilation of herms in, 108, 140, 172–73, 174, 180, 181; Nicias and, 21, 138, 147, 149, 167, 168; oligarchy in, 157–59, 161–64, 181; origins of